G000099958

To Valerie,

With very best dishes,

Tina Brown

PERCY'S
COOKBOOK
Tina Bricknell-Webb

First published in Great Britain by Merlin Unwin Books, 2009

Copyright text © Tina Bricknell-Webb, 2009
Copyright photographs © Matt Austin, 2009

All rights reserved, including the right to reproduce this book or portions thereof in any form or by any means, electronic or mechanical, including photocopying, recording, or by any information storage and retrieval system, without permission in writing from the publisher. All enquiries should be addressed to Merlin Unwin Books (see address below).

Published by:
Merlin Unwin Books Ltd
Palmers House
7 Corve Street
Ludlow
Shropshire SY8 1DB
U.K.

www.merlinunwin.co.uk

The author asserts her moral right to be identified with this work.

Designed and set in Helvetica by Merlin Unwin.
Printed on FSC approved paper by Butler Tanner & Dennis Ltd, UK.

FSC Mixed Sources
Product group from well-managed forests and other controlled sources
www.fsc.org Cert no. SGS-COC-005091
© 1996 Forest Stewardship Council

ISBN 978-1-906122-14-0

CONTENTS

FOREWORD

I am delighted to have been invited by Tina to write a brief Foreword for her book. I am an old fashioned Green, one who goes back to Rachel Carson's time when being green was about the joy of the countryside and how to live decently in it. To me, the countryside of England was then the face of Gaia, somewhere that humans and the natural world lived together in a seemly way. In the 1960s farmers turned to agribusiness and, except for a few places, made it an efficient food producing monoculture but as barren for the natural world as a biofuel plantation. As the old labour intensive farms died away so did the villages. With no employment the villagers sold their old cottages and moved to the nearby towns. The villages, now filled with city folk, were gentrified and made even more beautiful than before but their new inhabitants lived a suburban life and soon there was little difference between the village and the town life they had vacated.

West Devon was an exception to this change in agriculture and the local farmers still farm grass and cattle as they have always done. My wife, Sandy, and I have made it our home. We first met Tina and Tony Bricknell-Webb when they were starting their enterprise of a truly green restaurant about two miles from where we live. We and our friends from all over the world have watched as their restaurant, Percy's, grew to become world famous as a star quality place to eat the food grown on what has now become their own truly organic farm.

The word organic has been devalued along with most things green. Runner beans grown in Kenya and flown to wealthy markets were not quite what the Soil Association had in mind for organic vegetables. Tina will tell you just what is involved in growing the food, raising the livestock and the cooking of a wholly fresh and natural meal. Every stage of their organic enterprise is hard worked with love and care. No wonder it tastes so good.

James Lovelock
Coombe Mill

August 2009

INTRODUCTION

My mother Catherine was the eldest girl in a family of eleven children. Her role was to shadow her mother and to assist in bringing up her numerous brothers and sisters. Her own father had emigrated from Sicily to New York at the age of 17 to work on the railroads. There he met my grandmother and they eloped when she was only fifteen. She had her first child at the age of 16 and with little family support and a very meagre income, resourcefulness was the order of the day.

As a child, my mother taught me, in culinary terms, how to make a silk purse out of a sow's ear. Having trained as a nurse, her knowledge of dietary nutrition was spot-on. Offal featured on the menu regularly, as did tertiary cuts such as neck of lamb, oxtail and sprats dusted with seasoned flour in a brown paper bag. A favourite childhood dish was a huge thick hearty soup she called minestrone into which she threw everything but the kitchen sink, including pork belly, haricot beans and a varied selection of vegetables.

She kept goats and when visiting the greengrocer she would ask for any trim (they used to trim cauliflower almost to order years ago) carrots past their sell by date and the stalks from Brussels tops to feed the pet goats. The car was reversed into the loading bay and all these boxes were neatly packed into the rear of the old estate car. Needless to say, the best of that lot was set aside for family consumption before the goats were given the opportunity to enjoy the rest.

In a nutshell, my mother gave me my passion for food. Everything was homemade and delicious. The kitchen was truly the heart of the home as is at Percy's – spacious, clean with a huge stainless steel induction hob which doubles as a breakfast bar or place for friends to sit and watch the cooking as they sip a glass of wine. These recipes have been chosen with love and dedication. My mother was my inspiration and I sincerely hope that I can be yours.

Tina Bricknell-Webb
August 2009

To my dear flock of ewes, especially Tinkerbell, Pink Tag and Little William
– and to Tony, my long suffering husband, with love

ACKNOWLEDGEMENTS

I would like to thank all the wonderful people who have helped me to put this book together: Anthony Blake and Kyle Hayes, without whom this book would not have come to fruition, my dear friends James Lovelock and David Woodfield for their support and encouragement, Philip Warren for being so generous with his time and knowledge, mentoring me on the butchery front. Maynard Davies who set me firmly on the road to bacon curing. Heather Holden Brown, my agent, for her patience. Angela and Robert Orme, Jon and Charlotte Price and Liz and Paul Cleghorn for recipe testing and proof reading; and lastly, Karen McCall and Merlin Unwin for having the confidence in the project and nursing me through my first publication, and to Jo and Gillian too.

I am indebted to Matt Austin for his wonderful photography in this book and to Richard Austin for allowing me to add some of his pictures to fill the gaps.

Tina Bricknell-Webb
August 2009

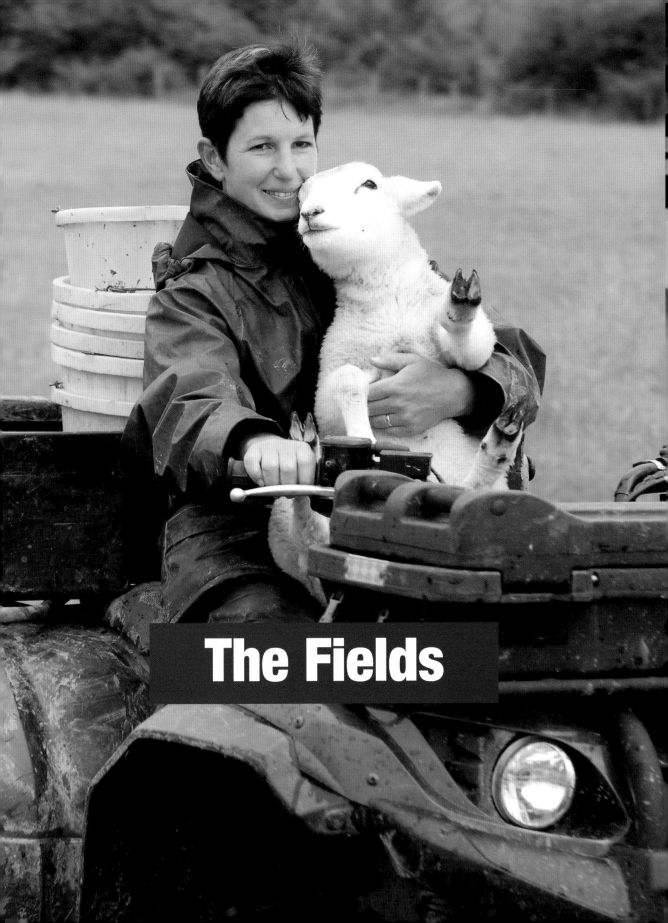

The Fields

The Fields

When we first completed on the Devon property on July 1st 1990, the then-owners introduced us to a local farmer called Roy, who had sheep, and was interested in having 'the keep' (renting the land for grazing). At first, we visited our new estate at Coombeshead only one or two days a week, and soon after Roy had installed his flock on our land, we were told by our neighbours that on the days we left for London, Roy would open all the gates to let the hungry beasts have the run of the property. These woolly hooligans were slowly destroying the hedges, as they managed to get everywhere. The final straw was when my newly-planted orchard was attacked by a horde of sheep. I summoned Roy and told him to remove them immediately.

Having little farming knowledge, Tony and I then discussed how we might best put the pasture to good use. 'Well,' I said, 'if Roy can farm sheep, then so can I.'

We purchased six Jacob ewes and a Jacob ram. This was the start of our own flock of sheep, now 200-strong.

We had more than enough pasture for seven sheep, so we bought ourselves a couple of horses and very soon found ourselves breeding thoroughbreds for flat racing. I had always yearned for a couple of pigs, so, following a win at Lingfield by our homebred filly 'Lady Chef' at the age of two, we invested some of the winnings in the purchase of two pregnant sows, 'Doreen' and 'Lucky'. They duly farrowed twenty-six piglets between them, and set us firmly on the road to bacon curing and sausage making.

It is now difficult to imagine not knowing the provenance of the meat I cook – if I do take on a new supplier, I always try the product first and then visit the farm. The information I look for from the farmer concerns general animal welfare, feedstuffs, minerals, quality of forage, stocking density etc. Having said that, it is pretty easy to purchase good quality meat direct from source, either from farm shops or food markets.

If you can get to know the farmer well enough to be shown around the farm, you will know he is proud of the way he looks after his stock. Contented animals, properly fed, result in great tasting meat.

Tina's Unique Method of Cooking Meat

Over a period of time, I have developed a unique method of cooking meat, which I refer to as 'pulse cooking'. With this pulse technique, I introduce the meat to a fairly high heat for a brief time and then remove it from the heat for a set time, usually by taking the roasting tray from the oven and 'resting' it. I repeat the process (in/out/rest, in/out/rest) until the piece of meat or joint is done. The benefit this has to all cuts of meat, whether chicken breast, rump of lamb or topside of beef, is that the heat that has been introduced to the outside of the meat has a chance to migrate slowly towards the centre of the cut during the resting time. This way, the temperature of the meat gradually equalises and the end result is that the meat is evenly cooked all the way through, thereby avoiding the dryness and toughness a high or prolonged heat can cause. Pulse-cooked meat remains moist, retaining all the wonderful, flavour-some juices. For the host or hostess, it means that meat can be 'resting' while you socialise with your guests or get on with another part of the cooking.

Loin of Lamb: Marinated with Lavender, Garlic, Lime Juice and Olive Oil

outdoor summer dinner party

Having successfully mastered the breeding of my own lamb for the table, I soon found that simplicity was the order of the day, since I was initially quite slow to butcher, which left me precious little time to spend actually cooking the food. Another thing I discovered is that although 'Spring Lamb' is very tender, slightly older lamb is a good deal tastier. And as this dish uses the loin or canon (which is the least-used muscle on the animal), a loin from a more mature carcase does not compromise the tenderness of the meat.

This is a dish for an outdoor summer dinner party, as it is delicious lukewarm, and pure, lean meat!

Serves 4

Ingredients

750g/25oz boneless loin of lamb, all fat and sinew removed
240ml/8 fl oz/1 cup good quality olive oil
Handful fresh lavender, leaves and flowers in bud, finely chopped
60ml/2 fl oz/¼ cup lime juice
90ml/3 fl oz/2 tbsp honey (preferably lavender), warmed
4 cloves garlic, peeled and finely chopped

Method

1. Pre-heat the oven to 200°C.
2. Combine the oil, lavender, garlic, honey & lime juice.
3. Whisk well to dissolve the honey.
4. Add the lamb loin. Leave to marinate for 20 minutes, turning occasionally.
5. Place a heavy roasting tray in the oven to heat for 10 minutes.

6. Take the lamb loin out of the marinade and place directly in the hot roasting tray. Shake briefly to prevent it from sticking.
7. Place in the oven for 3 minutes.
8. Take out of the oven, turn the meat over and rest for 8 minutes. Turn the meat over again, place back in the oven and roast for a further 3 minutes. Remove from oven.
9. Turn then rest again for 8 minutes. The meat should feel slightly springy to the touch and should at this stage be cooked through to an even pinkness whilst retaining a delicious juicy, mouth-watering texture.
10. Slice against the grain and serve with a crisp green salad and new potatoes.

Ease of cooking: ★☆☆
Surprisingly simple.
Preparation & cooking time: 50 minutes

Tina's Tip

Once the lamb has been removed, the marinade can be put to good use. One suggestion is to place the marinade in a roasting tin, place the tin into a hot oven for 15 minutes, then add some par-boiled potatoes, cherry tomatoes and peeled Jerusalem artichokes. Baste, then place back in the oven for 20–30 minutes until the vegetables are golden and cooked through. Delicious!

Moist & Succulent Roast Loin of Pork with Sage & Juniper

simple and easy to cook

When the provenance of your pork is abundantly clear, and the quality faultless, it is not necessary when cooking to virtually annihilate it (as the government advised us to do during the 1960s). The golden rule with most meat is that much of the flavour is contained in both the fat and the meat juices, and, if you remove the fat or cook the meat until it is dry, the taste and texture can be markedly compromised. Watch out, as many modern pig breeds are very lean indeed and the meat often lacks the flavoursome fat-covering that is essential for keeping the joint nice and moist during cooking.

Serves 6

Ingredients

1080g/36oz loin of pork, rind removed & reserved, fat trimmed to about 1cm depth
Sea salt
Handful of sage leaves
1 tbsp juniper berries, crushed and chopped
Quantity of pork gravy (page 29)

Method

1. Pre-heat oven to 200°C. Score the fat on the loin (take care that you do not cut through the meat or the juices will escape). Sprinkle with some of the sea salt and rub it into the fat (for crispness).
2. Heat a wok or a large skillet until hot.
3. Place the pork, fat side down and cook gently for about 5–10 minutes to render the fat. Pour off the fat and then turn the pork over to brown on the other side for a further 5 minutes. Turn back to the fat-side and render a few minutes more. Reserve the fat (this can be used as a roasting fat for potatoes or other vegetables).
4. Take the pork out of the pan, place in a roasting tray and rest for 8 minutes.
5. Place the tray in the oven and cook for 6–8 minutes depending on how thick the meat is. Remove from the oven, rest for 8 minutes, cook for a further 5 minutes, rest again for 8 minutes and then check for done-ness (the meat should feel reasonably firm to the touch but not hard).
6. Crush the juniper berries and chop them with the sage. Add to the gravy and simmer gently for 8-10 minutes before serving.

Ease of cooking: ★☆☆
Not at all difficult, just make sure you have a timer in good working order.
Preparation & cooking time: 45 minutes

Tina's Tip

For perfect crackling, score the rind (a Stanley knife makes an easy job of this) place in a colander and pour some boiling water over it, then rub with sea salt and roast in a medium oven until crisp. Cut into strips and serve with the pork.

A great accompaniment to pork is of course apple sauce, but for a change, and especially if you are cooking a cut from a rare breed, then try my cranberry and orange relish (page 183).

Lamb Shanks Braised with Onions & Red Wine

deceptively easy, can be pre-prepared

A very simple, achievable dish with only about half an hour preparation time which may well earn you disproportionate compliments for the time and effort taken to prepare.

Serves 4

Ingredients

4 large shanks of lamb,
(about 350–450g/12–16oz each)
3 tbsp olive oil
2 large onions, finely sliced
1 tbsp garlic purée
8 sprigs thyme
½ large celeriac diced to 1cm cubes
6 bay leaves
2 tbsp cornflour
1400ml/2 pints 9oz lamb or chicken stock, or water
560ml/¾ of a bottle red wine
Thyme leaves and chopped parsley
Sea salt
Black pepper

Method

1. Pre-heat oven 150°C.
2. In a wok or heavy frying pan, heat the oil or fat and fry the shanks quite well until browned all over.
3. Remove from pan and set aside.
4. Add oil to the pan with onions and garlic and fry until golden. Drain, place in a heavy casserole, and arrange the herbs over the base followed by the shanks and lastly the diced celeriac.
5. Cover with the stock or water and the wine ensuring the shanks are fully submerged.
6. Place in the oven and cook for approx.

2–3 hours or until the meat falls away from the bone.

7. Drain the liquor from the casserole into a pan, reduce by half, season, then thicken with the cornflour, pour back over the meat, and place back in the oven for 20 minutes and then serve.

8. Sprinkle with thyme leaves and coarsely chopped parsley.

Ease of cooking: ★ ★ ☆
Preparation & cooking time: 3–3½ hours

Tina's Tip

This is a dish that both freezes and keeps well. It is worth doing more than you need, as the jellied sauce will preserve the dish for several days in the fridge. Knuckles of lamb from the shoulder can be substituted for the leg shanks but will be smaller so reduce the cooking time accordingly. Can be cooked a day or two in advance and chilled.

Moroccan Lamb Tagine

jeans & jumper supper party

Slowly braised chunks of succulent lamb cooked in a dazzling fruity sauce with a plethora of Moroccan spices, dried fruits and tomato – this is probably my favourite way of preparing a lamb stew. One of the best things about this recipe is that (like most spiced dishes), it tastes better the next day. With this in mind (and the prep done in advance) it is certainly my preferred choice for a 'jeans and jumpers' supper party of eight or more, with a stone jug or two of light red wine to wash it down. Shoulder, shank or neck fillet meat are all equally suitable. If you can procure well-hung mutton, so much the better.

Don't be put off by the seemingly endless list of ingredients, or by the fact that it takes time to cook. Cook a day or two before you need it and then just simply re-heat and spend time with your guests or family.

Serves 8

Ingredients

2kg/4lb 6oz diced lamb shoulder, shank or neck fillet
1½ cups plain flour
Salt and freshly ground black pepper
1 cup olive oil
2 sticks of cassia bark or cinnamon
4 cloves
6 cloves garlic, finely chopped
4 large onions, finely sliced
200g/7oz organic, non-sulphured dried apricots, sliced
200g/7oz jumbo sultanas
125ml/4½oz lemon juice
100g/3½oz ground almonds
2 litres/3½ pints lamb or chicken stock
Large bunch fresh coriander or flat leaf parsley

For the spice:

10g paprika
2g turmeric
2g ground cumin
5g ground coriander
10g ground cardamom
2g saffron
50g freshly grated root ginger
50g sun-dried tomato paste or tomato purée
1 tbsp harissa paste or chilli sauce

Method

1. Mix together all the spice ingredients.
2. Soak the sultanas in the lemon juice, cover with cling film, prick the cling film in several places and microwave for 4–5 minutes until the sultanas plump up and the lemon juice is absorbed. Alternatively, soak overnight.
3. Pre-heat the oven to 140°C.
4. In a large casserole, heat half the oil.

5. Sieve the flour with the salt and pepper.

6. Dust the lamb pieces in the seasoned flour, shake to remove any excess and fry gently in the olive oil until golden brown on all sides.

7. Remove and set aside.

8. Add the rest of the olive oil to the pan and then fry the garlic and the onion. When almost cooked, stir in the spice mix and cook for a further 5 minutes.

9. Add the sliced apricots and the soaked sultanas.

10. Add the ground almonds and stir to combine.

11. Add the lamb back to the casserole; add the cinnamon and the cloves.

12. Mix all the ingredients together and cover with the stock.

13. Cook for 2–3 hours or until the meat is tender and just starts to fall apart.

14. Serve on a bed of couscous or rice, sprinkle with the coriander or parsley and a bowl of plain yoghurt to dollop on top.

Tina's Tip

Halfway through cooking, taste the sauce. If you have overdone the heat, pop in a few raw carrots, as they will absorb the spice and then remove them before serving. Alternatively, stir in some of the yoghurt just before serving. Best to plan ahead and cook in advance. That way, the tagine can chill overnight and any surplus fat that rises to the surface will set and can then easily be removed.

Ease of cooking: ★★☆
Preparation & cooking time: 4–5 hours
Freezes well.

Cull Ewe & Vegetable Broth

comfort food, freeze any excess

There comes a time when the breeding life of an ewe draws gently to a close. For the economics of animal husbandry, it pays for the farmer to send these ewes to slaughter – the carcasses are then sold on to the general public as mutton.

As a cook with her own flock of homebred ewes and a substantial kitchen garden, I usually have an abundance of both well-hung mutton and an ample supply of root vegetables. The following recipe combines both of these ingredients in a warming, robust and satisfying broth ideal for days when there is a chill in the air, served simply with some homemade rustic bread.

Serves 6–8

Ingredients

500g/18oz neck fillet, lean shoulder or leg of mutton, cut into 1½ cm dice
3 litres/5 pt water, fresh lamb stock or stock made with good quality cubes
60g/¼ cup pearl barley or rice or oatmeal
180g/6oz carrot cut into 1 cm dice
180g/6oz parsnip cut into 1 cm dice
180g/6oz turnip cut into 1 cm dice
200g/7oz celeriac cut into 1 cm dice
200g/7oz onion, cut into 1 cm dice
60g/2oz peeled, finely chopped garlic
1 generous bunch flat leaf parsley
6 sprigs fresh thyme
2 tsp sea salt
1kg/2lb 3oz lamb bones if available, sawn into 20 cm lengths

Method

1. Place the diced mutton in a large bowl together with the salt and the bones if you have them.
2. Cover with clean cold water and leave to soak for 1½ hours to remove the blood.
3. Rinse and place in a large saucepan covering with all the water or stock. Add the barley/rice/oatmeal together with the thyme sprigs and cook on a very gentle heat for approx. 1½ hours, skimming as any froth rises to the surface.
4. Add the onion and garlic and cook for a further 10 min. Add the rest of the vegetables and simmer until they are half cooked i.e. they still have a bite to them. Take off the heat. (At this point the vegetables will carry on cooking slowly).
5. Add salt and freshly ground black pepper to taste. Just before serving, check the vegetables for done-ness; cook a little more if required. Add the freshly chopped parsley and serve with warm crusty bread and butter.

Ease of cooking: ★☆☆
A good recipe to make in bulk and then freeze.
Preparation & cooking time: 2½ hours

Tina's Tip

If you are going to make this to freeze, wash out some used milk bottles, fill ⅔ with cold water and freeze. When you have reached step 3, take the pan off the heat and set the frozen bottles into the pan to arrest the cooking process. This will cool the broth quickly and retain enough crispness in the vegetables to leave a bit of 'bite' when you come to reheat. At this point, add the seasoning and parsley. Lamb can be substituted for the mutton, but it will not need quite as much cooking.

Pork Escalopes

easy and delicious

The pork I use is from our own home reared pig herd of rare breed, organic, pedigree Large Blacks. Allowed to develop at their own pace, stress-free on fully organic land, they live an idyllic existence beneath their own tree canopy. Foraging from a woodland floor dense in acorns, brambles, roots and natural goodness to produce superbly flavoured succulent meat. Traditionally bred pork is widely available at farmers markets and good quality butchers.

Serves 4

Ingredients

8 pork escalopes, each weighing approx. 70–80g/2-3oz
100g/3½ flour
Freshly ground sea salt & black pepper
⅓ cup olive oil or bacon fat
2 lemons, quartered

Method

1. Place the flour in a bowl and season.
2. Dust the pork escalopes in the flour and set aside.
3. Heat the oil or bacon fat in a frying pan or skillet.
4. Fry the escalopes for 2–3 minutes on each side.
5. Rest in the pan for 8 minutes before serving with a wedge of lemon.

Ease of cooking: ★ ☆ ☆
Preparation & cooking time: 40 minutes

Tina's Tip

The beetroot chutney (page 191) pairs very well with pork. If you want a piquant sauce, heat some pork gravy, whisk in some green peppercorns, a dollop of crème fraîche and a splash of lemon juice or brandy.

The Perfect Topside Roast
for Eating Hot or Cold

easy dinner party

This is a great way to cook beef for medium-sized gatherings – add garlic & rosemary if you like, or roast it plain. The secret to keeping the roast pink from top to bottom is not necessarily in the cooking, but **in the resting time**. Cooking the joint this way not only ensures that it remains pink, but also keeps it succulent and tender. Much of the pleasure of eating beef is in the texture – a huge chunk of thickly-sliced, over-done beef is not only quite a mouthful, but also can be a challenge to chew. Thin slices however, can feel almost silky to the touch and leaves you with a really good 'mouth-feel' – especially if chased with a slug of an exceptionally good red Burgundy or Claret!

Serves 6–8

Ingredients

1 well-hung boned & rolled topside of
beef weighing 2½kg/5½lb
(ask your butcher for the bones)
225g/8oz dripping to seal
Salt & pepper
6 sprigs of rosemary
6 cloves of garlic, peeled

Method

1. Pre-heat the oven to 220°C.
2. Rub the joint thoroughly with salt and pepper.
3. Cut the garlic into thin slivers.
4. Break the rosemary into 24 smaller sprigs, removing any surplus stalk.
5. Insert a knife into the meat then lever sideways slightly to create a pocket.
6. Slide a sliver of garlic down the blade of the knife, followed by a sprig of rosemary.
7. Repeat all over the meat until the garlic and rosemary has all been used.
(If you have the time to do this a day ahead of time, so much the better, as the flavours will have time to permeate through the meat).
8. Heat the dripping in a large roasting tray on top of the stove. Add the joint and seal thoroughly on all sides until nicely browned.
9. Remove the meat from the dripping (reserve) and transfer to a clean roasting tray, into which you have put the beef bones (this acts as a trivet).
10. Place in the oven for 20 minutes then take out of the oven and turn over the joint, taking care not to pierce the meat (this will let the juices run out). Rest for 20 minutes and then return to the oven and cook for a further 20 minutes. Remove from the oven and rest the meat for 20 minutes.
11. Turn the oven down to 150°C
12. Check the core temperature with a meat thermometer (we are looking for

about 55°C after resting time). Return the meat to the oven (reduced to 150°C) for a further 20 minutes, then rest once more and check the temperature.

13. Carve thinly and serve with horse-radish sauce and Yorkshire puddings (popovers) (p236).

Ease of cooking: ★☆☆
Not difficult, just keep a close eye on the timings.
Preparation time: 10 minutes
Cooking & resting time: 1¾–2½ hours

Tina's Tip

The cooking time will vary slightly depending on the size of the joint, how cold it is when you start and how well hung it is. The fresher and colder the meat, the longer cooking and resting will be required. Don't be tempted to cut into the meat before it is fully cooked and rested as this will break the seal and allow valuable juices to escape.

Homemade Breakfast Pork Sausages or Patties

children's favourite

Few of us make our own sausages, which is more the pity, as you have total control over the ingredients, the size and whether you want them in skins or not. It is much easier than you may think. If you choose not to have skins, you can simply roll them into shapes, or you can then cover them in caul fat as the French do, which they then call 'crepinettes'. For a small sum – around £50-60, you can invest in a manual 'sausage filler'. Alternatively, food mixers from manufacturers such as Kenwood and Kitchen Aid have mincing attachments as standard and also sell sausage fillers for around £15. Linking the filled skins is great fun – you can get chipolata skins, hog casings (normal sausage size) or hogs pudding skins to play with. Some years ago, I asked my butcher to teach me how to link and then I was off, making sausages of any kind at any opportunity, whether it be fish, faggot mix or otherwise. A regularly linked sausage cooks evenly and should taste (providing your pork is good quality) sublime. When purchasing your meat, ask for pork from one of the rare breeds. Ideally, you need 50% lean meat and 50% fatty meat (using pork belly or a whole shoulder with a good fat covering, gives the best results). The fat in the meat is essential as it contains much of the flavour and provides succulence. The breadcrumbs add a lightness of texture and help to prevent the fat (and therefore much of the flavour) from cooking out. This recipe is for a plain breakfast sausage/patty. However, if you want to experiment creating a sausage suitable for a brunch or supper dish for example, then why not add a little smoked garlic, blue cheese, herbs or even sun-dried tomato? One of my favourite combinations is pork, Harbourne Blue or Stilton cheese, and summer savory, which tastes great both hot or cold.

Serves 6

Ingredients

1 small shoulder of pork weighing approx. 2kg/4½lb
200g/7 fl oz ice cold water
200g/7oz white breadcrumbs
20g/1 tbsp sea salt
20g/2 tbsp freshly ground white pepper

Method

1. Remove all the skin from the pork shoulder and cut into 2 cm/1" cubes.
2. Sprinkle with the salt and pepper and combine well.
3. Cover with a damp cloth and place in the refrigerator for a couple of hours.
4. Pass through a mincer with a medium blade, directly into a mixing bowl.
5. Using the paddle attachment, add the water slowly and mix well.
6. Finally incorporate the crumbs thoroughly.

7. Cook a little of the mix to check the seasoning. If you are happy with both the taste and the texture, place a little of the mix at a time in the palm of your hand, roll into a ball and then gently flatten in to the shape of a patty.

8. Alternatively, the mix can be filled into sausage skins and then linked.

Ease of cooking: ★ ★ ☆
A good recipe for children.
Preparation time: 3 hours

Tina's Tip

This mix can also be used as a basis for a stuffing for turkey, to fill sausage rolls, to make into meatballs and then cook in a sauce (such as Satay) or into a burger to serve in a bun. When freezing, first place the sausages on greaseproof paper so they do not touch, cover with cling film and then place in the freezer. Once frozen, the sausages can be put in a bag or freezer-proof container and taken out individually or as required.

If you do not have a mincer, the pulse setting on a food processor can be used to chop the meat. Cooked rice, moist oatmeal or cooked polenta can be substituted for breadcrumbs.

For sausage-making supplies visit: www.scobiesdirect.com or www. sausagemaking.org or in the West Country: www.mkwholesale.co.uk

Whole Ham Baked with Lovage

tradition with a twist

The most ordinary of hams can be transformed into an extraordinary meal, simply by the addition of some carefully selected seasonings. Ham has probably spent several weeks in brine being cured, and can therefore be quite salty. Put the ham into a large container of cold water for several hours and change the water every couple of hours or so, in order to remove the excess salt.

Do not be afraid to cook a joint slightly larger than you think you will need. It is surprising just how quickly a cooked ham can disappear from the fridge – especially with a large family. Ham is a very versatile ingredient. It can be sliced and served with eggs for breakfast, chopped to add to omelettes, delicious with salad and freshly-dug new potatoes, or boiled and served with white sauce and capers (page 219).

Left-overs can be combined with mushrooms and cheese to create a dish cooked with cream and eggs, or can be successfully paired with green split peas and lovage to make a delicious soup.

Serves 12–30
(depending on the size of the ham)

Ingredients

1 whole ham, of your choice, either on the bone or boned and rolled
Large bunch of lovage
6 large carrots
4 large parsnips
3 large onions
Bunch of fresh thyme, rosemary or summer savory
Generous tbsp juniper berries, crushed
Generous tbsp white peppercorns, cracked
½ cup soft brown sugar or grated jaggery
1 tbsp ground ginger
1 tbsp ground cardamom

Method

1. Place the herbs, vegetables, juniper berries and peppercorns into the bottom of a large pan.
2. Place the ham on top. Cover with cold water.
3. Bring to the boil. Turn down the heat and simmer for about three hours, or until the core temperature reaches 100°C.
4. Remove the ham from the pan, leave to cool slightly and then remove the string and the skin. Pre-heat oven to 180°C
5. Score the fat and then rub in the mixed sugar, ginger and cardamom thoroughly until all the sugar has dissolved.
6. Place on a roasting tray and then pop in the oven to roast for 1 hour.
7. Leave to rest for 30 minutes before carving if being used for a hot meal or leave to cool at room temperature and then chill in the fridge overnight before slicing.

Ease of cooking: ★ ★ ☆
Allow an extra ½ hour the first time you
attempt this recipe.

Preparation time: 1 hour
Cooking time: 4 hours

Tina's Tip

My favourite way of cooking ham is in a bag – there are special bags used in the
industry called Nalophan bags, which are suitable for roasting, boiling, freezing and
microwaving. The reason I have become so attached to this particular method of
cooking hams is that not only are all the juices from the meat kept in the bag, they are
also flavoured with the aromatics and herbs within the bag.

The second reason is that when the ham is cooled, it will absorb back some of the liquid
that has escaped during cooking, thereby giving it a nice moist and silky texture.

The third reason is that the liquid is both very tasty and gelatinous and can be used
as an aspic jelly for canapés, to set terrines or as a stock to make soups such as split
pea, ham and lovage.

Lamb Burger

great for barbeque, picnic or cold buffet

This is a truly delectable way to enjoy lamb. It is best made with freshly minced lamb and fresh herbs. I like to mince the meat relatively finely with some of the fat interspersed for moisture and flavour – it eats really well and ensures there are no gristly bits. This is a great favourite for a child's supper or a barbeque, and is even delicious cold. For a change, the mix can be pressed into a bread tin and cooked as a meat loaf, which can then be served hot with gravy or left to chill in the fridge and be used for picnics or a buffet.

Serves 8–12

Ingredients

1800g/4lb lamb mince
150g/1 cup fine breadcrumbs
200g/1 cup red wine or water
250g/1 cup tomato puree
1 cup roughly chopped sweet marjoram
3 eggs to bind
Salt and pepper to taste

Method

1. Combine all ingredients thoroughly in a bowl by hand.
2. Form into burgers about 140g/5 oz each in weight.

3. Cook under a medium grill, just enough to leave a little pink in the centre.
4. Serve with yoghurt, sultana & almond mint dressing (p216).

Ease of cooking: ★☆☆
Not at all difficult. Very rewarding.
Preparation & cooking time: 45 minutes

Tina's Tip

These freeze very well. For a fruity version, add half a cup of marrow, bean and onion chutney (page 176) to the mixture at Stage 1.

Boston Baked Beans

good value, easy meal

Authentic Baked Beans, just as the Indians created them three centuries ago – baked in earthenware pots. My grandmother frequently served this dish to her hungry family of 13. My mother was quick to include this in her own repertoire of 'recipes to feed a family of six on a very modest income'.

Serves: 8–10

Ingredients

1kg/2lb 3oz/5 cups haricot beans
450g/1lb salt pork
2 sliced onions
1/3 cup molasses
2 tsp salt
1/3 tsp pepper
1/2 tsp English mustard powder

Method

1. Soak the haricot beans in cold water overnight.
2. Place the salt pork in cold water, bring to the boil and simmer for 5 minutes.
3. Drain the pork and scrape the skin. Pat dry and cut into slices or cubes – whichever is your preference.
4. Place the beans in a large pot in cold water and simmer until tender (2–3 hours), strain, reserve liquor.
5. Pre-heat the oven to 140°C.
6. Place the beans in a large casserole together with the salt pork and the onions.
7. Add the molasses, salt, pepper and mustard to the beans and mix well. Add just enough bean liquor to cover the beans.
8. Cover with a lid and bake for 4–6 hours.
9. Check from time to time to make sure the beans do not dry out.
10. Serve with crusty brown bread and a large salad.

Ease of cooking: ★☆☆
Preparation & cooking time: 8½ hours
Freezes well.

Tina's Tip

If you are looking to cut down the preparation time dramatically, substitute the dried haricot beans for cooked tinned ones. For this recipe you will need to use 2½kg of tinned beans (drained weight).

If you have the opportunity, add a couple of pigs' trotters with the salt pork – these give a lovely gelatinous texture as well as bags of extra porky flavour and are great to eat.

How to Cure Bacon Traditionally

In the old days, curing was far more prevalent in everyday food preparation as there was little or no refrigeration. Much effort was spent perfecting specialist cures for different types of ham and bacon depending on the breed of pig, which area they came from and so on. Today, most butchers buy in ready-to-use cures that have been scientifically developed to keep the bugs at bay and give us a universally good tasting product at the same time. These cures work extremely well and cut the curing time dramatically. This however means that the bacon from most butchers' shops tastes pretty similar. If you want to try curing your own bacon at home and are looking for a unique flavour, here is a recipe along the lines of a 'traditional cure.'

Traditional Bacon Cure

Makes enough to cure approx. 70kg meat.

Ingredients

450g/1lb rock salt
450g/1lb sea salt
370g/13oz light Muscovado sugar
30g/1oz ground coriander
30g/1oz ground mace
30g/1oz ground nutmeg
85g/3oz saltpetre

Method

Combine all ingredients well. Store in an airtight container until needed.

1. The first step is to find out how much of the cure you will need. To do so, make sure the meat is neatly squared off and weighed. Then calculate 3% of that weight. This is the amount of cure you require.
2. Place the belly of pork skin side down in a galvanised or stainless steel container then sprinkle with the mix (away from any other fresh meat that you do not intend to cure) Rub the cure thoroughly into the meat. As a general rule of thumb, it will take approx. 1 day for every 450g/1lb of meat to cure, although if the belly is really thick, it may take a little longer.
3. After a couple of days the bacon should be sitting in its own natural brine. When the bacon is cured, rinse under cold running water, pat dry with a clean towel, wrap well and store in the refrigerator until needed. (it should keep for 10–14 days).

Ease of preparation: ★ ☆ ☆
Make sure the ingredient weights are accurate.
Preparation time: 30 minutes, plus 4–5 days

Tina's Tip

Don't make up too much in advance. It does keep, but is best made fresh, with freshly roasted and ground coriander, freshly ground mace and freshly grated nutmeg if you can spare the time. The saltpetre is available in small quantities from chemists (although you will have to explain what your intention is, as it is also used in bomb making!).

The ingredients can be interchanged for spices such as ginger, anise, cardamom, cumin etc. But do remember, the best pork needs little spicing, as the aim is to let the natural flavours shine through. The varying quality of pork available encompasses a very broad spectrum – the poorer the quality, the more seasoning is needed.

If you are thinking of curing on a fairly frequent basis, it is well worth getting a vacuum-packing machine. This will extend the shelf life of your meat considerably and can also be a blessing if you want to prepare food for several meals at a time.

The cured belly can be sliced thinly for bacon, sliced thickly for lardons, or sliced, rind removed and beaten between two sheets of plastic to create very thin bacon to wrap around other ingredients such as chicken or monkfish.

Faggots

nutritious and economical

A traditional English dish, faggots originated in the South West of England, Wales and the Black Country. Faggots are generally a product from the pig where the lights, livers, kidneys and spleen are minced and then combined with onions, breadcrumbs, sage, salt and pepper, formed into billiard-ball shapes, covered preferably with the pig's caul fat and then braised in the oven with a little stock. I love the rich depth of flavour of faggots, due mainly to the high mineral content. I make them from the trim and offal of both pork and lamb as I think it is a great way of presenting a really tasty dish from an otherwise under-utilised and inexpensive ingredient. If you like this recipe and are tempted to rear your own pork or lamb, rest assured that you will open up a lifetime of experimentation, using everything you can from a carcass.

Over the years the mainstream cuts of both red and white meats have become more affordable so that generations have not handed down the habit of eating offal. I feel that the resistance to offal is often psychological and once decided to prove my theory. One November, several years ago, my husband and I were invited to a fireworks party held by a local couple for their friends and staff. I offered to bring some food and made a large batch of faggot mix which I stuffed into sausage skins. These I simmered in salted water for 30 minutes to pre-cook and then left them to cool. At the party (in the dark, with only the glow of the fire for light) I popped these faggots onto the barbeque and roasted the skins as I heated them through. They were all eaten in half an hour as the bought-in cheap chipolatas languished on the side. I had a tremendous evening, supping gin & tonics as I watched these happy faces devouring ingredients they would never have knowingly chosen to eat!
P.S. I never did tell anyone.

Serves 24

Ingredients

510g/18oz pigs' or lambs' livers
3 medium onions
140g/5oz fresh breadcrumbs
100g/3½oz suet
1 tbsp chopped sage
Salt & pepper to taste

Method

1. Mince the liver and onions into a mixing bowl. Add the breadcrumbs, chopped suet and sage.
2. Season with salt & pepper (be generous with the pepper). Mix well, shape into balls (if the mixture is too wet, add a few more breadcrumbs), then place on a greased roasting tray and bake in a moderate oven (175°C) for about half an hour.

3. The balls can first be poached in salted simmering water or stock for 20 minutes, then drained, placed on a roasting tray, brushed with melted butter and placed in a moderate oven (175°C) for 20 minutes.
4. The juices on the tray, together with some of the cooking liquor, can be thickened with a little flour to make gravy.

Ease of cooking: ★ ★ ☆
Once tried, never forgotten
Preparation & cooking time: 3 hours

Tina's Tip

Heart, lungs and kidneys can be substituted for some of the livers. The dish freezes very well and the faggots, once cooked, can quickly be re-heated from frozen. The suet can be made from the hard fat surrounding the kidneys of either pork or lamb. To do this, chill the fat very well, together with the mincing attachments for your machine, then pass the chilled fat through slowly and onto a tray. Freeze, then break up and put into a container so that you have frozen free-flow suet at the ready for later use. These faggots, once cooked, are delicious eaten hot or cold, with chutney, or re-heated in gravy for a late breakfast or brunch.

Jellied Canine Meatballs

satisfying to make

Tinned dog food is skilfully designed to get a pooch's mouth to water. Succulent chunks of re-formed protein (some of it meat) are surrounded by a soft jelly to keep it nice and moist. This is something that someone with a little time on his or her hands can do at home.

Before dogs became domesticated, they would hunt for their food and eat it raw, benefiting from the minerals in the whole animal carcass, including the bones and the liver. These meatballs wholly capture that nutritive value. These minerals contain heaps of flavour, so there is no need for any seasoning. In fact, spices such as pepper can actually irritate the gut lining of a dog. I wouldn't recommend using any pork or wheat products, as some dogs can have unpleasant reactions to these ingredients, including dry skin and upset tummies.

Makes 24 meatballs

Ingredients

5kg/11lb bones (chicken, lamb or beef)
Bay leaves, parsley, carrots
1kg/2lb 3oz minced meat (can be chicken, lamb or beef)
3 medium eggs
2 cups oat or rice flour

Method

1. First make the stock. Place the bones into a large pan and cover with cold water. Bring to the boil, turn down the heat and simmer for 20 minutes, skimming the froth off the top as it appears. When most of the froth has been removed, add the bay leaves, parsley and carrots. Simmer for 3-4 hours, and then strain the stock.
2. To make the meatballs, mix the eggs, meat and oat or rice flour together, form small meatballs and place on a greased roasting tray.

3. Place in a hot oven and cook for 30–40 minutes or until nicely browned.
4. Transfer the balls to a large casserole or pot, cover with the stock and simmer for about 1 hour, or until the balls start to float.
5. Cool, then serve with the jelly or freeze as desired.

Ease of cooking: ★★☆
Preparation & cooking time: 5 hours
Freezes well.

Tina's Tip

Be ready for your pooch to ask you for second helpings. Most butchers usually have 'pet mince' for sale for a very reasonable price.

Lamb Gravy

Makes about 1 litre

Ingredients

2–3kg/4–6½lb lamb bones and trimmings
8 fresh bay leaves
2 tbsp black peppercorns
2 large onions
3 carrots
1 small celeriac
1 large leek
12 sprigs fresh thyme
6 sprigs fresh lavender
Small bunch parsley
2 tbsp cornflour

Method

1. Pre-heat oven to 160°.
2. Roughly chop the bones and trimmings and roast until well browned.
3. Drain the fat. Reserve.
4. Place the bones and trimmings into large saucepan.
5. Chop vegetables and add to the pot together with the herbs and peppercorns. Cover with clean cold water.
6. Bring to the boil, simmer gently for 3–5 hours, skimming as necessary.
7. Remove the bones and vegetables.
8. Pour the stock through a fine strainer and then through muslin.
9. Remove any fat that rises to the surface.
10. Bring the stock back to the boil and simmer until it has reduced to approx 25%. Taste frequently to assess strength of reduction.
11. Thicken the reduced stock with the cornflour mixed with a little cold water.
12. Season to taste.

Ease of cooking: ★☆☆
Preparation & cooking time: 4–5 hours

Pork Gravy

Makes about 1½ litres

Ingredients

4 litres good quality chicken stock
4kg/9lb pork bones and trimmings
1 head celery
3 large onions
4 medium parsnips
large bunch of fresh thyme
6 sprigs fresh sage
Small bunch parsley
⅓ cup juniper berries
½ cup cornflour

Method

1. Pre-heat oven to 160°.
2. Roughly chop the bones and trimmings and roast until well browned.
3. Drain the fat. Reserve.
4. Place the bones and trimmings into a large saucepan with the chicken stock.
5. Chop vegetables and add to the pot together with the herbs, juniper berries and peppercorns.
6. Bring to the boil, simmer gently for 3–4 hours, skimming as necessary.
7. Remove the bones and vegetables.
8. Pour the stock through a fine strainer and then through muslin.
9. Remove any fat that rises to the surface.
10. Bring the stock back to the boil and simmer until it has reduced to approx. 25%. Taste frequently to assess strength of reduction.
11. Thicken the reduced stock with the cornflour mixed with a little cold water.
12. Season to taste.

Ease of cooking: ★☆☆
Preparation & cooking time: 4–5 hours

Pork Terrine

Serves 6–8

Ingredients

1 whole cured pigs head
1 tbsp juniper berries
1 tbsp white peppercorns
Small handful of bay leaves
Large handful of parsley stalks
Generous bunch of thyme on the stalk
6 carrots
3 onions
1 large leek
Several cloves of garlic
1 tbsp coriander seed
Several sprigs fresh rosemary

Method

1. Soak the pig's head for several hours in clean cold water. Rinse and cover with more clean cold water. Leave in fridge overnight and then drain.
2. In a large stockpot, place all the vegetables, herbs and aromatics on the base followed by the pig's head. Cover with clean cold water and simmer for several hours until the meat gently falls away from the bone.
3. Lift the head out of the cooking liquor and leave to cool slightly.
4. Strain the liquor through a fine sieve, skim off the fat and simmer gently until reduced by half. Place a little in a chilled bowl to check that it will set.
5. Line a terrine mould with cling film or greaseproof paper and set aside. Alternatively the terrine can be kept in jars with rubber seals and clip down lids.
6. Remove all the meat from the pig's head, including the ear and the tongue (skin removed) and cut into even sized pieces.
7. Place in a large bowl, sprinkle with freshly ground black pepper, flat leaf parsley, finely chopped sage and some freshly picked thyme. Mix thoroughly. Taste to check seasoning.
8. Place in terrine mould pressing down gently. Leave meat slightly proud of the mould. Carefully pour the reduced liquor over the meat until it almost reaches the top of the mould.
9. Place terrine in a roasting dish or on a tray, cover with a board, place in the fridge with some weights on the board/tray.
10. Leave to set for 24 hours. If using jars, fill until level, pour over liquor and seal the lid.

The Sea

The Sea

Given the abundance of fish available to purchase from fishmongers, whether independent, in supermarkets, at a farmer's market or via the internet, it is often easy to forget that sea fish is the ultimate wild food: if the weather is bad then fresh fish will not be available. What is more, over-fishing means that certain species of fish are under threat.

The message is very simple: make friends with your fishmonger and shop with an open mind. If you have fallen in love with a recipe that demands sea bass and there is none, don't walk away. Find out what else they have in the same style of firm white-fleshed fish (grey mullet for example). Success in the kitchen – or in my kitchen at any rate – is based on being adaptable to whatever fresh produce is available.

Once you have made friends, follow your fishmonger's advice and experiment. For instance, I am a real fan of John Dory (St. Peter's fish). Here's a fish that is not widely used, as the spiny bones are really tricky to deal with. But next time you see John Dory fresh on the slab, snap it up and ask your fishmonger to fillet it for you. It has a fine delicate texture, and takes on flavours well. My favourite method is to treat it very gently: grill for just under one minute and serve with an elegant hollandaise sauce (p218) with finely chopped spring onions & chives. If you don't live near the coast, or a good fishmonger, then do investigate shopping via the internet. Ideally, choose the recipe once you have the fish, and not the other way round.

For a recipe to triumph, the key is quality of ingredient; if you have a limited selection of fish, find out what is freshest and then adapt a recipe to suit. Remember, fresh fish doesn't smell of fish, just of the sea. Use all your senses to choose your fish. The feel should be firm, the skin should be vibrant and the smell should be fresh and evoke thoughts of deliciousness.

The best place to learn about fish is at a fish auction. Plan to get up at dawn to travel to a market and reward yourself with a hearty breakfast in the traders' café once the early morning rush is over. These visits are a great way to get your 'eye in' to quality. Watch what the experts are buying – and rejecting – and look for the classic signs of superb fresh fish; the **bright eyes**, **glistening scales** and **deep red gills**. Londoners can make the trip to Billingsgate in the East End, and fish fans around the British Isles can find markets in such places as Bristol, Hastings, Lowestoft, Grimsby, Birmingham, Glasgow, Aberdeen, Newlyn, Plymouth, and Dublin and Cork in Ireland.

If you are serious about buying, take a pair of surgical gloves to wear and don't be afraid to touch the fish before you make a purchase. Show that you mean business but as always with a market, you have to be careful not to get in the way of trade! If you want to buy, you should be able to find someone who is prepared to sell you fish in small quantities, rather than by the box. I have learnt to look out for certain boats and skippers at our local auction just over the Cornish border at Looe. Just like buying beef from a particular herd, or cheese from a specialist cheese maker, so it's the same with fish. I like the *Cazadora* and *Hope* boats for squid and red mullet; *Temeraire* and *Lisanne* for ray and mackerel; *Kessenyans* for crab; *Mystique* for prime fish such as turbot and monkfish; and *Joanna* for scallops and my beloved John Dory.

I feel so exhilarated every time a selection of the freshest fish arrives, packed in ice, outside my kitchen door, knowing that it was caught only a matter of hours before. I can then start dreaming up recipes, while the fish it is still at its best. The essential point with fresh fish is that it tastes so wonderful; other ingredients on the plate should complement, not mask or compete with it. Follow my advice in the recipes that follow and you will be able to enjoy fish at its very finest.

Lightly Spiced Seafood Chowder

can be prepared ahead

This simple chunky soup is a personal favourite. Warming, homely and comforting with a real depth of flavour, the inspiration for this spiced chowder came from two wonderful Sri Lankan brothers (former employees), Upendra and Sampath, who used to bring me fresh herbs and spices from their garden in Colombo. Procuring a good fish stock is pretty essential in this recipe. If you are able to get hold of fresh lemon grass and curry leaves to flavour the stock it is well worth it – they give an altogether different dimension to the finished soup.

Serves 4

Ingredients

30ml/2 tbsp olive or avocado oil
2 tsp cumin seed
1 tbsp root ginger, chopped
1 tbsp garlic, chopped
1 red chilli, de-seeded and finely chopped
340g/12oz onion, finely chopped
340g/12oz leek, diced
1 tbsp ground turmeric
1150ml/2 pints good quality fish stock (p62)
¼ cup cornflour mixed with a little cold water
340g/12oz coconut milk or 1 x 200g packet of creamed coconut
510g/18oz mixed fish (whiting, red mullet, sole, plaice, prawns, haddock, gurnard, John Dory) filleted, small bones removed, cut into even-sized pieces (your fishmonger can do this for you)
½ cup chopped parsley & chives

Method

1. Pour the oil into a large thick-bottomed saucepan. When it's hot, add the cumin seeds and stir until lightly browned.
2. Add the ginger and stir for another minute, then the garlic and stir for a further minute.
3. Now mix in the finely chopped onion and chilli, cover with a lid and cook gently until the onions are almost opaque.
4. Add the turmeric and cook for about 5 minutes.
5. Pour in the fish stock and bring everything to the boil, then add the cornflour and water before setting the mixture to simmer for 5 minutes.
6. Add the leeks and allow to bubble away for a further 2 minutes.
7. Stir in the coconut and simmer for a further 5 minutes, or until the consistency of the soup is nice and thick with lots of body. Check the seasoning.
8. Finally, add the diced fish, cook for two minutes, then throw in the large handful of chopped parsley & chives and serve immediately.

Tina's Tip

The base (everything except the fish and the herbs) can be made in advance then re-heated or frozen. If you envisage needing this in a hurry, freeze in shallow containers to enable fast thawing.

Take particular care not to let the fish overcook or it will spoil the texture of the chowder. Also, it is important to chop the herbs at the last minute to ensure that you capture their flavour in the finished soup.

This recipe can be adapted to include potatoes, peas, corn kernels or baby broad beans – to make it either more substantial or to stretch to a few more portions.

Ease of cooking: ★ ☆ ☆
This is a doddle; just make sure the pan does not get too hot as it is quite easy to burn the onions and spices.
Preparation & cooking time: 40 minutes

Prawn, Skate & Haddock Pie

an unusual cold picnic dish

One summer weekend I had a group of four gentlemen attending one of my fish cookery workshops. A couple of them had tried to fillet fish before, but on the whole we had to start from scratch. Filleting isn't the easiest of jobs for any cook, as the initial results of my students demonstrated. Admiring the pile of 'fillets' before us, we decided that they might best be presented in a white sauce, and covered tactfully with a layer of pastry.

The full on flavour of this delicious pie is suitable for numerous occasions. Hot for a brunch, cold for a picnic or made into individual parcels for a dinner party. The use of gelatinous fish such as skate or conger eel adds a wonderful texture. It sets firm when chilled and slices extremely well.

Serves 6

Ingredients

Quantity of shortcrust pastry (page 239)
1 egg mixed with a teaspoon of water for egg wash

For the filling

340g/12oz skate wing, skin & bone-free (you can ask your fishmonger to help with this), cut into 2cm pieces
200g/7oz whole peeled prawns
200g/7oz haddock
60g/2oz butter
60g/2oz plain flour
300ml/11 fl oz good quality fish stock (p62) or alternatively use a fish stock cube
150ml/5½ fl oz white wine
3 tbsp parsley or tarragon, or a mix
Sea salt
Freshly ground black pepper

Method

To bake the pastry case

1. First pre-heat your oven to 200°C.
2. Using a rolling pin to roll the pastry, line a 20cm/8" flan ring, taking care to push the pastry into the corner at the base.
3. Trim the excess pastry and chill the lined flan-ring for 10 minutes.
4. Line with baking parchment or foil, fill with baking beans (ceramic beans to hold the sides of the pastry case up) and place in the oven to cook for 10 minutes.
5. Remove the baking beans and parchment or foil and prick the pastry base with a fork. Return to the oven and bake for a further 10 minutes.
6. Remove from oven and leave to cool.

To make the filling and assemble

1. Melt the butter in a saucepan and add the flour. Stir over a gentle heat for 5 minutes.

2. Little by little, pour in the fish stock and wine, beating the mix well to prevent any lumps forming. Add salt and pepper to taste and leave to cool for 5 minutes. Stir in the fish and herbs to the white sauce, taste to check the seasoning and pour the mix into the cooked pastry case.

3. Brush the edges of the pastry case with the egg wash, roll the remainder of the pastry to cover the pie, press the edges down firmly to seal, and trim excess pastry with a sharp knife.

4. Cut a few slits in the lid to allow steam to escape and bake for 30 minutes at 200°C or until the mix is bubbling gently from the centre of the pie.

5. Leave to settle for about 10 minutes before serving.

Ease of cooking: ★ ★ ★
The pastry case can be tricky, but well worth the effort.
Preparation & cooking time: 75 minutes

Tina's Tip

Almost any fish can be used for this pie, but if you are unable to source gelatinous fish and you want to make a pie suitable for a picnic, add a little dissolved gelatine (enough to set 570ml/1 pint liquid) to the fish stock and wine as you are making the filling. If you prefer a gluten-free fish dish, without pastry, simply place the fish mixture in a well-greased earthenware dish and cover with a spring onion, celeriac and potato mash. Again, bake for 30 minutes in an oven pre-heated to 200°C.

Gravad Mackerel

easy and light

Many moons ago, when I had just taken over the kitchen at Percy's wine bar and restaurant in north London and my assistant chef walked out unexpectedly, a Swedish man who was drinking at the bar heard of my plight and offered to give me a hand on his day off. He was a chef called Klaus and ran a Swedish restaurant in Belgravia. His help was a godsend, especially as we had a full restaurant and I was still trying to find my feet. He helped me again the next weekend and taught me how to make gravadlax (cured salmon). His other speciality was rolling pork meatballs – he could make 500 single-handed in one hour!

Curing salmon was so easy that it became a regular feature on the menu. This cure is a Swedish speciality, which is suitable for many different types of fish. It is a very healthy way to prepare a delicious dish for a starter, light lunch or even as a canapé. The salt-cured raw fish can also be lightly grilled and served hot.

For this recipe I have chosen mackerel, a common fish found in the North Atlantic and Mediterranean waters. Their season lasts from the autumn to midsummer but the fish are at their best during April, May and June. Mackerel are not in danger of extinction; in fact they are quite prolific, which is reflected in their low price. Not only is mackerel very tasty, it's extremely good for you, being full of essential omega 3. However, due to the relatively high oil content, this fish does spoil quickly and should ideally be eaten within 24 hours of leaving the sea.

Serves 4

Ingredients

1kg/2lb 3oz mackerel fillets
65g/2½oz/2 tbsp soft brown sugar
60g/2oz/1½ tbsp sea salt
15g/½oz/1 tbsp white peppercorns
15g/½oz/2 tbsp coriander seed
1 large handful of fresh dill, including the
young stems, coarsely chopped

Method

1. Place the peppercorns and coriander seed in a robust plastic bag and crush with a wooden mallet. Add to the sea salt and soft brown sugar, and mix thoroughly.
2. Sprinkle the mix onto a stainless steel, plastic or ceramic dish or tray, preferably perforated. Sprinkle the dill on top. Place the mackerel fillets skin side up on top of the mix. Leave them like this for two days but no longer (the aroma of the ingredients used for this recipe will stimulate your appetite and make you want to eat the fish way before it is ready). If the dish you use does not allow the liquid to drain, then check the fish after the first day and pour off the juices.
3. Remove from dish, pat dry, and slice at an angle. Use immediately, possibly served with mustard & honey dressing (p178).

Ease of cooking: ★☆☆
Preparation time: 20 minutes
Freezes well.

Tina's Tip

Try tarragon or chervil instead of the dill. Trout, salmon, cod and sea bass also work very well.

Squid, Scallop & Sweet Cure Bacon Salad

exotic and fast

When you are out to impress and need something light and exotic – and you need it fast – follow me...

There are two secrets to this simple dish: fresh ingredients and timing. The combination of textures is as exciting as the different flavours: crisp warm sweet-cured bacon, caramelized scallop meat and tender melt-in-the-mouth-squid all pulled together with the definitive flavours of coriander, mustard and honey.

Serves 4

Ingredients

4 small-medium squid, cleaned and sliced into even sized pieces
4 queen scallops per person, corals removed
2 large slices of middle back or streaky bacon, grilled (fat reserved)
Selection of salad leaves
Quantity of mustard & honey dressing (p178)
1 bunch of fresh coriander washed, drained and chopped
Sea salt & freshly ground black pepper

Method

1. First prepare a selection of mixed salad leaves of your choice and pop them in the fridge.
2. Next, warm a small amount of olive oil or bacon fat in a heavy frying pan or skillet. When this is hot and almost smoking (pour off any excess fat so that the pan has just a light coating) add the scallops and sear for no more than a minute on either side until golden brown, then draw the pan off the heat and rest.
3. In a separate frying pan heat a little more oil or bacon fat. Swirl the fat around the pan to coat the sides and pour off most of it, leaving the pan evenly coated. When this has had a chance to heat up, add the cleaned, well-drained squid and leave to sear for a couple of minutes. Sprinkle with a little sea salt and black pepper and then toss to sear the squid evenly on both sides. Draw the pan off the heat and rest.
4. Cut the cooked bacon into 2 cm slices and place under a grill until crisp and hot.
5. Assemble the salad by sprinkling the salad leaves with a little of the chopped coriander. Drizzle the dressing over this, place the squid on top followed by the scallops and lastly the bacon.

Ease of cooking: ★★☆ Quite easy
Preparation & cooking time: 45 minutes

Tina's Tip

It is important that the pan is hot and the squid is quite dry when it goes in – if it isn't, it may boil, which can alter the texture and toughen the squid. For best results prepare the squid the day before, drain in a colander and then leave overnight in a container lined with a dry cloth. Small squid are much more tender than large and need far less cooking. If only large squid is available, freeze it overnight and then thaw slowly (allow 48 hours if you can) in the coldest part of the fridge before preparing, as the freezing helps to tenderise the flesh.

For non-meat eaters the bacon can of course be dropped from this recipe.

Steamed Tarragon Turbot & Asparagus, Celeriac Mash, Béarnaise Sauce

easy, impressive dinner party

This is such a great treat when entertaining friends. It is a combination of the king of all sea fish – the turbot – and the king of the vegetables – English asparagus. The turbot has a great-tasting meaty texture and the slow-growing English asparagus has the best flavour in the world with a fine, tender texture. It is also very easy to cook and is truly delicious. The sauce can be made a little in advance, as can the mash, so you can just sit back and enjoy the company of your guests.

Serves 8

Ingredients

8 boneless turbot steaks, skin left on (optional)
Quantity of Béarnaise sauce (p218-9)
90g/3oz melted butter
500g/1¼lb fresh asparagus
Large bunch fresh tarragon
600g/20oz peeled potato of a floury variety such as King Edward
600g/20oz peeled celeriac root
Sea salt
Freshly ground black pepper

Method

1. Sprinkle the turbot steaks with a little sea salt. Set aside, skin side down.
2. Place a handful of the tarragon in the base of a saucepan, add the celeriac and potato then cover with cold water and add a generous pinch of salt. Bring to the boil and simmer for about 30 minutes or until cooked, then drain immediately, reserving the cooking water.
3. Mash the potato and celeriac with the melted butter. If too stiff, add a little potato water. Season, set aside and keep warm.
4. Place the turbot fillets skin side up in a steamer on top of a bunch of tarragon. (The flavour of the tarragon meanders right on through the fish as it is steaming).
5. Steam for 6–8 minutes depending on the thickness and the temperature of the fish. When the fish is cooked there should be a 'give' in the flesh when you touch it lightly.
6. When the fish is nearly ready, cook the asparagus in boiling salted water for 3 minutes, then drain. Serve the fish skin side down, or skin removed, with the mash, asparagus and Béarnaise.

Ease of cooking: ★☆☆
Relatively easy though careful planning is needed.
Preparation time: 40 minutes
Cooking time: 30 minutes

Tina's Tip

When purchasing turbot, ask for a mature male fish. Well-developed muscle has both a superior texture and flavour (because all the energy goes into the flesh and not into reproduction). Remember that turbot bones are the very best you can get for making fish stock, so, if your fishmonger has filleted your fish for you, bring the bones home and, if you don't have time to prepare them immediately, freeze them to make stock at a later date (page 62).

If you do not have a steamer in your kitchen, improvise by placing a colander over a saucepan filled with a little water and cover the colander with a lid.

Kedgeree

great celebration breakfast or hearty supper

Kedgeree (khichri) was first established in Britain as a Scottish breakfast dish in the C18th and consisted of cooked rice, hard-boiled egg and haddock, which were combined, heated, seasoned and garnished with parsley. The origins of kedgeree, however, lie in India – there it started as a dish based on rice, onions and red or green lentils. With the British Colonial influence in India, the dish was developed to include early morning-caught fish, turmeric powder, fresh chilli, root ginger and fried onion. When the dish migrated to Scotland, it coincided with the launch of stagecoach distribution for 'Finnan Haddock', which then was heavily salted in order to withstand long journeys, so the bland accompanying ingredients were a good way to dilute the impact of the strong, salty fish flavour. Nowadays there is scope to add a number of other interesting ingredients to the otherwise blank canvas of rice, egg and fish, such as freshly ground spices, fresh herbs, legumes and fresh chillies.

I like to use the following basic recipe for breakfast and a spicier version opposite for a meal later in the day. This dish is one to perfect to individual taste, so do experiment and make note when you have reached a winning combination for yourself!

Breakfast Kedgeree

Serves 6

Ingredients

450g/1lb smoked haddock.
6 hard-boiled eggs, roughly chopped
1 cup Basmati or long-grain white rice
90g/3oz unsalted butter
2 medium onions, chopped fairly fine
1 tbsp of turmeric
2 tsp mild curry powder
285ml/½ pint water
1 large bunch of parsley
Black pepper and salt
Pinch of paprika

Method

1. Place the smoked haddock in a saucepan with the water and some parsley stalks (for added flavour) and cook for approx. 8 minutes. Cool and then flake the fish into pieces, removing all the bones and skin. Reserve the cooking liquor.
2. Melt the butter in a pan, add the onions and cook gently until opaque. Add the turmeric and curry powder and cook for a further five minutes or so.
3. Add the rice, cooking liquor and a little cold water, put the lid on and cook for approximately 15 minutes or until the rice is tender.
4. Add the flaked smoked haddock and stir in gently until warmed through, taking care not to break up the fish pieces.

5. Roughly chop the eggs and the parsley, then mix it all up, gently and thoroughly. Check seasoning.

6. Sprinkle with a pinch of paprika and serve either hot or cold.

Spiced Kedgeree

Smoky fish, fragrant rice, vibrant green peas or beans and some skillful Anglo-Indian spicing make this racy version a more adventurous and spicier dish suitable for a hearty lunch, picnics or a hearty informal supper.

Follow the breakfast recipe above, omit the curry powder and then add the following, together with the turmeric:

1 tbsp minced garlic together with the onions

1 tsp cumin seed

1 tsp ground coriander

1 tsp fennel seed

1 tsp fenugreek seed

1 tsp onion seed

1 tbsp freshly grated root ginger

1 tbsp harissa paste

Ease of cooking: ★☆☆
Preparation time: 10 minutes
Cooking time: 35 minutes
Freezes well. Tastes great cold, straight from the fridge.

Tina's Tip

Use a few bay or curry leaves with the rice during cooking.

You can substitute coriander, sweet marjoram, leaf celery, lovage or tarragon for the parsley.

Freshwater elvers and eels, trout, salmon and pike can all be lightly smoked and used as a substitute for smoked haddock. Sometimes peas are added for a little sweetness – if you are growing peas, mange tout or even broad beans, try boiling a few in a little water for about 1 minute and then adding them to the dish. They will add vibrant colour, texture and superb flavour.

Fillets of John Dory in a Spring Onion and Coriander Batter, Tomato Salsa

classic with a twist

John Dory is a very underrated fish, often overlooked due to its incredibly ugly head and thorny spines. However, it has a marvellous delicate flavour and a nice firm texture; its fine delicate flesh lends itself to being steamed, fried, grilled or poached. Cooking the John Dory in batter encapsulates the sweet fish juices and adds a nice contrasting crunchy texture, whilst the acidity and the sweetness of the tomato salsa with the piquancy of the capers and saltiness of the pilchards balance the richness of the batter.

Serve with chips for a twist on the classic!

Serves 4

Ingredients

2 large or 4 small John Dory, filleted, bones reserved
90g/3oz butter for frying
Quantity of spring onion & coriander batter (see opposite)
Quantity of tomato salsa (p84)
Sea salt
225g/8oz plain flour

Method

1. Sprinkle the fillets with a little sea salt. Leave to stand for 10 minutes.
2. Heat the butter in a large heavy-bottomed frying pan.
3. Dust the fish fillets with the flour and then pass them through the batter.
4. Place in the heated frying pan.
5. Cook gently for 2–3 minutes on either side or until golden brown.
6. Serve accompanied by a bowl of the tomato salsa.

Ease of cooking: ★ ★ ☆
Organise the rest of the meal; so that when the fish is cooked it can be served immediately.
Preparation & cooking time: 50 minutes

Tina's Tip

Take care to cook the batter slowly and evenly – if the pan is too hot, you will end up burning the batter before the fish has a chance to cook.

Sole, hake, cod (skins left on), gurnard, small turbot and sea bass are all good substitutes for John Dory. Salting the fish not only seasons it, it helps to draw out some of the juices and firm up the flesh. This makes a difference if using very fresh cod for example, as you may find that the fish juices leach into the batter, preventing it from crisping up.

Spring Onion & Coriander Batter

Ingredients

225g/8oz plain flour
285ml/½ pint milk (room temperature)
Small ball of fresh yeast (size of a large marble)
1 bunch of spring onions, washed and trimmed
1 bunch of fresh coriander, washed and drained

Method

1. In a glass bowl, make a paste with the yeast and some of the milk.
2. Add some flour and mix, followed by some of the milk until all the flour and milk has been added and the mixture is smooth and lump free.
3. Add salt & pepper.
4. Chop the spring onions & coriander and add to the mix.
5. Leave to stand in a warm place for 20 minutes before using.

Herring Roes on Sesame Toast with Capers & Horseradish Crème Fraîche

unusual, inexpensive starter or light supper

As a child I can remember the time that I was just tall enough for my eyes to survey the fish counter, if I stood on tiptoe. At the front, nestling closely against the washable plastic parsley was always a tray of the silky, shiny, soft herring roes, which invariably sat next to a larger tray holding fresh sprats. I had no idea at the time that these roes (milts) were from male fish, but the way my mother prepared them was sublime. Cooking on a budget was not something I related to as a child, but I now know just what my mother achieved feeding us all such sumptuous, innovatively prepared, nutritious and delicious food at low cost. This incredibly inexpensive dish makes an excellent starter or light supper served with a salad and some crusty bread to mop up the delicious buttery juices.

Serves 4

Ingredients

450g/1 lb soft herring roes
170g/6 oz butter
1 tbsp lemon juice
Plain flour
4 slices sesame seed bread (p224), toasted
Large bunch of parsley, finely chopped
Freshly ground black pepper & sea salt
1 small tub crème fraîche
1 tbsp horseradish sauce
¼ cup of capers, drained

Method

1. In a large frying pan or skillet, melt the butter.
2. Dust the herring roes in the flour and shake off the excess.
3. Fry the roes in the pan until golden on all sides.
4. Place the warm toast onto four plates and spoon the roes onto the toast.
5. Add the lemon juice to the pan (from which you have removed the fish) and stir to incorporate all the juices.
6. Bring to the boil; add the capers, pepper and finally most of the parsley then drizzle over the roes.
7. Mix the horseradish and crème fraîche together and then spoon a dollop of it on the top.
8. Garnish with the remaining parsley and black pepper and serve hot.

Ease of cooking: ★☆☆ Very easy
Preparation time: 10 minutes
Cooking time: 10 minutes

Brown Paper Bag Sprats

easy and nutritious

Another childhood favourite – sprats are crunchy, crispy and very more-ish as well as being full of vitamins A & D, omega 3 and calcium. This complete little meal used to feature heavily in our diets as growing kids. My mother was a nurse, who knew the RDA's (recommended daily intakes of vitamins and minerals) and made sure we all got our fair share. 'Eat the heads and you can have a square of chocolate after dinner,' she would say (yes, a square!). It worked, and I am banking on living until well past 100. The other bonus is that they are very cheap, only costing a few pence each.

Serve with a large plate of roasted potato wedges, Mediterranean chutney and steamed courgettes or crunchy mange tout.

Serves 2

Ingredients

450g/1lb sprats
225g/8oz wholemeal flour
1 large lemon, cut into wedges
Salt and black pepper
Oil or butter for frying

Method

1. Put the wholemeal flour into a strong brown paper bag, add a generous pinch of salt and the sprats and shake vigorously until all fish is well coated.
2. Knock off the excess flour and shallow fry in oil or butter.
3. Grind some black pepper over the top and serve with crusty bread, lots of lemon wedges and a salad.

Ease of cooking: ★ ☆ ☆
Extremely simple.
Preparation & cooking time: 15 minutes

Tina's Tip

Sprats are in season from November to March. They freeze well and can be dusted and fried from frozen, so snap them up whilst they are plentiful and keenly priced. By the way, you don't *have* to have a brown paper bag for this recipe!

The Very Best Grilled Lobster

easy treat

Lobster flesh is more meaty than fishy, its outstanding flavour being directly related to its diet, which typically consists of crabs, clams, mussels, and an occasional sea urchin or slow-witted flat fish. Sometimes lobsters might catch a crab, and then drag it back to their home to bury it (just like a dog buries a bone). The lobster then stays in for the next few nights nibbling away at his catch!

Because lobster meat can go bad quickly, it's generally necessary to obtain a lobster while it's still alive.

To enjoy it at its best, first place your live lobster in a freezer for ½-1 hour (this numbs them). Then simply split it in half by inserting a knife firstly into its head (which is the most humane way) before turning the lobster on its back and cutting it lengthways in half. Then remove the intestine and the gills. That means you pick a blue lobster, but don't eat it until its shell turns red! Never eat a cooked lobster with its tail uncurled, as it died before it was cooked.

Once cleaned, spread garlic butter liberally over the flesh, sprinkle with coarse sea salt and freshly ground black pepper and grill for approx. 5–7 minutes or until half cooked. At this point, coat the lobster tails with a little pesto, sprinkle a handful of breadcrumbs and some finely grated Parmesan cheese on top and then grill lightly to gratinate and finish cooking (if you are preparing a number of lobsters and are short of grill space, a very hot oven can be used to roast them instead).

Serve hot with lots of lemon or lime wedges, freshly dug boiled new potatoes, a big bowl of green salad and a nicely chilled bottle of your favourite Chablis.

Ease of cooking: ★ ☆ ☆
Very easy, once you have managed to split the lobster.
Preparation & cooking time: 20 minutes

Tina's Tip

A freshly-caught, healthy lobster should have a claw that is full and fleshy, not atrophied. When prepared for selling, the lobster claws are generally held together with a strong elastic band to prevent injury to each other and to handlers. However, the inability to move their claws causes the muscle meat to start wasting away, which alters both its texture and flavour. Generally speaking, if you are looking to buy a lobster, don't be afraid to pick it up to ascertain the liveliness and the weight. The fresher the lobster, the heavier it will seem and the more it will struggle. To buy the very freshest lobsters, search for lobster pots on the internet and ask the craftsmen who make them, who uses them – track down the fishermen and see if you can buy a lobster or two straight off the boat and either collect them on-site or get them posted overnight. This way, you will know that they have not spent days in tanks waiting for someone to purchase them.

Sea Bass en Papillotte with Summer Vegetables

healthy – and can be prepared ahead

Baking in parchment or foil is a fabulous way to enjoy a fat-free flavoursome dish that can be prepared ahead of time and only takes minutes to cook. The fish can be served in its own little parcel for an interesting presentation.

Serves 4

Ingredients

1360g/3lb whole sea bass, scaled, gutted and filleted or four 170g/6oz boneless fillets
2 large turnips
12 asparagus spears
1 large carrot, peeled
4 large spring onions
1 large piece of root ginger, peeled or several pieces of crytallized ginger
Generous handful of parsley, chervil, coriander or tarragon
4 tbsp dry white wine
Olive oil or butter for greasing
Sea salt & freshly ground black pepper

Method

1. Sprinkle the flesh side of the fish with salt 10–20 minutes before cooking.
2. Lay out four large pieces of foil or baking parchment, greased and season.
3. Peel the base of the asparagus spears (unless just picked) and slice off the top 5cm/1" of the tips at an angle. Cut the rest of the stem into neat diamond shapes of the same length.
4. Cut the carrot and turnip into matchsticks. Slice the spring onion and either grate the ginger or cut into very fine strips.
5. Mix the vegetables together with the herbs and ginger and lay on the foil.
6. Place the fish on top of the vegetables, skin side up. Season.
7. Add a tablespoon of wine to each parcel and seal by crimping the edges together.
8. Pre-heat oven to 180°C.
9. Cook for approx. 10 minutes and serve with new potatoes, mange tout or beans.

Ease of cooking: ★☆☆
Preparation & cooking time: 30 minutes

Tina's Tip

If you get the chance, prepare this dish to stage 7 ahead of time, as it gives the fish the chance to absorb the flavours of its companion ingredients.

Tope Teriyaki

simple and quick to assemble

I first discovered Tope in the late 1980s, when its reputation was as a prized game fish as opposed to a culinary ingredient. It was incredibly inexpensive and a wonderful fish to experiment with. The texture of the flesh is quite meaty but soft; the flesh has a fairly strong flavour, tastes sweet and cooks up well, dusted in flour and pan-fried to get a nice crispy coating. This fish can take most sauces destined for chicken due to its meat-like texture and is exceptionally good with wild mushrooms, chicken stock, cream, lemon juice and tarragon (tope stroganoff). The recipe below is a nice one to start with when experimenting with tope. It works equally well on a barbeque, pan-fried or grilled and makes an excellent light easy supper.

Serves 8

Ingredients

8 tope steaks or skinned fillets, weighing approx. 170g/6oz each

For the sauce:
½ cup tamari or soy sauce
½ cup medium or dry sherry
¼ cup grated fresh root ginger
2 tbsp toasted sesame oil
2 tbsp honey or soft brown sugar
4 cloves garlic, chopped

Method
1. Combine all the sauce ingredients.
2. Add the fish and marinate for 20 minutes–1 hour, turning from time to time.
3. Drain. Pan fry, grill or steam.

Ease of cooking: ★☆☆
The cooking time will depend on the thickness of your steaks, how cold they are and which method you adopt, but as a rough guide, cook for 3–4 minutes either side or 6-8 minutes if steaming.
Preparation & cooking time: 20 minutes
Marinading time: 30 minutes

Tina's Tip

If tope is not available, alternative fish include swordfish, shark, and tuna (although the latter needs very little cooking at a high heat).

Cornish Crab Pasty

an unusual picnic idea

The pasty originally evolved in conjunction with tin mining. The story goes that the miners, covered in dirt from head to foot (including traces of arsenic, often found with the tin), could hold the pasty by the folded crust and eat the rest without touching it, discarding the dirty pastry, thereby avoiding poisoning themselves!

Serves 6

Ingredients

450g/1lb crab meat, cooked and flaked
225g/8oz cold mashed potato
Juice of 1 lemon
Bunch of parsley, chopped
Freshly ground black pepper

For the pastry:
4 cups plain flour
225g/8oz suet
½ tsp salt
Cold water to mix
1 egg, beaten with a little water

Method

1. Sieve the flour and salt into a bowl. Add the suet, combine and mix with just enough water to make a good paste.
2. Roll out to ¼ inch thick and cut into rounds about 6 inches in diameter.
3. Check and remove any broken shell. Moisten the crab meat with the lemon juice, mix with the parsley and combine with the potato and some freshly ground black pepper.
4. Take a round of pastry and put it on a floured surface. Brush the edges with egg wash, put a large spoonful of the crab mixture onto one half, then fold the other side over to make a semi-circular pasty.
5. Crimp the edges down neatly, brush with egg-wash and make a slit in the middle of the top to let out the steam.
6. Pre-heat the oven to 180°C. Bake the pasties on a greased baking sheet for about 20 minutes, or until golden brown.

Ease of cooking: ★ ★ ☆
Preparation time: 30 minutes
Cooking time: 20 minutes

Tina's Tip

If you are able to buy fresh crab, look out for a 2kg/4½lb cock crab (they are much fleshier and easier to prepare due to their size). Then cook in water that has been brought to the boil with lots of garden herbs (lovage is my favourite for shellfish), some whole white peppercorns, bay leaves, carrots and onions for approx 15 minutes. Leave to cool for about 10 minutes and then remove all the meat and juices into a bowl.

Red Mullet, Whiting & Chervil Fishcakes

ladies' lunch or child's supper

One of the most popular starter dishes I have ever prepared has been red mullet chipolatas. Some years ago, my friendly butcher taught me how to make sausages, which was great fun indeed. Then lateral thinking gave me the idea of making fish sausages. I asked my butcher if he would make some for me. He willingly took delivery of the fishcake mix I prepared (transported in a cool box), stuffed the mix into sausage skins and then returned them to me. If you happen to own a sausage filler, you will have tremendous fun stuffing and linking the sausages; if not, then just follow the recipe and form into fishcakes. Serve for a ladies lunch or child's supper with mashed potato and tomato salsa (page 84).

Serves 6

Ingredients

225g/8oz red mullet fillets, bones and skin removed
225g/8oz whiting fillets, bones and skin removed
80g/2 egg whites
¼ cup crème fraîche
2 tbsp flour or potato starch
¼ tsp cayenne pepper
½ tsp salt
Bunch of spring onions, finely sliced
Bunch of fresh tarragon, finely chopped
Quantity of herbed mayonnaise
170g/6oz butter for frying
Quantity of sausage skins

Method

1. Mince or chop the fish very finely.
2. Add the fish, tarragon and spring onions to the rest of the ingredients.
3. Fry a little of the mix in order to taste and to correct the texture and the seasoning if needed.
4. Stuff the mix into sausage skins or divide into 6 large or 12 small balls and then flatten to form patties.
5. Pan-fry the sausages or patties in butter for 2–3 minutes on each side. They can also be grilled, poached or steamed. Serve with herbed mayonnaise

Ease of cooking: ★☆☆
Simple to prepare.
Preparation & cooking time: 20 minutes

Tina's Tip

As a starter, simply shape small ovals of the mix between two dessert spoons (quenelles) and drop into simmering salted water or preferably fish stock. When the fish is cooked, the quenelles will rise to the surface. Serve with tagliatelle and white wine sauce.

Salmon

Salmon and other oily fish are excellent sources of the essential omega-3 fatty acids, which are important in the fight against cardiovascular disease and can reduce the likelihood of rheumatoid arthritis. It is also good for babies' brain development and it is therefore of great benefit for pregnant and breast-feeding women to include oily fish in their diet.

Now, to my mind, there's nothing wrong with eating ordinary farmed salmon but wild salmon definitely has a far superior taste and texture. I researched both conventionally and organically farmed salmon to identify the differences between them, which are:

There are no antibiotics, growth promoters, hormones or artificial colouring used in the rearing of organic salmon which results in the fish taking twice as long to reach maturity. Due to the fact that the stocking density is a great deal lower (8 kg per m^2 as opposed to 25kg per m^2), the fish have more room to display their natural behavioural traits, and the result is that the flesh of the salmon is of a totally different make-up, as it has developed properly and not been forced.

The organic salmon is reared in off-shore locations in areas of high tidal flow so that the fish are able to swim naturally and the result is that the flesh has a consistency more like that of wild salmon. The feed is all a bi-product of fish used for human consumption together with crushed prawn shells from processors. The feed has to be from the same geographical area, which in the case of salmon is the North Atlantic.

In contrast, conventionally farmed salmon has a lot of oil in the feed, in order to bulk out the flesh of the fish considerably, and in so doing the flesh retains far more water.

When curing salmon for smoking it is immersed in brine to draw out the liquid to dry out the flesh to inhibit bacterial growth. As the organic salmon contains less water within the flesh, it absorbs far less salt (up to 40% less in fact) than conventional salmon, which needs longer in the brine to draw out the extra water in the flesh. This is particularly helpful for those who need to keep their salt-intake to a minimum.

Smoked Salmon Pâté

has to be the easiest recipe ever

Something tasty to nibble on Melba toast, or a treat in a sandwich with some thinly sliced cucumber. This could be used as a tasty filling for puff pastry or filo parcels. Organic salmon tends to be paler than the strong pink we associate with farmed salmon. Do not worry, you are eating a creature which has not been fed artificial colouring.

Serves 4–6

Ingredients

225g/8oz organic smoked salmon, cut into small pieces
170g/6oz organic low fat cream cheese
1 tbsp lemon juice
Freshly ground black pepper

Method

Place all ingredients in a food processor and blend.

Ease of cooking: ★☆☆
Preparation time: 10 minutes

Tina's Tip

This will keep in jars in the fridge and also freezes well. If you have time on your hands just after Christmas or New Year and have a party coming up in the ensuing weeks, why not raid the post-festive season half-price offers and make this in bulk to store?

Cajun Salmon

unusual, easy standby

This is a first-rate recipe for when you are really under pressure. Make sure you have a jar of Cajun spice (which you can make yourself) in the fridge just for the occasions when you are short of time and ideas.

Serves 4

Ingredients

4 organic salmon steaks
Quantity of Cajun spice (see this page)
1 large lemon

Method

1. Coat the salmon with the Cajun spice.
2. Cover and leave in a cool place for 1–2 hours.
3. Heat a cast iron skillet or heavy frying pan which you have brushed very sparingly with a little oil or butter, then heat until the pan is almost smoking.
4. Add the steaks to the pan.
5. Cook for 3 minutes on either side.
6. Leave to rest in the pan for 3–4 minutes (to finish cooking).
7. Cut the lemon into wedges and serve with the salmon.

Ease of cooking: ★☆☆
Preparation & cooking time: 10 minutes

Tina's Tip

Salmon freezes beautifully due to its oily make up, so, when you are next chatting to your fishmonger, ask him when he normally gets a salmon delivery and to set aside some really fresh salmon steaks to freeze.

Cajun Spice

Ingredients

5g/1 tbsp ground bay leaf
5g/1 tbsp ground cumin
5g/1 tbsp ground coriander
110g/¼ cup garlic pûrée
10g/2 tbsp mustard powder
20g/¼ cup paprika
30g/⅓ cup dried or ground thyme
60ml/¼ cup brandy
45ml/3 tbsp sweet sherry
120ml/½ cup lemon juice

Method

Combine all ingredients and mix to a paste. Store in a jar in the refrigerator until needed.

Fish Stock

Makes 2 litres

Ingredients

510g/18oz fish trimmings (you can include heads and bones and skin of most types of fish, but try to avoid oily fish such as red mullet, salmon and mackerel)

3 leeks or 5 medium onions

1 bulb fennel, ½ a celeriac or 2 sticks celery

3 carrots

2 large handfuls fresh herbs: parsley, chervil, thyme, dill or tarragon

340ml/12fl oz dry white wine

Method

1. Rinse the fish bones and trimmings of any blood.
2. Roughly chop all the vegetables and herbs (including the stalks) and place into the stockpot.
3. Add the fish trimmings to the stockpot.
5. Pour in the white wine, then add enough cold water to cover the fish and vegetables (about 2 litres/4 pints).

6. Place the stockpot onto a high heat and bring the liquid to just below boiling point. Turn down to simmer. After five minutes, remove the scum that forms on the surface with a spoon and discard.
7. Cook for about 35 minutes, skimming as necessary.
8. At the end of cooking time, remove the stock from the heat and strain, discarding the fish trimmings and the vegetables.
9. Cool and store the stock in the fridge for up to three days. Alternatively, it can be frozen.

Tina's Tip

If you get the chance, soak the fish bones in cold salted water for a couple of hours, this will draw out any residual blood which could make the stock bitter and cloudy. To cool the stock quickly, add an ice pack made from filling a plastic milk bottle ⅔ with water and then freezing it. If you are short of freezer space, boil the fish stock until it is well reduced and then freeze it.

The Vegetable Garden

The Vegetable Garden

In 1990 we were awarded a Michelin 'Red M' for our London restaurant. We put this down not only to the cooking but the effort we put into sourcing fresh, top quality ingredients. At the time, we had a Peugeot pickup truck and used to do a twice-weekly eight mile run leaving at 4.30am to the fruit, vegetable & flower wholesale market near Hayes, in Middlesex. In the market, we were able to select the best quality fruit, vegetables and flowers for the restaurant. Our efforts paid off. The customer comments were positive, and our reputation quickly went from strength to strength.

Soon after, we bought the Coombeshead Estate in Devon, today Percy's Country Hotel and Restaurant, and we decided to employ someone local to grow vegetables for the London restaurant. Two or three times a week, Ann, the gardener, would pack several boxes of freshly harvested vegetables with chill packs, then bundle them into her truck and drive to a layby on the A30 where she met the fully stocked fish lorry from Looe, on its way to London. This way, we were able to supply our London restaurant with our own produce, which was delivered together with our fish order, at dawn. This gave us the ability to offer a far wider variety of superior quality vegetables to our clientele.

Harvesting our own produce is a joy, and I would thoroughly recommend to anyone who has not grown anything before to try doing so, even if it is a few chives and parsley in a window box. The flavour and aroma of freshly picked herbs and vegetables is so very much better than anything you can buy. I was so enthused by Ann, who would grow anything from mange tout to mooli (long white radish), cucumbers to physalis (cape gooseberry), and romanesco cauliflower to white sprouting broccoli, that it has spurred me to jot down a few notes about some of the more widely-used vegetables in our garden.

Potatoes

My current preferred potato variety is a red-skinned, yellow-fleshed tuber called 'Franceline'. The first potatoes I harvest are superb boiled and great in salads, but as the summer gets underway and the plants have a little longer to mature, the 'dry matter' content increases, which means that they are no longer waxy and are fantastic for mashing or roasting.

There is little that can beat a freshly-dug Franceline potato, cooked with a few sprigs of sage or lovage in the water, then crushed on a plate, sprinkled with freshly ground sea salt and white pepper, before being topped with a generous knob of unsalted butter or cream cheese. If left to dry in the sun in preparation for storing, the Franceline keeps well and the attractive red skin does not lose its colour when cooked.

Jerusalem Artichokes

Jerusalem artichokes are related to the sunflower, which is apparent when the plant flowers to display bright yellow daisy-like flowers. I grow these most years, and harvest them in time for Christmas. I generally make a terrine combining the artichokes with red peppers, Buffalo mozzarella, leeks, red onions, and perpetual spinach. Once peeled, the white vegetable tastes somewhat like water chestnuts, and can be an interesting addition eaten raw in salads.

A delicious soup can also be made by boiling some peeled tubers and combining them with a few roasted sweet chestnuts to enhance their mild, sweet nutty flavour (p86).

Parsnips

Before the introduction of the potato, parsnips and turnips were an important and nutritious staple food. Due to its high sugar content, parsnip was also used in industry to sweeten cakes and jams.

Cheap and simple to prepare, I love to cook these, especially roasted with meats, as the starch absorbs the meat juices and the sugars caramelise to give a nice warm sweet crunch. The first frost of the year converts the parsnip's starch to sugar and gives it a pleasantly sweet flavour, so watch the weather forecast carefully!

Beetroot

My favourite beetroot type is one called 'Choggia Barbietola', a variegated bright crimson beet, slightly less 'earthy' and a little sweeter that the dark red varieties.

I have had great fun serving this in my restaurant to non-beetroot fans (predominantly men), who would often call me over to the table to ask what the delicious vegetable was. 'Some type of radish?' they would enquire. What's more, little did they know that beetroot contains betaine, a mind relaxant used to treat depression;

tryptophan, which contributes to a sense of well-being; and lastly boron, which enhances male sex hormones! This truly is a vegetable to request, especially when away for the weekend to catch up on 'quality time together'.

Delicious either cooked or raw, the adaptability of beetroot is remarkable. Scrub well, bake like a jacket potato then split and eat with butter or cream cheese, or par-boil then roast in the oven, cube and fry in a little butter then add a small spoon of vinegar, a pinch of sugar and some freshly squeezed orange juice to make a delicious glaze.

Beetroot and chocolate cake is to die for (p88), and the beetroot and onion chutney (p191) works superbly well with grilled goat's cheese.

Celeriac

Giant Prague is the variety I have had most success with, although Snow White, Tellus and Marble Ball (good storer) are other recommended cultivars. Well-suited to damper, lightly shaded parts of the garden, celeriac is easy to grow.

Plant in February and you should start to lift the roots in October and, providing the plants are well protected from frost (with sheep wool, straw or bracken), your kitchen should have an ample supply to last you right the way through the winter months until the following April or May.

I am immensely fond of this incredible, multipurpose vegetable, as the bulb can be used for soups, stews, celeriac & potato rösti, cut into julienne for steaming with fish, it can be eaten raw as crudités, finely grated for a tasty addition to coleslaw, added to mash, and can even be made into a thirst-quenching drink (an alternative to tomato juice) – try using a lovage stalk with a leaf left on in place of a straw – it works well and can be very popular with children.

The celeriac leaves can be chopped and used in place of parsley and the stems can be peeled and chopped for salads or stir-fry.

Broad Beans

Broad beans are the oldest of all our beans, dating back to Stone Age times. They are a superbly versatile vegetable, have a lovely robust flavour, and can be put to many uses including soups, stir-fries, pasta and rice dishes, salads, pâtés and dips, or even added to omelettes.

They are very nutritious; full of phosphorous, vitamin A and C, and are notably rich in protein at 23%. Some varieties can be dried and used as pulses or roasted, ground and used as flour ("Fava Bean Flour").

The time to enjoy homegrown broad beans is during the months of May, June and early July. The pods should be pale green and feel soft and tender. The beans are best eaten shortly after picking as the sugars quickly turn to starch.

They do however freeze very successfully if frozen as they are harvested. Young beans can be cooked whole, rinsed and boiled for no more than 2 minutes. As the beans become older they develop quite a tough outer skin. The easiest way to tackle this is to boil the beans lightly for 1 minute, then plunge into iced water and remove the skins when the beans are cool.

There are two classic herbs to accompany the broad bean. One is parsley, added to a white sauce if serving the beans as a hot vegetable, and the other is summer savory (a companion herb to the broad bean plant, which helps to discourage black fly when planted between the rows) mixed with the beans in a salad with other ingredients such as tomatoes and cheese.

Cabbage

Cabbage belongs to the cruciferae family (to which broccoli, brussels sprouts, cauliflower, kohlrabi, radish and turnip also belong). Crucifers have very valuable cancer-fighting properties – the more you eat, the less likely you are to develop the disease. To get the most benefit from your cruciferous vegetables, choose organically grown and be sure not to overcook.

Chard

Chard is a member of the beet family and has crunchy stalks and spinach-like leaves. The leaves have a slightly bitter, earthy flavour and are excellent either raw or cooked. It's an excellent source of iron, vitamin C and magnesium (essential for the absorption of calcium). The main chard season in the UK is from June to August although there are a number of frost-resistant varieties available making it a useful crop during the cold weather. Its earthy taste is a little stronger than spinach and its vibrant multi-coloured stems provide an ornamental centrepiece in any garden.

Chard's crinkly leaves can be prepared as you would spinach, although they will need longer cooking due to the sturdy structure of the leaves.

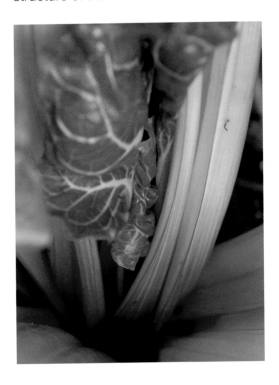

For the larger leaves, I find it best to cook the leaf and the stem separately. Wash well and remove the ribs. Then steam or stir-fry leaves until wilted (a little garlic may be added to the pan and browned with the butter). Cut the ribs into squares and steam, boil or fry gently until tender. Serve together with a little light Tamari sauce drizzled on top.

Another quick and tasty dish can be created by simply cutting the chard stems into large pieces, blanching them in boiling, salted water for about 5 minutes, draining well and then layering them in a well-buttered baking dish with sautéed garlic, leeks, black pepper, sea salt, sliced boiled potatoes, some grated Parmesan cheese and fresh thyme. Bake at 190°C until browned and soft.

Squashes and Pumpkins

As autumn approaches and the swallows are winging their way back to warmer climes for the winter, the garden is a sea of ripening golden squashes. Just a few seeds planted each year on a redundant muckheap provide several hundred fruits. My favourite of all squashes is the Golden Hubbard and as soon as they are ripe they appear on the table in different guises: soups, breads, risottos, ice cream, mash, quiches and the like, not forgetting, of course, the hazlenut, mace and squash cake (p73).

Winter squashes are very easy to grow, are pretty hardy and disease-resistant, although the fruits do like a little sun to help them ripen before harvesting. Ripe fruits sound hollow when gently tapped.

Turnip

Turnips are not fussy about the soil they grow in; they thrive in a cool climate and are a great crop for cleaning up the soil.

I grow turnips for their delicate, peppery flavour and amazing creamy whiteness of the interior flesh. They are delicious raw: grated in salads, mixed with herbs and mayonnaise, or sliced as an alternative to radish. A young, freshly-picked root, lightly boiled with a little water and sea salt, then tossed in butter with some herbs and black pepper, is a delight to look at and just bursts with flavour.

Turnip leaves can be eaten and resemble mustard greens. In general, the smaller the turnip, the sweeter the taste.

Leeks

At its best from November to April, the British leek is a fantastically versatile vegetable that adds flavour and bite and tastes superb in all sorts of disciplines: steam with fish; bake with cider, bacon and cream; dice and add to soups; stir-fry with other vegetables and a light soy sauce; or combine with cheese such as Caerphilly or chicken to make a delicious pie.

Peas: Pod, Shoot and Seed

I find peas exciting to grow. They are especially enchanting for the first-time gardener. Choose a disease-resistant variety such as Markana or Onward, sow in a well-prepared, well-manured soil in a sunny, sheltered position with good airflow.

Once the plants are established, check daily and wait for the shoots to appear. The time to pick them is just as the flower starts to emerge. The flowering shoots are delicious whole in salads, or chopped at the last minute and added to soups. Once they have flowered, the pods start to appear. Picked young, the pods can be treated as mange tout (boil or steam lightly for 30–40 seconds, then drain).

When the pods get larger, it is worth waiting for them to grow to maturity before harvesting in order to enjoy the best peas you have ever eaten. The peas can be added to risotto, vegetable terrines, added raw to salads, or blanched briefly and then frozen for later use.

Asparagus

Asparagus is one of my very favourite seasonal vegetables.

Available for just six weeks of the year from the beginning of May to the middle of June, this fantastic vegetable is a 'must' when absolutely fresh and in season (asparagus loses 40% of its flavour two days after picking). English asparagus has the best flavour in the world, due to the fact that the stems grow slowly in the English climate, enabling them to develop a much fuller flavour and fine, tender texture.

Low in calories with no fat, no cholesterol, low in sodium, a good source of potassium, high in folic acid, vitamins A and C, and thiamine – this vegetable does not just taste good!

Avocados

Despite the fact that they do not grow the UK, I have chosen to include avocados because they are such a valuable source of a wide spectrum of nutrients; they are virtually the only fruit that has mono-unsaturated fat, are a good source of fibre, and contain over 25 vitamins, minerals and phytonutrients including lutein (which is especially valuable at preventing eye disease such as macular degeneration).

Roasted Garlic, Thyme & Butter Bean Pâté

Butter beans (or lima beans) are normally thought of as a dried bean. Given a good, well-drained soil, and a nice sunny aspect, fresh butter beans are in fact quite easy to grow. They are one of those vegetables that can double as a dried bean later in the season when the mature pods are left to shrivel and dry in the autumn sun. Try planting a pole variety such as King of the Garden or Florida and leave plenty of pods to grow to adulthood, before harvesting and storing.

Butter beans are one of my preferred winter store cupboard ingredients. Their versatility as a soup ingredient, deep-fried snack, curried with vegetables or used in salads always surprises me – I even make a butter bean purée and add it to my vegetable bread (page 238). When sautéed with bacon fat, they become crisp and nutty and are truly delicious. This pâté keeps well and tastes fabulous spread on bruschetta (grilled bread rubbed with extra-virgin olive oil), thinly sliced toast or pitta bread at any time of the day, but especially in the early evening with a nice glass of dry sherry or white wine!

Serves 6 as a starter or snack

Ingredients

2 cups dried butter beans, soaked overnight in cold water and drained
1 whole head of fresh garlic
1 tbsp olive oil
½ teaspoon chopped fresh thyme
Sea salt to taste
Freshly ground black pepper to taste

Method

1. Put the pre-soaked drained beans in a large saucepan and add water to cover the beans by 3 inches (check the water level during cooking – you may need to top up).
2. Bring to a boil, cover, and simmer until very tender, 1 to 1½ hours then drain and set aside reserving the cooking liquor.
3. Heat the oven to 200°C.
4. Break the garlic heads into cloves, leave the peel on and roast until soft in the oven for about 10 minutes. Leave to cool and then remove the peel.
5. Put the drained beans in a food processor, then add the roasted cloves of garlic, the oil and a little of the reserved cooking liquor and blend until you have the consistency of smooth mashed potato.
6. Season with salt and pepper.
7. Add the thyme leaves and serve at room temperature.

Ease of Cooking: ★☆☆
Soaking & cooking time
for the beans: overnight plus 1–2 hours
Preparation time: 20 minutes
Will freeze or can keep in a jar in the fridge covered with a little olive oil for a couple of months.

Hazelnut, Mace and Squash Cake

a modern twist on a classic

Have you ever made a carrot cake? Well, this is a re-work of that age-old classic recipe but using a slightly different orange vegetable with an interesting spice. A really good autumn recipe, especially for the smallholder with an overflowing muckheap of squashes.

Serves 10

Ingredients

6 whole eggs
375g/13oz melted butter
660g/1lb 7oz white caster sugar
1 tbsp vanilla extract
475g/17oz self-raising flour
1 tbsp bicarbonate of soda
1 tbsp baking powder
¾ tsp salt
1 tbsp ground mace
2 tsp ground cardomom
685g/1½lb grated squash, ideally
Golden Hubbard, or pumpkin
175g/6oz chopped hazelnuts

For the icing
125g/4½oz butter, softened
225g/8oz cream cheese, softened
515g/18oz icing sugar
1 tbsp lemon juice
115g/4oz chopped hazelnuts

Method

1. Preheat oven to 160°C.
2. Grease and line a large baking tray with greaseproof paper 15½" by 10" by 3" in size.
3. In a mixing bowl beat together eggs, butter, sugar and the vanilla extract.
4. Sieve the flour, bicarbonate of soda, baking powder, salt, mace and cardamom together and add to the mix.
5. Stir in the grated squash. Fold in the nuts.
6. Pour into a greased baking tray. Bake for one hour, or until cooked.
7. Let it cool in the baking tray for 10 minutes, and then turn out onto a wire rack and cool completely.

To make the icing

1. In a bowl, combine butter, cream cheese, icing sugar and lemon juice.
2. Beat until the mixture is smooth and creamy. Stir in the chopped nuts.
3. Ice the cooled cake.

Ease of Cooking: ★★☆
Preparation & cooking time: 2 hours

Tina's Tip

This cake is easy to make and, as it freezes exceptionally well, make large batches in the autumn and keep in the deep-freeze. It will thaw in no time, keeps its moisture and tastes good with or without the icing. Its scrumptiousness belies the fact that it is quite high in fibre; so don't feel too guilty when reaching for a second helping! Pumpkin or squash of any kind can be substituted for the Golden Hubbard.

Spiced Pumpkin & Ginger Soup with Coriander and Yoghurt

freezes well

Rich, nutty sweet flavours combine beautifully with the warmth of the spice and the creaminess of the yoghurt.

Serves: 4–6

Ingredients

60g/¼ cup butter or vegetable oil
2 cloves of garlic, peeled and crushed
2 medium onions, peeled and roughly chopped
2 fresh red chillies, seeded and chopped
1 tbsp cumin seed
1 tbsp ground coriander
1 large piece root ginger, peeled and grated
570ml/1 pint/2½ cups good quality chicken or vegetable stock
450g/1lb pumpkin, peeled and cut in to 2cm/1" cubes
1 bunch fresh coriander
1 small tub of thick plain yoghurt
Salt & pepper

Method

1. In a large pan, heat the butter/oil. When hot, add the garlic and onions and sweat until soft.
2. Add the cumin seed, chillies, ginger and ground coriander and cook for a further 5 minutes.
3. Add the chicken stock and pumpkin and cook until the pumpkin is tender.
4. Blend in a liquidiser or push through a sieve. Return to the pan and bring back to the boil.
5. Taste, season with salt and pepper. Just before serving, chop the coriander and add.
6. Ladle into bowls adding a generous dollop of yoghurt and serve immediately.

Ease of cooking: ★ ☆ ☆ Soupersimple
Preparation & cooking time: 45 minutes

Tina's Tip

The root ginger is best soaked in cold water to soften the skin, which can then be scraped rather than peeled. Make sure you add the juices from the grated ginger – they are full of flavour.
Do not add the coriander or yoghurt prior to freezing.

Avocado, Broad Bean, Thyme & Smoked Bacon Salad

wonderful year-round starter

This is a nutritious and amazingly appetising dish. It combines the smoky, salty juices of the bacon, the succulent and slightly crunchy broad bean with the smooth delicious avocado flesh, all of which are enhanced by the freshly picked thyme and the sharp vinaigrette which checks the bacon fat.

Serves 4

Ingredients

2 ripe medium-sized avocados
Quantity of avocado vinaigrette (p193)
8 rashers of smoked streaky bacon, rind removed
450g/1lb broad beans, fresh or frozen
Selection of salad leaves
24 pea shoots (optional)
1 crisp lettuce of your choice (Webb's wonder, iceberg, little gem)
Bunch of fresh thyme, stems removed
Sea salt and freshly milled black pepper

Method

1. Pre-heat the grill and cook the bacon until crisp. Leave to cool and then cut into pieces about 1cm/½" wide. Set aside.
2. Place the shelled beans in a large pan of boiling salted water. Bring back to the boil and cook for 1 minute (or slightly longer if the beans are large).
3. Remove the beans from the water and plunge into a bowl of iced water. Stir to chill as rapidly as possible.
4. When cool, drain the beans then remove the outer skin (this isn't necessary if the beans are really young).
5. Arrange the lettuce and salad leaves on to four plates.
6. Sprinkle some of the thyme leaves over the salad.
7. Drizzle some vinaigrette over the top.
8. Cut the avocados in half and peel carefully. Slice and place on top of the salad.
9. Warm the cut bacon through under the grill and then add the shelled broad beans to the tray (to warm through and combine with the bacon and the juices).
10. Spoon the bacon and beans over the avocado together with a little more of the dressing, place the rest of the thyme leaves over the top, arrange 6 pea shoots onto each salad and serve.

Ease of cooking: ★★☆
Preparation & cooking time: 30 minutes

Tina's Tip

Pea shoots are available commercially, but are also really easy to grow. Just buy some ordinary pea seeds such as Markana or Onward from a garden centre and pop into weed-free soil, water well. Pick off the shoots just before they flower.

Celeriac, Ham & Haricot Bean Soup

hearty winter soup

Perfect for those crisp frosty winter days when being outside stimulates a healthy appetite, the nourishing, warming, ingredients re-stock the spent reserves.

Serves 6–8

Ingredients

4 medium celeriac
1 large or 2 small knuckles of ham, soaked overnight in cold water
225g/8oz dried haricot beans, washed and soaked over-night in cold water
Generous handful of lovage
4 large leeks, washed
8 bay leaves
1 tbsp white peppercorns
1 large bunch flat leaf parsley

Method

1. Peel and wash the celeriac.
2. Dice the celeriac into ¼" cubes. Slice the leeks. Reserve the trimmings from both.
3. Rinse the soaked ham and the haricot beans under clean cold running water.
4. Place in a large heavy-bottomed pan and cover with cold water to 3" above the top of the ham knuckle.
5. Add the lovage, bay leaves and peppercorns.
6. Simmer gently until the ham is falling away from the bone and the beans are cooked through (2–3 hours).
7. Lift out the ham, discard the herbs and peppercorns then strain the beans and reserve the cooking liquor.

8. Discard the fat and the bones from the ham and cut into small dice. Set aside.
9. In a large pan, place the vegetable trimmings together with half the haricot beans and enough cooking liquor to cover.
10. Bring to the boil and cook until tender. Liquidise and strain into a clean saucepan.
11. Add the sliced leeks, diced celeriac and ham together with the remainder of the beans and simmer until the celeriac has just a little bite left.
12. Check the seasoning.
13. Chop the parsley and add at the last moment.
14. Serve with a big basket of crusty bread.

Ease of cooking: ★★☆
Make sure you allow yourself enough time.
Preparation & cooking time: 2½–3½ hours

Tina's Tip

This soup is also great with butterbeans and a few cloves of chopped, roasted garlic added just before serving.

Layered Leeks & Potatoes with Cheese & Cream

easy vegetarian meal to pre-cook

There comes a time in the life of anyone who has an allotment or kitchen garden, when your family or guests get thoroughly bored of leeks. To re-kindle their unconditional adoration of this vegetable, bring this dish out for real comfort. It is very easy to put together and is excellent to teach teenagers before they leave home, and of course, it's vegetarian. This is easily multiplied to serve 16 or 32, so remember it when New Year's Eve comes. At that time of the year I like to serve it with a crisp sweet/bitter salad of sugar loaf chicory, radicchio and lardons of smoked bacon.

Serves 4

Ingredients

900g/2lb floury potatoes (such as King Edward, Maris Piper, Wilja, Ailsa and Golden Wonder)
6 small leeks, trimmed, split and thoroughly washed to remove grit
285ml/10 fl oz double cream
butter (for greasing)
3 eggs, beaten
Sea salt & freshly ground black pepper
1 tbsp chopped garlic
225g/8oz Gruyère, Raclette or Emmenthal cheese (or a local cheese of your choice), grated
Bunch of tarragon, chopped

Method

1. Cut peeled potatoes into ¼" slices.
2. Place in boiling salted water to scald for 4 minutes. Drain well.
3. Butter a shallow earthenware dish thickly.
4. Beat together the garlic, eggs and cream. Season with salt & pepper.
5. Blanch the leeks in boiling salted water for 4 minutes. Drain well and gently squeeze out the excess moisture using a clean tea towel, without crushing the leeks. Pre-heat oven to 190°C
6. Arrange half the potato slices in an overlapping pattern in the bottom of the dish, season well.
7. Pour half the egg & cream mixture over and sprinkle with half the cheese and half the tarragon.
8. Arrange the leeks over this, then the remaining potatoes with more seasoning.
9. Pour the other half of the egg & cream mixture and the rest of the tarragon over the top, followed by the last layer of cheese.
10. Bake approx. 1 hour.

Ease of cooking: ★☆☆
Preparation & cooking time: 1½ hour
Freezes well. Will keep in the fridge for up to 1 week when cooked.

Thyme-Scented Mash

an easy sophisticated touch

Unless you are fortunate enough to grow your own potatoes or have a good local supplier, most of the varieties available to purchase are grown for properties other than flavour, such as resistance to diseases. By noting a few of the following simple guidelines, you will learn how to lift the taste of an ordinary potato enormously.

Method

In the bottom of a saucepan place a large bunch of thyme – stems included. Place the peeled potatoes on top together with several cloves of garlic and a good pinch of sea salt.

Cook until the potatoes are tender, remove the thyme, strain the water, and mash the potato and garlic with some butter and freshly ground black pepper. If the mash seems a little tight, add some of the cooking water to slacken.

Tina's Tip

Thyme is a very good hardy winter herb, though winter savory, sage or rosemary all harmonize with mash n' meat dishes very well. Should you want mash for a fish dish, then try cooking the potato with tarragon, coriander, lovage or dill as an alternative to mint.

The water that is drained from the potatoes is full of flavour and vitamins and is well worth keeping for soups, gravies, sauces or even as cooking water for pasta or other vegetables such as cabbage or winter greens, for instance chard or kale.

Asparagus with Avocado Oil, Black Pepper & Garlic Salt

quick romantic starter

Each year, for about six weeks from the end of April to the middle of June, the asparagus season is in full flow. The three most important things to remember with asparagus are to *purchase it as fresh as possible*, to *cook it as little as possible,* and to *consume it as quickly as possible.* This is dead easy to do *(especially the last one)*, and amazingly flavoursome.

A great starter for two, especially for a first date or anniversary.

Serves 4

Ingredients

2 large bunches of asparagus
2 tbsp avocado oil
Freshly ground black pepper
Good quality garlic salt

Method

1. Drizzle the avocado oil on to a large roasting tray.
2. Sprinkle some garlic salt and black pepper over the oil.
3. Plunge the asparagus into a large pan of boiling salted water and cook for one minute.
4. Remove the asparagus, drain and place on the tray.
5. Shake gently to roll the asparagus coating it evenly with the seasoning.
6. Devour.

Ease of cooking: ★☆☆
Preparation & cooking time: 10 minutes

Tina's Tip

As asparagus is a marsh plant and normally grown in very fine alluvial soil, I cook it in water as opposed to steaming it as it allows any residual sand to sink to the bottom of the pan.

To make the dish slightly more substantial you can place some goat's cheese or pesto over the asparagus and then grill lightly. Great with warm Ciabatta bread (p232) to soak up the seasoned avocado oil.

Cauliflower and Sweet Parsley Fritters, Warm Mediterranean Chutney

different light summer lunch

In Cornwall, cauliflowers are grown in abundance, but most of the crop is quickly transported out of the region to be sold at markets further afield. The popularity of cauliflower among British diners has waned recently, although they are widely used in Asian cuisine – here is a lightly spiced recipe to make your mouth water and think twice next time you walk past a stack of the creamy curds. Serve with tossed salad.

Serves 6

Ease of cooking: ★ ☆ ☆
Preparation & cooking time: 25 minutes

Ingredients

140g/5oz plain flour
1½ tsp ground cumin
1½ tsp ground coriander
½ tsp turmeric
¼ tsp cayenne
Pinch salt & freshly ground black pepper
140ml/5 fl oz of your favourite beer
1 large egg, beaten
6 spring onions, sliced
140g/5oz cauliflower florets
Large bunch of fresh flat leaf parsley, roughly chopped
Vegetable oil for frying

Method

1. Sift together the salt, spices and flour.
2. Add the beer and the egg. Mix well.
3. Stir in the onions.
4. Add the cauliflower florets and coat well with the batter.
5. Heat the oil and deep-fry the mixture by the spoonful until golden brown.
6. Drain on paper and serve accompanied by Mediterranean Chutney (p175)
7. Garnish with the parsley.

Tina's Tip

If the cauliflower does not readily mix with the batter, dip into water and then flour first.

Tomato Salsa

great with fish

The word 'salsa' is an Italian derivative of the Latin word salsus, meaning 'salted'. In this case the salted ingredients are the pilchard fillets. This tomato sauce lends itself beautifully to fish, especially oily fish such as bass or grey mullet. The acidity of the tomato, capers, and vinegar balances well with the heat of the chilli, the salty, oily fish and is further complemented by the garlic and herbs.

Serves 6

Ingredients

450g/1lb ripe plum tomatoes, de-seeded and finely chopped
⅓ cup baby capers (soaked & drained)
1 green chilli, de-seeded and finely chopped
1 slice of white bread, crusts removed
4–6 spring onions finely sliced
2 tsp minced garlic
4–6 finely chopped salted pilchard fillets
⅓ cup olive oil
½ cup finely chopped chives and flat leaf parsley
¼ cup good quality white wine vinegar and/or lime juice
Sea salt & freshly ground black pepper

Method

1. Pound the garlic, capers and pilchard fillets together in a mortar and pestle.
2. Soak the bread in the wine vinegar then pound it and the herbs and green chilli into the mixture.
3. Add the black pepper and salt and then stir in the olive oil and then finally add the tomatoes and spring onions.

4. Taste, adjust the seasoning if necessary, and serve.

Ease of cooking: ★ ☆ ☆
Preparation time: 20 minutes

Tina's Tip

Any spare salsa will keep well in the fridge (covered with a layer of oil to prevent it oxidizing) and makes a great sauce for last-minute improvisation with pasta or rice, or perhaps stuffed into courgettes or peppers. Coriander or basil can be used instead of parsley. Balsamic vinegar makes a nice alternative to white wine vinegar.

Jerusalem Artichoke and Sweet Chestnut Soup

winter comfort

Jerusalem artichokes are one of the best ingredients that winter has to offer. The humble ingredients of this blissfully simple recipe are transformed into a sweet, earthy delight. This soup has outstanding flavour: I guarantee you 'love at first slurp'!

Serves 4

Ingredients

1½kg/3lb Jerusalem artichokes
100g/3½oz butter
1 large onion chopped
1 large leek, roughly diced
½ celeriac root, roughly diced
4 cloves of garlic, crushed
350g/12oz roasted sweet chestnuts
(available pre-prepared)
2 litres/3½ pints of vegetable/chicken stock
Salt and pepper
100ml/3½oz double cream
1 tbsp cumin seeds
8 rindless rashers of smoked streaky
bacon, grilled
2 handfuls of chopped flat leaf parsley

Method

1. Scrub the artichokes thoroughly then place them in a steamer and cook for 5–10 minutes (depending on the size of the tubers), just enough so that you are able to peel the cooked skin away from the crunchy interior flesh.
2. Melt the butter in a large saucepan, add the cumin seed and stir for 1–2 minutes.
3. Add the leeks, onions, garlic and celeriac and cook gently until they soften.
4. Add the jerusalem artichokes, chest-nuts and the stock.
5. Bring to the boil, then simmer for 30 minutes or until the jerusalem artichokes are totally soft.
6. Take off the heat, put the soup into a blender (you may need to do this in batches) and whizz until smooth.
7. Sieve the soup into a clean pan, bring back to the boil and then turn off the heat.
8. Cut the cooked bacon into ⅛" shreds.
9. Season, stir in the cream and parsley, sprinkle the bacon on top and serve.

Ease of cooking: ★ ☆ ☆
Preparation & cooking time: 45 minutes

Tina's Tip

A few roasted garlic croutons are a nice addition. If you want this soup to aspire to the 'big bowl league', reserve some of the whole jerusalem artichokes, at stage 1, cook them a little more then cut into chunky slices and add to the whizzed soup before bringing it back to the boil. For a dainty dinner party 'amuse bouche' to be served in small cups, omit the cumin seed and cook the bacon with the rest of the ingredients before sieving (to get the bacon flavour without the chunks). Add a few drops of white truffle oil if you have any.

Warm New Potato & Cabbage Salad

great barbeque side-dish

This is one of those dishes that just 'happened' – all the ingredients were dotted around the kitchen and I somehow felt encouraged to put them together. I found the combination quite delicious, so much so, that I am writing it down so that you too can enjoy this inspirational summer concoction. This also makes an excellent brunch or light supper.

Serves 6

Ingredients

900g/2lb new potatoes
900g/2lb sweetheart cabbage
3 tbsp. avocado oil
1½ tbsp white wine vinegar
3 large stems of lovage
3 individual goat's cheeses
8 rashers smoked bacon
1 bunch asparagus
450g/1lb cherry tomatoes
Few sprigs of tarragon
Sea salt
Black pepper

Method

1. Place the lovage and potatoes in a large saucepan, cover with cold water and add a teaspoon of sea salt.
2. Bring to the boil and simmer gently until cooked. Remove the lovage, drain the potatoes and set aside.
3. Separate the cabbage leaves, then tear the leaf away from the central rib. Place the cabbage into a saucepan with the tarragon, fill with 2 cm of cold water and a pinch of salt. Bring to the boil and cook for 30 seconds. Drain. Set aside leaving the lid slightly ajar.
4. Grill the bacon until crisp; cut into strips.
5. Place the cherry tomatoes on a greased tray and roast in a fairly hot oven for approx. 30 minutes. Set aside.
6. Put the asparagus into a pan of boiling salted water and cook for 1 minute. Drain and set aside.
7. Drizzle the avocado oil onto a large roasting tray. Add the vinegar and some salt and pepper. Cut the goat's cheese into pieces and arrange evenly on the roasting tray. Place in a hot oven for 5 minutes or so until the cheese has melted.
8. Place the potatoes and cabbage in the roasting tray on top of the cheese; add the bacon, asparagus and cherry tomatoes. Toss all the ingredients to mix. Combine oil and vinegar, season and drizzle over.

Ease of cooking: ★ ☆ ☆
Preparation & cooking time: 20 minutes

Tina's Tip

The cabbage needs to barely wilt, so keep an eye on the cooking time. Should you have any of the finished salad left over, it will keep and can be re-heated in a hot oven for 5–10 minutes.

Dark Chocolate Beetroot Cake

a cake with a difference

This amazing deliciously moist beetroot cake has an intense flavour that simply urges you to 'devour'.

Serves 10

Ingredients

225g/8oz self-raising flour
225g/8oz caster sugar
2 tsp ground cardamom
100g/3½oz dark chocolate, minimum 60% cocoa solids
140g/5oz butter
225g/8oz cooked beetroot, grated
4 medium eggs

Icing:
500g/18oz dark chocolate, grated
300ml/11 fl oz double cream
30ml/2 tbsp dark rum

Method for the cake

1. Preheat oven to 180°C.
2. Grease and line a deep 9"/25cm round cake tin.
3. Sift the cardamom and flour together.
4. Melt the chocolate and butter together in a bowl over warm water.
5. Remove from the heat, add the sugar and stir until dissolved.
6. Add the eggs one at a time and whisk in thoroughly.
7. Add the grated beetroot and mix in well.
8. Fold in the flour carefully.
9. Pour into the prepared cake tin.

10. Bake for 50 minutes or until a wooden stick inserted in centre comes out clean.
11. Remove from the oven and leave for about 15 minutes before turning out on to a wire rack to cool.

Method for the icing

1. Combine the dark chocolate and the cream in a bowl and heat gently over a pan of warm water.
2. Leave to cool slightly, add the rum then spread over the cake as it starts to set.
3. Serve with crème fraîche.

Ease of cooking: ★ ★ ☆
Preparation & cooking time: 1½ hours
Freezes well.

Tina's Tip

White chocolate and white rum can be used for the icing with some beetroot juice added for a splash of extra colour. Thinly sliced wedges of beetroot can be brushed with 20g sugar dissolved with the juice of one lemon and then popped into a slow oven to cook for 20 minutes until sticky to use as a garnish.

Roast Tomato and Basil Soup

delicious use of your excess crop

Most of us love tomato soup. This recipe uses oven-dried tomatoes that are slowly baked in the oven to create a more intense flavour.

Serves 6

Ingredients

60ml/2 tbsp olive oil
1 onion, chopped
10 cloves of garlic, crushed and roughly chopped
4 rashers of streaky bacon, diced
1 stick of celery
8 large tomatoes
60ml/2 tbsp balsamic vinegar
1 litre/35 fl oz of chicken stock
90g/3oz tomato puree
Handful of fresh basil, leaves and stalks separated
Coarse salt and black pepper

Method

1. Pre-heat the oven to 130°C.
2. Grease a roasting tray with some of the oil.
3. Remove the core from the tomatoes using a small sharp knife.
4. Cut the tomatoes in half and place on the tray, cut side uppermost. Sprinkle with a little of the vinegar and some coarse sea salt and slowly roast them for 2–3 hours or until they are half their original size.
5. Heat the rest of the oil in a saucepan and slowly sauté the onion, garlic, diced bacon, basil stalks and celery. When they have been gently browned add the stock, tomatoes and tomato puree.
6. Bring the soup to the boil and simmer for about half an hour.
7. Place the soup in a blender and whiz until smooth. Sieve, place back in the pan, season with salt and pepper, add the finely chopped basil leaves and serve.

Ease of cooking: ★☆☆
Preparation & cooking time: 2½-3½ hours

Tina's Tip

To use as a sauce to serve with chicken, fish or omelettes, simmer the strained soup for 15 minutes to reduce until a thicker consistency is reached.

Broad Bean, Watercress, New Potato, Summer Savory and Feta Cheese Salad

easy summer salad

This simple yet stunning summer dish is easy to assemble, visually appealing, highly nutritious, and really gratifying. One May, I was thinking of seasonal ingredients that could be quickly combined to inspire an audience watching a cookery demonstration. I wanted them to go home and embark upon just a little of the 'good life': to dig up the garden and have a little veggie patch. To this end, I handed out packets of broad bean seed and summer savory (companion herb) as encouragement.

Serves 4

Ingredients

450g/1lb new potatoes, scrubbed
225g/8oz feta cheese (organic Vrai is my favourite and is widely available)
450g/1lb broad beans, shelled
1 large bunch of fresh watercress
¼ cup summer savory or thyme leaves
90ml/3 tbsp olive or avocado oil
30ml/2 tbsp white wine vinegar
1 tsp sea salt
1 tsp freshly ground black pepper

Method

1. Place the watercress in a bowl of iced water for 20 minutes to crisp up.
2. Take the watercress out of the water, and pinch off and discard any damaged leaves along with the coarse stem.
3. Place the new potatoes with the thyme/summer savory stalks in cold salted water. Bring to the boil and simmer for 20–30 minutes until cooked. Drain the water and cover the potatoes to keep them warm (don't let the potatoes stand in the water once cooked, as they will become gloopy).
4. Blanch the broad beans by cooking them in a large pan of boiling salted water for 1 minute.
5. Remove the beans from the pan and plunge into a bowl of ice-cold water. Stir the beans in the water in order to cool them as fast as possible. Drain and set aside.
6. In a large bowl combine the watercress, potatoes, summer savory, feta cheese and beans.
7. Whisk together the oil, vinegar, salt and pepper and pour over the salad.
8. Toss gently to coat evenly and serve.

Ease of cooking: ★☆☆ simple
Preparation time: 40 minutes

Tina's Tip

If you have any summer savory or thyme to spare, add a small bunch to the potatoes whilst cooking. You might also like to reserve the water as this can be used for soups and sauces or for cooking pasta.

Salad & Herb Garden

Salad & Herb Garden

The salad and herb garden is an incredibly rewarding area as young seedlings grow very quickly, and can be harvested in about eight weeks. In the spring and early summer, seeds are planted for butterhead, cos, crisp and loose-leaf types of lettuce. During the months of June, July and August the sowing gets underway for the hardier types including chicories, parella red and green, winter imperial and a host of other varieties. The pattern is similar for the herbs; for example, dill, coriander, fennel, chervil, summer savory, lovage and tarragon are perennial and need to be planted at the earliest opportunity to maximize the growing season.

Hardy winter herbs such as sage, rosemary, winter savory and thyme come into their own as the nights draw in and the temperature starts to drop. Preserving is one way to extend the use of herbs, for example by making pesto, or by pickling eggs or onions with tarragon vinegar. Infusions such as rosemary water made into syrup are delicious drizzled onto fruits. Ice creams can capture the wonderful aroma of summer lavender, and baked egg custard flavoured with thyme is heavenly – and can stimulate some interesting conversation!

Radicchio and Bitter Leaf Salad with Orange and Ginger Dressing

colourful winter salad

One of the reasons I adore this salad is that these slow-growing, bitter lettuces are resistant to the cold and provide a welcome sea of colour on dark and dismal days throughout the winter. They are robust in both texture and in taste, and are packed with antioxidants. The chicory family (which also includes curly endive, batavia and escarole) rates very highly amongst salad fans not only for their flavour but also their crunch, and is definitely one to be added to the ever-growing list of superfoods.

Serves 6

Ingredients for the dressing

1 small bunch of thyme, leaves picked from the stem
1 tbsp ginger syrup (from a jar of preserved stem ginger)
1 clove garlic, finely chopped
1 tsp Dijon mustard
Juice and grated zest of 1 orange
2 tbsp white wine vinegar
130ml avocado or sunflower oil
Freshly ground black pepper
Sea salt

Ingredients for the salad

1 head lettuce from the chicory family
1 head radicchio
2 whole oranges (blood oranges by preference)
1 large bunch of watercress (I harvest mine from the wild)

Method for the dressing

1. Combine all ingredients and chill until needed.

Method for the salad

1. Crisp up the lettuces by placing in ice-cold water for 1–2 hours.
2. Drain and pat dry with a tea towel.
3. Combine all the leaves in a large salad bowl.
4. Segment or slice the oranges and add to the salad leaves.
5. When ready to serve, add the dressing to the salad and toss gently.

Ease of preparation: ★☆☆ Easy
Preparation time: 30 minutes

Tina's Tip

A great way to transform this salad into a meal is to add a little cubed feta cheese and some cooked lardons of bacon.
A little freshly ground cardamom from seeds removed from cardamom pods, placed into a pepper mill, will have your guests guessing the mystery ingredient for hours!

Bacon, Egg and Potato Salad with Lovage

delicious light lunch

This salad is also a great addition to any barbeque.

If you do not have new potatoes, try pan-frying some old boiled potatoes and put the dressing on them whilst still warm.

Serves 6

Ingredients

900g/2lb new potatoes
450g/1lb red onions, finely sliced
1 tbsp cumin seed
1 tbsp onion seed
¼ cup avocado oil
2 tbsp red wine vinegar
5 large stems of lovage
9 pickled eggs (p181)
110g/4oz butter
12 rashers streaky bacon
Sea salt
Black pepper

Method

1. Strip the lovage leaves from the stems. Put the stems in a large saucepan with the potatoes and a generous pinch of salt. Cover with cold water.
2. Bring to the boil and simmer gently until cooked. Drain the potatoes, set aside and keep warm.
3. Melt the butter in a large frying pan and when sizzling gently, add the cumin and onion seed and stir for 1 minute (this helps to bring out the flavour).
4. Add the finely sliced red onion and fry until crisp.

5. Take off the heat but leave in the pan to keep warm.
6. Grill the bacon until crisp, leave to cool then slice into 2cm/1" strips.
7. To make the dressing, combine the avocado oil and red wine vinegar in a bowl and season with salt and pepper.
8. Quarter the eggs.
9. To finish the salad, put the potatoes in a bowl and drizzle the oil and vinegar mix over so that the warmed potatoes can absorb the dressing (this tastes ten times better than using cold potatoes).
10. Chop the lovage leaves and add three quarters to the potatoes.
11. Add the bacon and the fried onion with cumin seed.
12. Mix thoroughly, divide onto six plates or tip onto a wide serving dish.
13. Place the quartered eggs on top, sprinkle with salt and pepper and finally the rest of the lovage and serve.

Ease of cooking: ★★☆ very satisfying
Preparation & cooking time: 40 minutes

Cornish Potato Salad

summer buffet staple

Cornish potatoes are the very first potato to be harvested in the UK each year. They hit the shops and menus from late April and throughout May. The potatoes are sold unwashed in an effort to preserve the quality, taste, freshness and goodness. Delicious freshly made and served warm, this salad also keeps very well in the fridge and is well suited to being prepared in advance. Ideal for picnics, out-door lunches, barbeques, buffets or even in a lunch box as a welcome treat.

Serves 6

Ease of cooking: ★☆☆ Easy
Preparation & cooking time: 40 minutes

Ingredients

900g/2lb Cornish new potatoes, scrubbed, cooked, drained & kept warm
Sea salt & freshly ground black pepper
180ml/6 tbsp thick mayonnaise
30ml/2 tbsp French dressing
30ml/2 tbsp crème fraîche
1 clove garlic very finely chopped
8 spring onions, thinly sliced
60ml/¼ cup chopped tarragon, chives or coriander

Tina's Tip

Thinly sliced red onion, bacon or red peppers may be added for extra substance, flavour & colour. If you add potatoes while they are still warm they will act as a sponge and draw in the flavours beautifully.

Method

1. In a large bowl, combine the mayonnaise, dressing, crème fraîche, garlic and seasoning.
2. Halve or quarter the potatoes or leave whole if small.
3. Add to the mayonnaise mix while still hot.
4. Add the herbs and spring onions and toss well.
5. Cool slightly and serve on a bed of mixed salad leaves.

Buffalo Mozzarella and Tomato Salad

simple, clean-flavoured salad

The texture of mozzarella should be creamy and the taste should have a mild fresh tang to it.

About three miles from my Devon restaurant, the Greenaway family set up a 150-strong herd of water buffalo in 2004. Mike Greenaway and his wife experimented with their buffalo milk, making everything from cheese to kulfi (an Indian version of cardamom ice cream). I was fortunate enough to sample the fruits of their labour, and so came up with this simple recipe that highlights this quality ingredient. This makes a great open sandwich using soda bread (p228), add some oregano to the mix, make flatbreads by rolling to 2cm thick, split when cooked and pile the salad on top.

Serves 4

Ease of cooking: ★☆☆ very easy
Preparation time: 10 minutes

Ingredients

150g/5oz mixed salad leaves
8 vine-ripened tomatoes, quartered
1 garlic clove, finely chopped
500g/18oz buffalo mozzarella, diced
Handful of oregano leaves
Sea salt and freshly ground black pepper
¼ cup olive oil
2 tbsp white wine vinegar

Tina's Tip

Bitter leaves such as chicory, endive and radicchio also taste delicious with this cheese. A slightly richer dish can be achieved by adding some Parmesan shavings.

Method

1. Place the tomatoes in a bowl; add the garlic and a little salt and pepper.
2. Mix together and leave to stand while you make the dressing.
3. Add the salad leaves, mozzarella and oregano to the tomatoes.
4. Combine the oil and vinegar, pour over the salad and combine gently, using your hands.

Caesar Salad

brunch, starter or healthy meal

This must be one of the wickedest ways to indulge in salad. The texture of the crunchy croutons, the crisp salad leaves, the saltiness of the bacon and the anchovies, are brought together beautifully with the rich creaminess of the Parmesan dressing. This makes a great starter for about 6 people, or decent brunch for 4; alternatively, combine it with a soft poached egg, smoked red peppers or some white meat such as chicken and you have a pretty substantial meal suitable for any time of day or night.

Serves 4

Ingredients

For the salad

6 baby gem lettuce, cos, romaine, crisp heart lettuce, or the heart of a Webb's Wonder, washed and drained
1 x 2oz tin of anchovy fillets (drained, oil reserved) cut into 2cm/1" pieces
400g/14oz smoked bacon, grilled then cut into 2cm/1" pieces
4 slices of bread cut into 2cm/1" cubes
75ml/5 tbsp olive oil
15g/½oz/1 tbsp grated Parmesan cheese

For the dressing

1 heaped tsp English mustard powder
½ teaspoon Worcestershire sauce
60ml/4 tbsp olive oil
250ml/9 fl oz sunflower oil
2 cloves of garlic, peeled
3 tbsp white wine vinegar
5 egg yolks
60g/2oz grated Parmesan cheese
Sea salt and freshly ground black pepper

Method

1. To make the croutons combine the bread cubes, olive oil, and half the Parmesan cheese in a bowl.
2. Season liberally with salt and pepper and mix thoroughly.
3. Transfer to a baking tray and bake for 10 minutes at 150°C. Leave to cool.
4. To make the dressing, put the egg yolks into a food processor together with the garlic, mustard powder, vinegar, Worcestershire sauce, and half the anchovy fillets.
5. Blitz for 2–3 minutes and then (with the motor still running) add the anchovy oil and then the sunflower oil until all combined.
6. Add the Parmesan cheese and season with salt and pepper to taste.
7. To put the salad together, place half the lettuce, croutons, bacon and anchovies on to a plate, drizzle with a little dressing then repeat with another layer and some more dressing.
8. Serve at once.

Ease of cooking: ★ ★ ☆
Once mastered, the prep time can be cut to 20 minutes.
Preparation & cooking time: 30 minutes

Tina's Tip

I like to add some dark green to this salad such as rocket leaves or watercress, which adds a slightly more peppery dimension. The addition of fresh herbs such as oregano, chives, sweet marjoram or thyme offer a delicious fragrance and enhance the whole eating experience.

Sauce can be made in advance and stored in the fridge. The fat from the bacon can be reserved and used to replace some of the oil. Pecorino cheese (made from sheep's milk) can be substituted if one of your diners has an intolerance to cow's milk.

Tina's Tip

Fill an empty milk carton with water, freeze, then place in a sink with cold water and the lettuces to crisp them up. Leave for one hour and then drain.

Braised Knuckle of Honey Roast Ham & Chicory with Parsley Sauce

a change from a Sunday roast

Chicory (also known as endive) is a forced salad leaf crop (encouraged to grow by keeping in a dark, warm environment) and the crisp leaves have a mildly bitter taste. The UK season is from January to March, although imported chicory is available all year round.

This is a great vegetable to grow. It is especially useful for salads and as a vegetable in winter when supplies are scarce as it is not only delicious but it is high in oxidative nutrients.

The tender nature of this vegetable, along with its pleasing crunch and mild bitterness, lends itself well to salty, smoked and/or fatty meats, such as duck, ham, bacon and chicken. It also pairs well with something sweet such as redcurrant jelly, ginger syrup or honey glaze. The addition of something acidic, such as cider, orange or lemon juice, completes a delicious quartet of flavours.

This is beautifully demonstrated in the following recipe where the flavours of the salty ham, the honey, the lemon juice and the chicory marry exceptionally well to provide a substantial and satisfying meal. A great family meal.

Serves 4

Ingredients

4 heads of chicory
2 tbsp honey
110g/4oz butter
2 cured ham knuckles
Bay leaves, peppercorns, rosemary & thyme sprigs
1 head celeriac, celery, 5 carrots
sea salt & freshly ground black pepper

For the sauce:
Béchamel sauce ingredients (p219)
Small bunch of finely chopped flat leaf parsley

Method

1. Place the knuckles into a large saucepan with the vegetables, herbs and peppercorns.
2. Cover with cold water and a lid and bring gently to the boil.
3. Simmer for 1½–2 hours or until the meat falls away from the bone.
4. Remove from the cooking liquor and place in to a greased roasting tray.
5. Strain the liquor and discard the herbs and vegetables. Skim any fat from the liquor.
6. Place the chicory into a small saucepan and barely cover with some of the liquor. Simmer gently for about 7–10 minutes or until half cooked.
7. Remove from the pan and add to the

ham in the roasting tray. Brush with butter, bacon or ham fat; grind some black pepper on the top and then drizzle the honey over both the ham and the chicory.

8. Place into a hot oven for 20 minutes or until the chicory has caramelised slightly and the ham has browned.

9. To make the sauce, attach the bay leaves to the onion by using the cloves as studs and place in a pan. Pour over the milk and heat to scalding point.

10. In a separate pan, melt the butter, then add the flour and cook to a sandy texture over a medium heat, taking care not to colour (as this is a white sauce) – about 5–6 minutes.

11. Add the warmed milk little by little to the flour and butter mixture. Stir well each time you add more milk to prevent lumps forming. When all the milk has been added, transfer the onion to the sauce and leave to simmer gently for 10 minutes. Strain if necessary, season to taste and add the chopped parsley just before serving.

Ease of cooking: ★ ★ ★
A tad convoluted, but the pain is definitely worth it!

Preparation & cooking time: 3 hours

Tina's Tip

Great with boiled potatoes – if the ham stock is not too salty, use some for cooking the potatoes. Serve with cranberry & orange relish (p183).

Lovage can be a good substitute for parsley in the sauce.

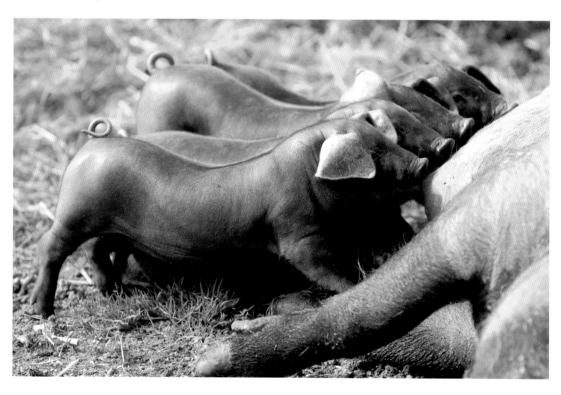

Chicory Braised with Bacon, Cider, Leeks, Ginger & Crème Fraîche

informal light meal

This little number is a great winter brunch dish – the chicory absorbs the whole spectrum of flavours and tastes. Perfect with a Pilsner, a glass of cider or dry white wine, and a hunk of warm crusty bread.

Serves 2

Ingredients

4 heads of chicory
4 thick rashers of streaky bacon
2 leeks, washed and cut into lengths to match the chicory
2 large pieces of crystallized ginger, finely sliced
1 small tub crème fraîche
1 x 330ml bottle dry cider
570ml/1 pint chicken stock
1 large bunch of fresh thyme
Freshly ground white pepper

Method

1. Pre-heat oven to 200°C.
2. Grill the bacon, cool and cut into 2 cm/1" pieces.
3. Pour the bacon fat into a thick-bottomed casserole or skillet; add the ginger, leeks and chicory.
4. Fry for 8–10 minutes or until nicely caramelized.
5. Add the bacon and the thyme.
6. Whisk the cider, chicken stock and crème fraîche in a pan, bring to the boil and simmer until reduced by almost half then pour over the leeks and chicory.
7. Place a lid on the top and bake in an oven at 200°C for 10 minutes.

Ease of cooking: ★★☆
Preparation & cooking time: 20 minutes

Coriander Pesto

versatile flavour-enhancer

If you love coriander this is another brilliant way to find an excuse to eat it. Once you have made this pesto there are many different ways of using it: brush onto grilled salmon, toss with mussels in white wine with a little coconut milk and lime juice, baste a joint of lamb and roast potatoes, place under cheese for welsh rarebit, add to sweet chilli and potato soup, and of course eat it with pasta!

Makes one large or two small jars

Ingredients

12 peeled garlic cloves
110g/4oz/1 cup fresh coriander
110g/4oz/1 cup fresh flat leaf parsley
170g/6oz pine nuts
110g/4oz grated Parmesan cheese
425ml/¾ pint organic olive oil
Freshly ground black pepper

Method

1. Combine all ingredients in a food processor and blend until smooth.
2. Decant into a jar, pour a layer of olive oil on the surface, cover with a tight-fitting lid and refrigerate until needed.

Ease of cooking: ★☆☆
Bottling quickly will capture the fresh flavours.
Preparation time: ½ hour
Freezes well

Tina's Tip

If you grow your own herbs, or benefit from a neighbour's glut, try making different flavoured pesto with the classic herb basil and also try tarragon, dill and chervil.

Cashew nuts can be used to replace the pine nuts or breadcrumbs can be used as a more frugal option.

Lavender and Hazelnut Shortbread

a classic re-visited

I find the element of surprise is good for the soul. Watching these biscuits being devoured does not disappoint.

Makes 8–12 biscuits

Ingredients

115g/4oz butter, softened but not melted
60g/2oz sugar
60g/2oz roasted ground hazelnuts
1 tbsp dried lavender flowers or 2 tbsp. fresh flowers
170g/6oz plain flour, sieved

Method

1. Preheat oven to 160°C.
2. Cream butter and sugar together.
3. Add the flour, lavender flowers, and the nuts slowly until incorporated well.
4. Lightly chill in refrigerator until easy to roll out without sticking.
5. Roll out to 1 cm thickness. Cut out biscuits with a 5.5cm round cutter.
6. Place on a greased tray. Bake for 15–20 min.
7. Cool on a wire rack. Stored in an airtight container they will keep for 1–2 weeks. Should they go stale, place the biscuits on a tray and heat through in a medium oven for 20–30 minutes to refresh them.

Ease of cooking: ★☆☆
If you have difficulty rolling these due to warm hands, chill the rolling pin and dip your hands in to iced water several times.
Preparation & cooking time: 45 minutes

Lavender Crème Brûlée

summer-scented classic with a twist

Lavender has a magical way of transforming recipes, and this crème brûlée, with its contrast of smooth, rich creaminess and bittersweet crunchy burnt sugar, is no exception. The floral aroma as the sugar is gently caramelising conjures up images of a typical English summer: the bees collecting nectar from colourful sweet-scented blossom to make honey, and baskets of fresh ripe berries oozing with juice and bursting with flavour.

Serves 4

Ingredients

8 egg yolks
15 lavender flowers & stems 5" long
850ml/1½ pints whipping cream
170g/6oz sugar

Method

1. Pre-heat oven to 130°C.
2. Put whipping cream, lavender stalks and flowers into ceramic bowl or pan and heat gently for 6 mins, (can use microwave or stove). Then cover, place in fridge and leave to infuse overnight.
3. Lightly whisk together the yolks and the sugar in a large bowl, then pour on the warmed cream and stir until the sugar has dissolved.
4. Strain, then pour into 4 ramekins.
5. Cook in the oven for about 1-1½ hours or until set.
6. Chill. Spread 2½ tsp of Demerara sugar evenly on to each brûlée and grill until the sugar has thoroughly melted.
7. Chill for 20 minutes and serve with lavender shortbread biscuits (p106).

Ease of cooking: ★ ★ ☆
Keep a close eye on these during cooking. To ensure even results turn the tray around and move shelves once or twice.
Preparation & cooking time: 1½ hours
Freezes well

Tina's Tip

These brûlées are delicious accompanied by fresh fruits, especially blackcurrants and can also be served hot.
Dried non-toxic organic lavender flowers may be used to replace the fresh lavender.
A drop of pure lavender oil (check suitability for culinary use) can further enhance the lavender aroma.

The Game Larder

The Game Larder

One bright morning in November, I was walking my two Dobermans in the local forestry commission when one of the dogs ran off and disappeared. I called and called, but to no avail. On returning to my pickup truck, accompanied only by my one bitch Kim, I was met by two men holding rifles. They asked me if I had another dog similar to the one walking beside me. I nodded. At that moment my other dog appeared, covered in blood. He had savaged a flock of sheep grazing in pasture adjacent to the woods, killing eight of them. One of the men with the guns was the father of the owner of the flock. It turned out that the other man, Mike, was a game dealer. I was ushered into an all-terrain vehicle and driven slowly around the field to survey the damage to the sheep. Details were exchanged and I then drove slowly to the local vet where I had my beloved dog 'Simon' destroyed.

The two men had been out stalking red deer. And so, by this stroke of misfortune, I was introduced to game. Since that unfortunate affair, Mike has supplied me with venison. A few years after that fateful day, Mike bought the local abattoir and now slaughters all our sheep for us, and our pigs as well.

The popularity of eating game is on the rise, and for good reason. Game is among the most natural food available. In the wild, the animals graze and forage freely, eating a very varied diet that not only keeps them healthy, but also gives the meat considerable nutritive value and a wonderful depth of flavour.

Coombeshead Estate boasts 60,000 trees, planted with a 'food from the forest theme'. The resident deer love to strip the bark, which kills the trees, so we try to keep the deer population to a minimum and whatever we cull ends up on the table.

If you have never eaten game, try some of the simple recipes that follow. Game can be quite easy to prepare and cook. Younger game is very tender and best cooked pink, while older animals are well suited for casseroles, braising, or other slow cooking. The meats featured in the recipes that follow are widely available through local butchers' shops, supermarkets, and via the internet. Pheasant, partridge, pigeon, snipe, woodcock, and mallard are generally very lean game birds with superb flavour, which can help boost our moods with a 'feel-good-factor', due to naturally high levels of selenium (almost five times that of lamb).

The ensuing recipes often call for the meat to be wrapped in bacon. This is because game is very lean, and needs the addition of fat for both basting, and also to protect the delicate nature of the meat. Most of the recipes suggest streaky bacon, as this is the most widely available fattier variety. If you are able to get hold of 'fat bacon' (pure cured back fat with no meat interspersed) so much the better, as this will add just a little more moisture during cooking.

Venison Goulash

one-pot comfort food

The first job I had when I left school at the age of 18 was as a kitchen helper/waitress in a family-run establishment called Hotel Garni Falch in St. Anton, Austria. My lasting memory of the food there was a brimming bowl of warming Gulyasuppe (made with veal and potato), which instantly made us feel quite replete. It was incredibly delicious, especially after an afternoon of energetic skiing. On the Coombeshead Estate, we have plenty of deer, some of which are culled for the table. The following recipe is a successful adaptation of the Austrian soup to a main meal of Goulash by using young venison shoulder and shank meat.

Serves 6

Ingredients

1360g/3lb venison shoulder and/or shank diced into 2cm/1" cubes
Olive oil for frying
3 large onions, peeled and thinly sliced
2 red peppers, thinly sliced
2 large potatoes, diced into 1cm/½" cubes
sea salt and black pepper
4 tbsp/¼ cup tomato purée
570ml/1 pint beef stock or a dark beer
½ cup fresh or ¼ cup dried marjoram
6 tbsp/⅓ cup Hungarian sweet paprika
Small bunch flat leaf parsley, chopped
570ml/1 pint soured cream

Method

1. Heat a heavy based casserole or pan on the stove, add some olive oil, and then brown the venison (in small batches), remove from the pan and set aside.
2. Add a little more oil, the onions and peppers and fry for 5–10 minutes.
3. Add the tomato purée and paprika then pour in the stock and bring to the boil. Add the venison and cook for 20 minutes.
4. Add the diced potatoes and cook for a further 20 minutes or until both the potatoes and the meat are cooked.
5. Taste, check the seasoning. Serve with potatoes or rice.
6. Garnish with the soured cream and the flat leaf parsley.

Ease of cooking: ★☆☆
Simple one-pot meal.
Preparation & cooking time: 30 minutes
Freezes well.

Tina's Tip

This dish is especially warming and comforting on a cold day. If you like spice, add a little more paprika and chop a medium hot chilli into small pieces to soften with the onions and peppers. (In Austria, this dish would be served with Spätzle). This recipe also lends itself well to pork. To adapt the recipe to make a soup, cut the meat into smaller cubes and add some more stock. Serve in deep bowls.

Loin of Venison with Rowanberry Jelly

superb dinner party main course

An incredibly simple dish to cook, the skill in the preparation lies in sourcing a well-hung piece of meat in perfect condition, so talk to you butcher when buying your meat.

Serves 6

Ingredients

1360g/3lb whole boned venison loin (red deer preferably)
Olive oil or pork fat for frying
Game gravy (see lamb gravy p29)
Rowanberry jelly (p188)
Sea salt & black pepper

Method

1. Pre-heat the oven to 200°C. Trim the venison of all sinew.
2. Heat the oil or fat in a heavy roasting tray on the stove until very hot, then brown the venison on both sides.
3. Leave to rest for 8 minutes, turn the meat over, then place in oven for 2 minutes.
4. Take out of the oven, turn over, rest for 8 minutes and then check to ascertain the 'doneness' by pressing gently with your finger (the more 'give' the rarer the meat). If more cooking is needed, turn the meat once again, and then roast for a further 2 minutes before resting for a further 8 (this is the most tender cut of the animal and is best enjoyed quite rare).
5. Carve against the grain at a slight angle; serve with the game gravy and rowan-berry jelly.

Ease of cooking: ★☆☆ Easy
Take care not to overcook, as venison cooks surprisingly fast.
Preparation & cooking time: 30 minutes

Tina's Tip

The resting time is important because it gives the juices time to settle once the meat is no longer subjected to heat. Once settled, the juices will remain in the flesh and not end up all over the carving board. The juice contains much of the flavour and nutrients and keeps the meat nice and moist. A good light Burgundy style wine is an excellent match for this meat.

Venison Haunch Steaks
Thyme & Wild Mushroom Sauce

glamorous but inexpensive venison

The benefit of using this cut of venison is that a well-hung haunch muscle can cook up just as nicely as loin, can also have more flavour and it is much less expensive! Allow 175–230g/6–8 oz meat per person. Both the texture and flavour of venison is better quite rare, so don't be tempted to overcook!

Serves 4

Ingredients

4 x 225g/8oz venison haunch steaks
450g/1lb mixed wild mushrooms
Large bunch of fresh thyme
2 litres/3½ pints chicken stock (p240)
1 small tub of crème fraîche
1 tbsp lemon juice
2 tbsp cornflour, mixed with a little water
120g/4oz pork fat or oil for frying
Sea salt and freshly ground black pepper

Method

1. Pick the thyme leaves from the stalks and set aside.
2. Place the thyme stalks and the chicken stock into a large pan and bring to the boil. Simmer until reduced by two-thirds then strain and set aside.
3. Brush steaks on both sides with the oil and season.
4. Heat a heavy based frying pan or skillet; add the steaks and cook for just under two minutes on each side.
5. Draw off the heat and leave to rest.
6. Place the mushrooms in a pan with a little fat or oil and fry gently for 5–6 minutes.

7. Add the chicken stock and cornflour, and boil with the mushrooms for 6–8 minutes to reduce by half.
8. Add the crème fraîche and cook until the sauce is thick and glossy.
Taste, season with salt and pepper.
Add the lemon juice, and spoon the sauce over the steaks.

Ease of cooking: ★ ★ ☆
It is important that the steaks are room temperature before cooking and that they are cooked rare for best results.
Preparation & cooking time: 1 hour

Warm Salad of Pigeon Breast

early autumn light, easy meal

Wood pigeon is Europe's most common pigeon. They live in wooded country, farmland, parks and gardens and are not at all fussy eaters, feeding on flowers, acorns, shoots, seeds, herbs, grasses and berries (and unfortunately farm crops as well). Because of their rich and varied diet, their flesh is very tasty. Pigeon meat is at its best from the end of August to the beginning of October, when the weather is mild and there is plenty for them to forage.

Squab is the West Country word for pigeon, although it is also a name used for farmed pigeon, which is a delicious alternative to wild pigeon but can be quite expensive. A squab can also be young pigeon, about 25 to 30 days old, not yet able to fly and fed solely on pigeon 'milk'. At this age it has reached its maximum degree of growth, plumpness and delicacy. Its rich and dark flesh is very tender, has a full-bodied slightly gamey flavour, and requires minimal cooking to retain both moisture and flavour. Older birds need hanging in a well-ventilated area and are best suited to slow cooking methods, such as braising or casseroling. This is a wonderful dish for a delightfully different light lunch or a starter.

Serves 4

Ingredients

8 young, tender plump wood pigeon breasts, skin removed
8 thin slices of smoked streaky bacon, grilled, fat reserved
Sea salt and freshly ground black pepper
Selection of bitter salad leaves for four (radicchio, panacalleri, endive, sugar loaf chicory, frisée etc.)
Quantity of red wine vinaigrette (p193)

Method

1. Cook the bacon in a thick-bottomed frying pan or skillet, then remove from the pan, leaving the fat in the pan.
2. Add the pigeon breasts and fry for one minute on each side.
3. Take off the heat but leave in the pan and rest for one minute on each side. They will keep cooking with the residual heat – when done they need to have a little 'give' to the touch. The aim is to cook the meat through but to leave it rare.
4. Arrange the salad leaves on four plates and drizzle with some of the vinaigrette.
5. Slice the breasts thinly at a 45° angle and arrange neatly on top of the leaves together with the bacon (warm through if necessary). Coat with a little more of the vinaigrette, sprinkle with sea salt and freshly ground black pepper and serve whilst still warm.

Ease of cooking: ★ ☆ ☆
Timing and touch is crucial for a perfect result.
Preparation & cooking time: 40 minutes

Oven Roast Wood Pigeon

impressive, inexpensive

This is a clever way to serve an inexpensive bird and will win you much applause from your guests. I cook grouse (the king of game birds) in the same way, which is also delicious but will probably cost you about ten times as much.

Serves 6

Ingredients

6 oven-ready pigeon (approx. 425g/14–16 oz each)
6 thickly sliced rashers of smoked streaky bacon, rind removed
6 sprigs of thyme and sage,stalks removed
225g/8oz lard or bacon fat (reserved from breakfast cooking)
Freshly ground black pepper
String for tying

Method

1. Pre-heat the oven to 190°C.
2. Place the bacon or fat bacon between two sheets of plastic and beat with a mallet evenly until thin all over.
3. Sprinkle the thyme and sage onto each of the beaten pieces of bacon.
5. Grind some black pepper on top.
6. Wrap one piece of bacon around each of the pigeons, taking care to cover the breast meat well, and tie with the string.
7. In a wok or heavy-bottomed frying pan heat the lard or bacon fat.
8. Fry off the tied pigeons until lightly

browned all over (approx. 6 minutes).

9. Remove from the fat and rest for 8 minutes.

10. Place the pigeons into the oven, breast down and cook for 3 minutes. Take out and rest for 8 minutes. Repeat. Then tip the bird after the second resting time to see if the juices run clear.

11. When cooked and well rested, remove the string, pull the legs away from the carcass, arrange on the plates, remove the breasts from the bone (leaving them whole), and place on top of the legs. The remaining carcass can be used for stock.

Ease of cooking: ★ ★ ☆
Preparation & cooking time: 1 hour

Tina's Tip

After having been wrapped with the bacon, the flavour of the pigeons will benefit from resting a couple of days in a fridge so the flavour of the salty, smoky bacon and the herbs can diffuse into the meat.

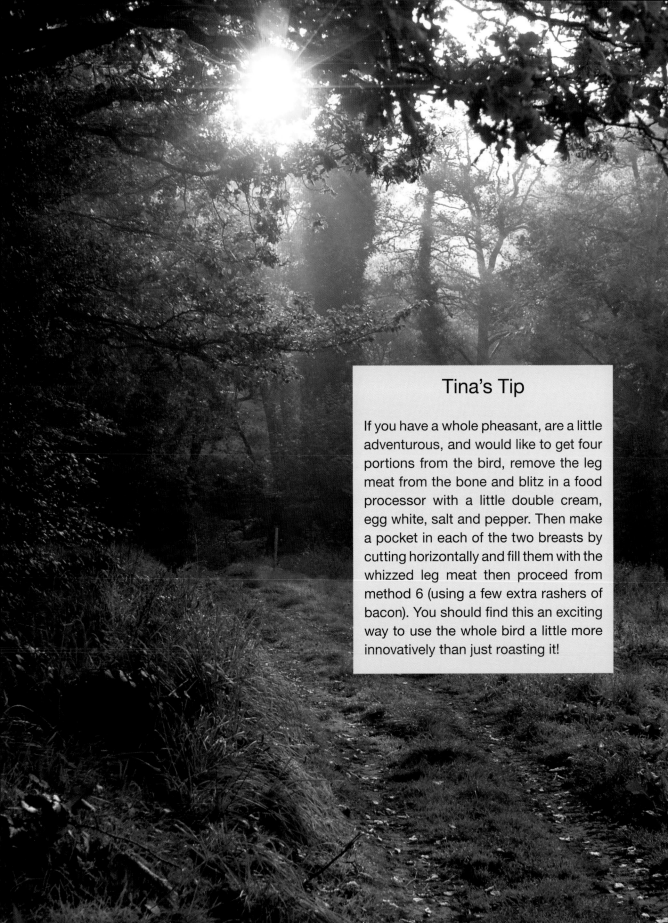

Tina's Tip

If you have a whole pheasant, are a little adventurous, and would like to get four portions from the bird, remove the leg meat from the bone and blitz in a food processor with a little double cream, egg white, salt and pepper. Then make a pocket in each of the two breasts by cutting horizontally and fill them with the whizzed leg meat then proceed from method 6 (using a few extra rashers of bacon). You should find this an exciting way to use the whole bird a little more innovatively than just roasting it!

Bacon-Wrapped Breast of Pheasant

can be pre-prepared and freezes well

Pheasants are available in abundance during the shooting season (1st October to 31st January), and because they have been introduced and bred specifically for shoots, there is no danger of over-hunting these birds. Pheasant meat is incredibly adaptable and, should you lay your hands on a brace or two, they can be turned into sausages, terrines, pâtés and broths, or they can be roasted whole. Just be careful of the shotgun pellets!

Serves 4

Ingredients

4 large rashers of smoked streaky bacon
4 tender, young pheasant breasts
(90–110g/3–4 oz each)
Salt & freshly ground black pepper
¼ cup fresh thyme leaves
Fat for brushing
Rowanberry & juniper jelly (p188)

Method

1. Pre-heat the oven to 200°C.
2. Remove the rind from the bacon, place between two plastic sheets and beat with a mallet until evenly thin.
3. Sprinkle some thyme leaves and black pepper onto the beaten bacon.
4. Butterfly the pheasant breast to open it up. Sprinkle with a little salt, pepper and the remaining thyme leaves.
5. Roll into a sausage shape, tucking the thin end of the breast towards the middle of the sausage to create an even thickness.
6. Wrap the bacon around the pheasant starting with a 45° angle, taking care to cover as much of the breast as evenly as possible.
7. Wrap with cling film and tie both ends.
8. Place in boiling water for 6 minutes (less if the meat is room temperature).
9. Remove from water and rest for 8 minutes.
10. Remove the cling film, brush with the fat and place in oven, for 4 minutes.
11. Remove from oven, turn over, rest for 8 minutes.
12. Turn again, place in oven, for 4 minutes.
13. Remove, turn, rest again for 8 minutes.
14. The meat should have just a little give and be served slightly pink.
15. Serve either whole or sliced at an angle with rowanberry and juniper jelly.

Ease of cooking: ★ ★ ☆
A delight to prepare, and can be prepared to stage 7 several days in advance.
Preparation & cooking time: 50 minutes
Freezes well at stage 7.

Wild Rabbit, Mango, Chilli & Coconut

exotic spicy dish

Introduced by the Romans into Britain, rabbits can devastate crops, but they also offer a nutritious and welcome meal. Although rabbit is included in the 'game' category, hunting is not restricted as it is deemed a pest. One day, whilst walking with a journalist around the Estate, my most portly black lab Tommy shot off across the fields into the woodland and disappeared. About 15 minutes later, he dropped a young rabbit at my feet. The meat was very tender. I made rabbit ravioli and served it for dinner the same evening! Domestic rabbit is available from some butchers and can be substituted, but it will be a good deal larger than the wild variety. Rabbit is not too dissimilar to chicken in many ways. It is very lean (the wild variety having a hint of gamey flavour) and can be successfully used as an alternative in most chicken recipes. Variety is the spice of life, and when you are in the mood for a 'fix', this could be the one for you!

Serves 4

Ingredients

2 wild rabbits, jointed
1 large or two small ripe mangoes, peeled and diced
1 x 200g/7oz packet creamed coconut, finely chopped
2–4 mild red chillies, seeds removed and cut in to small dice (wash your hands after chopping the chillies)
¼ cup ground turmeric
1 tbsp cumin seed
225g/8 oz flour
450g/1lb onion, finely chopped
850ml/1½ pints chicken stock
Small handful of curry leaves
1 bunch of fresh coriander
125g/4½oz oil or pork fat
Salt & freshly ground black pepper
1 tub plain Greek style yoghurt

Method

1. Pre-heat oven to 170°C.
2. Combine a little salt and pepper with the flour.
3. Dust the portioned rabbit pieces in the seasoned flour.
4. Heat the oil or fat in a flameproof casserole and sear the rabbit pieces gently on all sides until golden brown. Remove from the casserole and set aside.
5. Cook the onions in the remaining fat for several minutes.
6. Add the turmeric, chillies and the cumin seed and cook for a further two minutes.
7. Add the chicken stock, and bring to the boil.
8. Simmer gently for 3–4 minutes
9. Add the curry leaves and then the rabbit pieces, cover with a tight fitting lid and cook for 1–1½ hours or until the meat is almost falling off the bone. Plate the rabbit.

10. Remove the curry leaves and then add the chopped coconut and stir until dissolved.

11. Add the diced mango, check the seasoning, chop the coriander, add to the sauce and spoon the sauce over the rabbit.

Ease of cooking: ★★★
Check that the rabbit bones are cut clean and not splintered as they can be quite sharp.

Preparation & cooking time: 2 hours

Tina's Tip

If you prefer more spice, add a couple more chillies. On the other hand, if the sauce is a little too warm for you, spoon a dollop of plain yoghurt over the dish as a cooler. The lactic acid in the yoghurt also helps to counterbalance the creaminess of the coconut.

Roast Woodcock

a treat for two

The woodcock's diet is very rich which gives this game bird the characteristic flavour it is famed for. It is truly delicious, and every mouthful should be thoughtfully savoured, preferably in-between a few sips of an excellent light bodied wine such as a fruity Pinot Noir.

I have recommended this recipe for two, as it is a real treat. Firstly, woodcock is pretty expensive, and secondly, we should not be eating too many of them as their numbers are currently in decline.

Serves 2

Ingredients

2 large rashers of smoked streaky bacon
2 oven-ready woodcock
Salt & freshly ground black pepper
Thyme leaves
Fat for sealing
Game gravy (see page 126)
Crab apple jelly

Method

1. Pre-heat the oven to 200°C.
2. Remove the rind from the bacon, place between two plastic sheets and beat with a mallet until evenly thin. (Beating the bacon improves the texture of the bacon when eating and also helps it to cover more of the bird)
3. Sprinkle some thyme leaves and freshly ground black pepper onto the beaten bacon.
4. Wrap the bacon around the woodcock, taking care to cover as much of the bird as possible, especially the breast. Tie with the string.
5. Heat the fat in a heavy frying pan or wok and brown the woodcock on all sides. Remove from the heat and rest for 8 minutes.
6. Place in oven, breast side down for 4 minutes.
7. Remove from oven and rest for 8 minutes.
8. Place in oven, breast side down for 4 minutes. Remove and rest for 8 minutes.
9. Tip the bird to allow the juices to run into the pan. When the juices run clear, the bird is cooked, add to game gravy. When done, remove the string, and serve with crab apple jelly.

Ease of cooking: ★★☆
Preparation & cooking time: 1 hour

Tina's Tip

Snipe is a good substitute for woodcock. It is just as tasty, but a good deal smaller, so at least two are required per portion.

Mallard Breast & Orange Sauce

great small-portion dinner

The Mallard and the Muscovy duck are believed to be the ancestors of all domestic ducks. However, unlike the fatty domestic ducks we are accustomed to, the (much smaller) mallard has a dense, dark, rich-tasting crimson flesh which is very satisfying. Include in a three or four-course meal, where small flavour-packed servings are the order of the day.

Serves 4

Ingredients

4 mallard breasts, 90–110g/3–4oz each
Sea salt and freshly ground black pepper
2 litres/3½ pints of duck or chicken stock (p240)
1 small tub of crème fraîche
Few drops of oil or fat for frying
570ml/1 pint freshly squeezed orange juice
Freshly picked thyme, rosemary, winter savory or sage, finely chopped

Method

1. Pre-heat the oven to 200°C.
2. Heat the oil or fat in a thick-bottomed wok or frying pan.
3. Add the duck breasts skin side down first and fry gently for two minutes either side. Take off the heat and place onto a roasting tray. Rest for 8 minutes. Turn.
4. Place into the oven for 3 minutes.
5. Remove from the oven, turn and rest for 8 minutes.
6. To serve, carve at an angle and place on a warm plate with vegetables of your choice. Coat with the sauce and enjoy

To make the sauce:

Place the stock and the orange juice in a large pan and boil until it has reduced by ¾. Add the crème fraîche and simmer further until a nice thick consistency is reached. Add some freshly ground black pepper, taste, add the herbs and serve straightaway.

Ease of cooking: ★ ★ ☆
To cook to perfection, touch and timing is essential
Preparation & cooking time: 50 minutes

Tina's Tip

The breasts may need a further three minutes in the oven at stage 5, depending on how large they are and how cold they were when you started cooking. It is best to have the breast slightly too rare than overdone as mallard is quite lean and can toughen easily.

Add a few drops of orange peel oil or some finely chopped orange zest to the sauce for an additional dimension.

Game Gravy

Makes about 1 litre/1¾ pints

Ingredients

2–3kg/4–6½lb game bones & trimmings
8 fresh bay leaves
2 tbsp black peppercorns
2 large onions, 3 carrots
1 small celeriac, 1 large leek
12 sprigs fresh thyme
6 sprigs fresh lavender
Small bunch parsley
2 tbsp cornflour

Method

1. Pre-heat oven to 160°C.
2. Roughly chop the bones and trimmings and roast until well browned.
3. Drain the fat.
4. Place the bones and trimmings into large saucepan.
5. Chop vegetables and add to the pot together with the herbs and peppercorns. Cover with clean cold water.
6. Bring to the boil, simmer gently for 3–5 hours, skimming as necessary.
7. Remove the bones and vegetables.
8. Pour the stock through a fine strainer and then through muslin.
9. Remove any fat that rises to the surface.
10. Bring the stock back to the boil and simmer until it has reduced to approx 25%. Taste frequently to assess strength of reduction.
11. Thicken the reduced stock with the cornflour mixed with a little cold water.
12. Season to taste.

Ease of cooking: ★ ☆ ☆
Preparation & cooking time: 4–5 hours

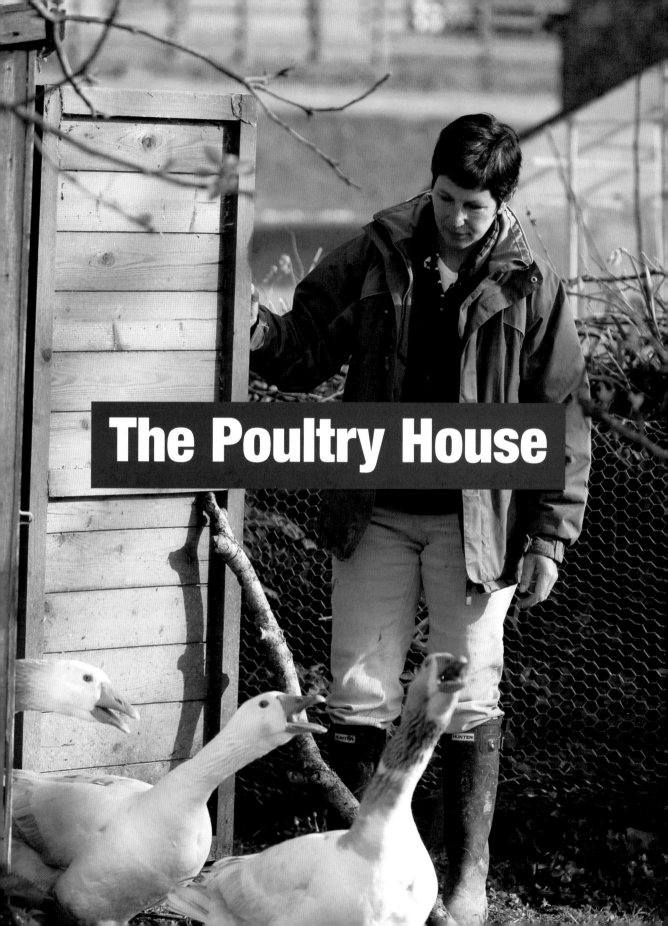

The Poultry House

The Poultry House

It is thought that chickens were domesticated around 10,000 years ago, and now there are more chickens in the world than any other bird. Chicken meat lends itself to a plethora of different styles of world cooking. Goose and duck were introduced to the table many years after the chicken and also prove to be extremely popular, but perhaps for more special occasions.

My preference for chicken is free range and organic (preferably sourced from small producers), as I am of the firm belief that it tastes significantly better. I like to go direct to source and order my chickens well in advance. The benefit here is that I am usually able to request that they are hung for 5–7 days before being plucked and eviscerated, which tenderises the chicken and improves the flavour ten-fold.

Chicken Thighs in a Herbed Parmesan Crumb

family recipe

This is a very easy and inexpensive dish. Any part of the chicken is suitable to crumb but I prefer the thigh. I find it has bags more flavour and is less likely to become dry, especially if inadvertently cooked for a little too long.

Serves 4

Ingredients

8 small chicken thighs, bone and skin removed
110g/1 cup plain flour
4 eggs
2 tbsp cold water
225g/8oz/1 cup grated Parmesan cheese
2 tbsp paprika
½ tsp cayenne pepper
150g/2 cups breadcrumbs
½ cup chopped thyme
Butter or chicken fat for frying
Sea salt and ground black pepper

Method

1. Sieve the flour together with a pinch of salt and pepper.
2. Whisk the eggs with the water.
3. Mix the chopped thyme, paprika, cayenne, Parmesan and breadcrumbs together with a generous pinch of salt and some ground black pepper.
4. Dust the chicken thighs in the flour, then dip the meat into the egg wash coating the whole surface thoroughly. Shake off the excess egg wash and dip into the crumb mixture. Coat liberally, pressing down so that the crumb adheres to the chicken.
5. Place on a tray until needed.
6. To cook, melt the butter in a heavy frying pan (a cast iron skillet is best). Add the chicken pieces and cook over a medium heat until golden brown on all sides.
7. Place in an oven pre-heated to 150°C and cook for 10 minutes.
8. Serve with a generous wedge of lemon.

Ease of cooking: ★☆☆
Very easy – the crumb can be made the day before.
Preparation & cooking time: 30 minutes
Freezes well

Tina's Tip

The removed skin from the thighs can be roasted in an oven tray at about 100°C. This will allow the fat to render, which can then be used instead of butter to cook the chicken. The chicken fat is full of chicken flavour, and it costs you nothing extra! Smoked paprika adds a fantastic aroma.

Cajun Chicken Wings

barbeque favourite

This is a fantastic barbeque recipe, and tastes almost better cold, should you have any left over. The combination of spice with the odd bit of char washes down equally well with a glass of beer or wine. Really simple to put together, the spice mix will keep for ages in the fridge and can be made well in advance so that on the day you are planning to prepare this dish, all you need to do is mix up the chicken with the spice and you are ready to cook. This recipe is certainly very moreish; I would recommend that, when preparing it, you err on the side of plenty! Good also for a finger buffet.

Serves 8 plus

Ingredients

60 chicken wings, tips removed
1 tbsp ground bay leaf
1 tbsp caraway seeds
1 tbsp cayenne pepper
1 tbsp ground coriander
1 tbsp ground cumin
20 cloves garlic, finely chopped
2 tbsp dry mustard
3 tbsp paprika
1 tbsp dried thyme
¼ cup brandy
½ cup sherry
½ cup lemon juice

Method

1. Combine all the dry ingredients.
2. Add the wet ingredients and mix to a paste.
3. Add the chicken wings to the paste and coat thoroughly.
4. Cook over a gentle heat on a barbeque, in the oven (150°C for ½ hour), in a heavy pan or a cast iron skillet on top of the stove.

Ease of cooking: ★ ☆ ☆
The most challenging element of this recipe is the shopping!
Preparation & cooking time: 45 minutes
Freezes well

Tina's Tip

This works well with chicken drumsticks (below), although the cooking time will need to be a little longer.

Rillettes

tasty economical snack

Rillettes is a preparation of meat similar to pâté. Originally made with pork, and not dissimilar to confit, the meat is cubed or chopped, salted heavily, and cooked slowly in fat until it is tender enough to be easily shredded (by pounding in a mortar), and then cooled with enough of the fat to form a spreadable paste. Rillettes can be successfully adapted to include chicken or duck meat, as in the recipe below.

Traditionally, rillettes are placed into stone jars, topped with a layer of fat, covered with white paper or a lid and stored in a cool dry place until needed. The end result is an economical, satisfying, great to make in advance rustic paste. This paste is perfect for a party canapé spread, or delicious spread on warm toast for a quick bite.

Serves 6

Ingredients

250g/9oz pork belly
4 duck or chicken legs, skin intact
400g/14oz rendered pork fat
Coarse sea salt
Handful of bay leaves
1 tbsp peppercorns
Handful of rosemary
Bunch of thyme

Method

1. Pre-heat oven to 120°C.
2. Slice the pork belly and place together with the duck or chicken legs into a thick-bottomed casserole.
3. Add the salt, peppercorns and herbs.
4. Cover with the liquid fat and place in the oven for 3–4 hours until the meat is falling off the bone.
5. Pour the contents of the casserole into a sieve placed over a bowl (to catch the fat).
6. Place all the meat in another bowl.
7. Remove the skin and the bones and then shred the meat loosely, using a fork. Place the meat into jars and cover with the fat it was cooked in, allowing a good layer on the top to seal. Cover with a lid.
8. Refrigerate.

Ease of cooking: ★ ☆ ☆
Stores well for several months refrigerated.
Preparation & cooking time: 4–5 hours

Tina's Tip

The texture is all-important in the eating. Remember to allow enough time for the rillettes to come to room temperature before use.

Duck Confit

a great store-cupboard item

Confit is a term loosely used to describe the slow cooking and preservation of anything from onions and chicken, to prawns and salmon. Making the confit begins by a process of curing, then long, slow cooking, and finally preserving by burying it under a thick, airtight seal of fat. The result is meltingly tender, succulent and flavoursome, and the prepared confit can be turned into a meal or a snack at the drop of a hat. The meats used to make confit are traditionally fatty ones – pork belly, goose, chicken and duck, although preserving game birds and rabbit is also popular. However, the lean meat needs to be combined with a fatty one. Try pork belly and pheasant, or duck and rabbit – the combination is entirely your choice!

Serves 8

Ingredients

8 whole duck legs, thighs attached
2 cups coarsely ground sea salt
8 cloves garlic, peeled
Large bunch of fresh thyme
16 sprigs of fresh rosemary
2 tbsp juniper berries
8 bay leaves
2 tbsp whole black peppercorns
½ litre/1 pint olive oil, chicken or pork fat

Method

1. Place the juniper berries and black peppercorns in a plastic bag and tap gently with a mallet.
2. Carefully crush the garlic cloves with the flat side of a large knife.
3. In a stainless steel or ceramic dish, sprinkle the base with half the salt, pepper, garlic, juniper, thyme and bay leaves.
4. Place the duck legs onto the herbs, skin side up, and sprinkle the remainder of the dry ingredients on top.
5. Cover and refrigerate for 36–48 hours.
6. Pre-heat the oven to 120°C.
7. Remove the duck from the fridge and brush off all the salt and aromatics.
8. Place in a high-sided baking dish (with a heatproof lid), just big enough to squeeze the legs into. Pour the oil or fat over the duck legs, ensuring that they are totally immersed. Cover the pot with a tight-fitting lid and cook gently for approx. 4 hours or until the meat almost falls off the bone.
9. Remove the duck from the fat.
10. To store, place the duck leg portions snugly into a jar, pour the oil through a fine strainer or muslin, then over the duck until it is totally covered, taking care not to add any of the duck juices from the bottom of the dish (this can be frozen and used for sauces at a later date). Seal the container well and refrigerate until ready to reheat.

Ease of cooking: ★ ★ ★
Needs planning but worth the effort
Preparation time: 2 days
Cooking time: 4 hours
Assembling time: 30 minutes

Tina's Tip

The excess oil/fat is packed with flavour and can be re-used if stored in an airtight container in the refrigerator. Re-boil periodically to refresh. Use for the next batch of confit (or rillettes – see page 131) or try it as an alternative to butter or oil, as a frying medium for eggs, mushrooms, courgettes etc.

Ideally, it is best to leave the confit for at least a week or two to allow the flavours to develop, although it can be eaten straightaway. When needed, either fry, roast or grill the legs in a bit of the fat until they are well browned and crisp. Use a little of the fat to roast some potatoes as an accompaniment. Another classic dish to serve with the duck confit is red cabbage braised with apples, a little brown sugar, vinegar and smoked streaky bacon – the sweet and sour nature of this dish partners the duck exceedingly well. Pairs well with spicy bramley apple chutney (page 173).

Roast Goose

a festive treat

As an alternative to turkey, goose is an exciting culinary adventure. It has shallow breasts and thick, meaty legs, which present different challenges whilst cooking. When purchasing your goose, make sure it has been hung for a while, as this ensures both tender and succulent meat. I love this dish for festive occasions, such as Christmas, birthdays or anniversaries. It is rich meat, and I find it best to eat around lunchtime or early evening when you might be able to take a stroll before bedtime.

Serves 8

Ingredients

1 Oven-ready goose 5½–6 kg/12–13lb
2 leeks
Olive oil
Salt and pepper
Lemon juice
Ground cardamom
4 sprigs rosemary
Bunch of thyme
Handful of sage leaves, chopped
200ml/7 fl oz liquid honey

Method

1. Pre-heat oven to 220°C.
2. Remove the breastbone with the point of a sharp knife (this allows for easier carving).
3. Remove any giblets and fat pads from the cavity of the bird, and season the inside lightly with salt and pepper. Insert the leeks, thyme and rosemary.
4. If the bird has been trussed, remove the string and free up the legs and wings, to allow better air circulation during cooking.
5. Prick the fat gland under the wing of the goose and by the parson's nose and then carefully score the breast (take care not to cut into the meat).
6. Rub the outside of the bird with some olive oil, salt and pepper.
7. Combine the chopped sage, salt, pepper, cardamom, honey and lemon juice to make a glaze. Set aside.
8. Place the goose in a roasting tray on its side, resting on one of its legs.
9. Place in the oven for 30 minutes.
10. Turn the goose to rest on the other leg, baste and roast for a further 30 minutes.
11. Turn the oven down to 190°C. Place the goose breast side down, baste and roast for 1¼ hour basting another three times (to prevent the meat from drying out).
12. Turn the oven down to 170°C.
13. Turn the goose breast side up.
14. Brush the skin liberally with the glaze.
15. Cook for a further 20 minutes, then brush with the glaze again.
16. Cook for a further 20 minutes.
17. Remove from the oven, cover with a damp tea towel.
18. Rest for 30 minutes, and then carve.
19. Serve with apple sauce.

Ease of cooking: ★★☆
Preparation time: 40 minutes
Cooking time: 3–3½ hours
Resting time: 30 minutes

Tina's Tip

If, at any stage, you find the goose browning too quickly, cover it with some aluminium foil.

Geese are normally sold complete with giblets. These can weigh anything up to 20% of the weight of the bird, so it is important to take that in to consideration when calculating how many people you are planning to cook for and the cooking time. Allow approx. 20 minutes per kg for a small bird (4–4½ kg) and 30–35 minutes per kg for a large bird (6kg +). Domesticated geese are fairly fatty, hence the long cooking time at a relatively high heat. You may find that after the initial hour or so of cooking, quite a bit of fat has rendered into the base of the roasting tray (the fat is exceptionally delicious, and you can expect roughly 1 litre from each bird). At this stage, the fat can be poured off into another tray for roasting potatoes, parsnips and carrots etc. or you may find it easier to remove the bird to another roasting tray and then use the one with the fat for the vegetables.

The fat pads found inside the cavity can be scored, salted and rendered, to be used to rub over the bird instead of the olive oil. Any additional fat is best kept in a jar in the fridge for later use.

If you keep horses, goose fat is invaluable as an aid for countless dermatological conditions. It can also be used to prevent foot rot in sheep, combined with copper sulphate and plastered in-between the hooves.

Chicken Liver and Wild Mushroom Parfait

fabulous wedding party starter

An inexpensive and thoroughly rewarding dish, suitable for a starter, light lunch, a quick nibble, or as a spread in sandwiches. This freezes well, but can also be success- fully stored for several months (in a dry cool place or in the refrigerator) in kilner jars with a little clarified butter poured over the top.

Fills 3 x 2lb bread tins

Ingredients

1250g/2¾lb organic chicken livers
900g/2lb clarified butter, pork or chicken fat, melted then cooled
5 whole eggs, whisked and sieved
3 bottles/2½ litres red wine
8 fl oz/1 cup dessert wine
680g/1½ lbs finely chopped onion
1 tbsp chopped garlic
⅔ cup mushroom powder (see tip)
¼ cup fresh thyme, finely chopped

Method

1. Sweat the onion and the garlic with some f the fat until opaque.
2. Add the thyme, the red and dessert wine and cook until it has reduced to a jam-like glaze.
3. Mince or blitz the raw livers and then pass through a sieve or moulin together with the glaze.
4. Blend the sieved eggs and the cooled butter gently into the livers.
5. Stir in mushroom powder.
6. Pour into bread tins lined with grease-proof paper.
7. Cook in water bath in the oven for 1 hr 25 min at 150°C.

Ease of cooking: ★ ★ ★
Make sure you have plenty of counter space.
Preparation & cooking time: 2½ hours
Freezes beautifully if cooked in tins.

Tina's Tip

To make your own mushroom powder, place mushrooms of your choice (wild or cultivated) onto some kitchen paper and place in a warm oven, or in the bottom of an Aga, until thoroughly dried. Place in a blender (covered with a damp tea towel) and whiz until a powder is reached. Sieve and store in a jar until needed.

Potted Chicken

good snacking dish with a bottle of rosé

This is a classic way to serve chicken with toast as a first course. It can also be used generously in sandwiches.

Serves 8

Ingredients

1 x 1.8kg/4lb chicken
12 slices streaky bacon cut into 1cm pieces
340g/12oz shallots or onion
285ml/10 fl oz chicken stock
225g/8oz pork fat, clarified or melted butter
10 sprigs tarragon
Generous bunch thyme or summer savory, leaves removed and set aside.
1 large head of garlic, broken into cloves
2 tsp ground mace
Salt & freshly ground black pepper

Method

1. Pre-heat the oven to 200°C.
2. Grease a heavy-bottomed casserole with the butter or use a chicken brick and arrange the tarragon, thyme, or summer savory stalks and garlic over the base.
3. Rub chicken over with the salt & pepper.
4. Place the chicken in the casserole or brick, drizzle with butter.
5. Place in the oven and roast for ½ hour.
6. Turn the heat down to 150°C, add the chicken stock, cover with a tight-fitting lid and cook for a further ½ hour or until done.
7. Remove from the casserole or brick. Strain the juices and set aside (the stock can be used as a delicious base for sauces or soups).
8. Leave to cool and then remove the meat from the bones.
9. Season with the salt & pepper.
10. Place a little butter or oil with the onions and bacon and sweat until cooked. Add mace.
11. Mince the cooked chicken, onions, bacon and herbs finely or place in a blender until the mixture resembles a coarse paste. Check seasoning.
12. Pack into an earthenware pot, cover with the pork fat or clarified butter and chill well, preferably overnight. The meat can be kept for two to three weeks in the coldest part of the refrigerator.

Ease of cooking: ★ ★ ☆
Best made in advance to allow flavours to 'marry'
Preparation & cooking time: 2 hours

Baked Chicken & Ham Pie

pre-prepared standby

This is a good little number to put together in two stages. Spend half an hour or so making the pie, then refrigerate and bake later on in the day, perhaps when you return from a day's shopping, or come home from work.

Serves 4

Ingredients

680g/1½lb diced, raw chicken
90g/3oz diced cooked ham
2 tbsp/¼ cup plain flour
1 large leek, chopped
½ medium celeriac, diced
1 onion, chopped
3 cloves garlic, finely chopped
1 tbsp ground coriander
1 bunch flat leaf parsley or lovage
3 sprigs thyme, thick stalks removed
30g/1oz butter
60ml/2 fl oz chicken stock
1 beaten egg for glazing
Quantity of short crust pastry
Salt & pepper

Method

1. Pre-heat the oven to 165°C.
2. Grease a suitable baking dish with the butter.
3. Sieve the flour, salt, pepper & ground coriander together into a bowl
4. Coat the chicken thoroughly and shake off the excess.
5. Cover the base of the baking dish alternately with the leeks, celeriac, onion, garlic, herbs and the ham and chicken.
6. Pour over the stock.
7. Roll out the shortcrust pastry (p239) to about 2cm/½" thick.
8. Brush the sides of the dish with a little of the egg wash to help the pastry stick.
9. Place the pastry on top of the meat and vegetables.
10. Crimp the side of the pastry firmly.
11. Brush the top and sides with the egg wash, make two crosses with a sharp knife in the pastry to allow the steam to escape during cooking (otherwise the filling may escape), and place into the oven to cook for 1 hour.
12. Serve hot.

Ease of cooking: ★★☆
A quick version can be achieved by purchasing ready-made pastry and cooked chicken, although the cooking time will need to be reduced to ½ hour at 200°C.
Preparation & cooking time: 1 hour 40 minutes

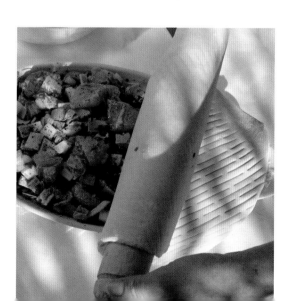

Breast of Barbary Duck, Cooked Pink with Sage & Juniper Gravy

impressive dinner party dish

Once slaughtered and butchered, the Muscovy duck becomes referred to as Barbary Duck. This species is used to mate with other species because they grow fast, are similar in texture and colour to Mallard and have a lighter fat covering than the Aylesbury duck. This is my favourite breed because not only are they fun to keep and very colourful to have around the yard, but also because if they are hung entire for a few days after killing, the flavour is improved enormously. This dish is definitely one to earmark for a dinner party – and will get you full marks and lots of compliments from your guests.

Serves 6

Ingredients

6 female (300g/7oz each) or 3–4 male (450g/10oz each) breasts of Barbary duck
Sea salt
1 small bunch of thyme
2 tsp juniper berries, crushed
½ tbsp cracked black peppercorns
20 sage leaves, chopped
2 tbsp cornflour, mixed with a little cold water
2 litres/3½ pints chicken stock

Method

1. Boil the chicken stock, crushed juniper berries, cracked peppercorns, thyme and half the sage leaves together until reduced to about a third of the original volume. Thicken with the cornflour, strain, add the remaining sage leaves and check the seasoning and the consistency. Keep warm.
2. Score the fat side of the duck breasts, taking care not to cut through the meat.
3. Rub a generous pinch or two of salt onto the cut surface.
4. Heat a wok or heavy frying pan.
5. Place the duck breasts skin side down into the hot pan.
6. Cook until most of the fat has rendered – pour this off periodically into a glass bowl and reserve to use at a later date (for roasting potatoes perhaps).
7. Turn the breasts over to seal.
8. Remove from the pan and place on a baking tray, skin down.
9. Leave to rest for 8 minutes, turn.
10. Pre-heat the oven to 200°C. Place in the oven for 4 minutes.
11. Remove from oven, turn and leave to rest for 8 minutes.
12. Return to oven and cook for 4 minutes.
13. Remove again, turn and rest for 8 minutes.

Ease of cooking: ★★☆
Preparation & cooking time: 1 hour

Tina's Tip

This method should have given the breasts enough time to cook through, whilst remaining deliciously succulent and pink. While the duck is resting for the final time, cook your vegetables and plate up. Serve the duck sliced thinly against the grain, add the sage leaves to the sauce at the last minute and pour over the duck.

Yoghurt-baked Chicken Breast with Ginger and Paprika

easy and unusual

This exceptionally tasty dish (with its roots firmly in Asia) was introduced to me by one of my Sri Lankan kitchen assistants in my London restaurant. Not only is it tasty, it is also relatively low in fat. Easy to prepare, the chicken is best marinated overnight.

Serves 6

Ingredients

6 medium chicken breasts bone and skin removed
570ml/1 pint plain yoghurt
¾ cup oil
⅓ cup grated fresh root ginger
2 tsp ground cardamom
2 tsp ground coriander
1 tsp salt
2 tsp black pepper
2 tbsp paprika
Bunch of fresh coriander

Method

1. Combine all the ingredients except the fresh coriander.
2. Place the chicken breasts in the marinade, cover and leave for a couple of hours or in the fridge overnight.
3. Pre-heat the oven to 200°C.
4. Place the chicken breasts on a well-greased baking tray. Cook for 15 minutes.
5. Turn oven down to 150°C and bake for a further 10 minutes or until cooked.
6. Sprinkle with the freshly chopped coriander and serve with a nice tossed avocado, rocket & watercress salad.

Ease of cooking: ★ ☆ ☆
Marinating time aside, this is both quick and easy to assemble and cook.
Preparation & cooking time: overnight plus 40 minutes.

Tina's Tip

Chicken thighs can be used but will need a longer cooking time. The flavour improves on re-heating. Good cold.

The Orchard & Fruit Garden

The Orchard & Fruit Garden

In the year 2000, sixty acres of the Coombeshead Estate were landscaped with trees. A 'food-from-the-forest' theme was adopted and species such as rowanberry, cobnut, hazel, cloudberry, crab apple, juniper and walnut were planted. These trees not only provide a wide selection of edible ingredients but also attract much beautiful wildlife. In summers past, some of the wild birds helped themselves to our cultivated ripe blackcurrants (in the fruit garden) and then inadvertently seeded some fruiting black-currant bushes along the rides within the woodland, which have become a welcome addition to the living larder.

Adjacent to our woodland plantation, we have established an apple orchard boasting local varieties such as the Cornish Mother, the Plympton Pippin, the Tom Putt and the Woolbrook Pippin. In the centre stand ten trees grafted from the Bramley family's original rootstock. Celia Stevens donated them to us in 2003. Celia is the great great granddaugher of Henry Merryweather who introduced the Bramley in 1865.

Blackberry & Apple Pie

a celebration of autumn

Juicy blackberries and tart apples, cinnamon, brown sugar and perhaps a hint of clove. These autumn ingredients evoke a warm, homey sensation; the mouth waters and the taste buds anticipate devouring the first forkful, slowly.
The ratio of apples to blackberries should be roughly 60:40.

Pick the berries when dry, otherwise they will exude too much liquid, have a diluted flavour and make the pastry soggy. This typically British dish is perfect for Sunday lunch. I like to make a large pie as it is equally good to eat cold the next day – if you have any left!

Serves 8

Ingredients

Quantity of sweet pastry (p239)
1360g/3lb/6 large bramley apples
800g/1¾lb/approx. 5 punnets of black-berries (cultivated or wild)
Sugar to taste (+/- 10%) therefore approx. 200g according to the tartness of the apples and blackberries
1 tbsp ground cinnamon

Method

1. Pre-heat the oven to 220°C.
2. Peel, core and quarter the apples, cutting them into fairly large pieces. Place in a bowl, add the sugar and cinnamon, and toss well. Add the blackberries and combine lightly with the apples and sugar.
3. Place in a large well-greased pie dish.
4. Roll the pastry to ¼" thick, just wide enough to lay over the edge of the dish.
5. Brush the rim of the pie dish with a little milk to help the pastry to stick to it. Gently lift pastry and place over the fruit.
6. Press down the edges firmly, crimping the pastry with your fingers all the way round. Brush the pastry with some milk,

sprinkle with some sugar and then cut a few slits in the pastry to allow steam to escape. If you have a pie funnel, now is the time to use it.
7. If there is any pastry left over, let your artistic talents shine and cut shapes of your choice to decorate the pie with.
8. Place in the oven and cook for just under 1 hour, or until the pastry is a light golden colour and the apple and black-berry juices are just beginning to bubble through the slits.
9. Serve with lightly whipped double cream, fresh egg custard (p217), cardamom or cinammon ice cream (p212).

Ease of cooking: ★☆☆ Simple.
Roll the pastry only once, to ensure you don't toughen it.
Preparation & cooking time: 1½–2 hours

Tina's Tip

Don't be tempted to add water to the fruit; the cooked pie will be juicy enough, especially if the apples and currants have been freshly harvested, as their water content will be fairly high.

Baked Blackcurrant Cheesecake

perfect mid-morning with fresh coffee

This is an absolute must in July when the currants start to ripen. Choose the plumpest, juiciest currants – they are nearly always the ones at the top of the bushes occupying the sunniest, most sheltered spot. The depth of fruit flavour and acidity of the black-currants just begs for the richness of the cream and crème fraîche base.

Serves 8/10

Ingredients

For the crust
1 large packet/300g/10½oz of unsweet-ened digestive biscuits
100g/3½oz soft brown sugar
2 tsp cinnamon
225g/8oz butter, melted

For the filling
600g/20oz cream cheese
510g/18oz low fat cream cheese, fromage frais or quark
400g/14oz soured cream or crème fraîche
300g/10oz caster sugar
2 tsp cinnamon
9 beaten eggs
Zest and juice of one lemon or two limes

For the fruit topping
900g/2lb ripe blackcurrants
450g/1lb sugar
8 leaves of gelatine or enough powder to set 2 litres/3½ pints of liquid

Method

To make the crust

1. Crush the biscuits (use a thick plastic bag and a rolling pin) and mix thoroughly with the melted butter, cinnamon and soft brown sugar.
2. Place on the base of a 26cm/10" spring form tin and press down firmly with the back of a fork.
3. Chill for 10 minutes.

To make the filling

1. Pre-heat the oven to 150°C
2. In a bowl, blend the cream cheese, quark, sugar and cinnamon.
3. Add the eggs a little at a time until thoroughly incorporated. Fold in the soured cream/crème fraîche and the lemon/lime juice and zest.
4. Pour into the prepared tin and bake for approx 1 hour or just until the centre of the cheesecake still has a slight wobble to it (check after 45 minutes to make sure you don't overcook).
5. Turn off the oven. Leave in the oven to cool slowly as this helps to prevent cracking. When thoroughly cool, remove from the oven and refrigerate for 2–3 hours.

To make the topping

1. Place the blackcurrants and sugar in a saucepan and cook over a gentle heat until the currants start to burst (5–7 minutes).

2. Take off the heat and spoon about half a pint of the liquid into a bowl.

3. If using gelatine leaves, soak them in a bowl of cold water until soft, then squeeze out the excess water and dissolve in the hot blackcurrant liquid. Add the dissolved gelatine to the blackcurrants and leave to cool for about 1 hour.

To assemble

1. Take the cooked cheesecake out of the fridge.

2. Pour the fruit over the cheesecake and place back in the fridge for 1 hour or until set.

3. To serve, heat a thin bladed knife under hot water and slide it around the cheese-cake to release it from the tin. Slice into portions and serve (heat the knife after each cut to ensure a smooth finished edge).

Ease of cooking: ★ ★ ☆
This is a very good recipe to make in advance as it keeps well, refrigerated.
Preparation & cooking time: 2 hours
Chilling time: 3–4 hours or overnight
Freezes well.

Tina's Tip

Try making the topping with different fruits such as apricot, raspberry, mango logan berries or gooseberries.

Bramley Apple, Fig and Hazelnut Flapjacks

a nutty, sustaining snack

Hazel is a hardy shrub. We have many of these planted that border the rides (paths) in between the trees of our woodland. The nuts taste fantastic when freshly harvested. It is quite a battle however, to get to them before the squirrels do, although as soon as they start to help themselves, at least you know that the nuts are ripe and in perfect condition! A tasty snack is enjoyable at any time you are looking for a nibble. Commercially cultivated hazelnuts are usually labelled as cob nuts and are considerably larger than their wild cousin.

Makes 30

Ingredients

900g/2lb Bramley apples, quartered, cored, peeled and sliced
330g/12oz butter
90g/3oz golden syrup
280g/10oz soft brown sugar or jaggery
170g/6oz oat flakes (whole)
220g/7½oz oat flakes (blitzed in food processor)
100g/3½oz cob or hazelnuts, roasted, skins removed and crushed
1 tbsp ground ginger
½ cup fig paste (from health food shops)
pinch of salt

Method

1. Simmer the apples gently in a covered pan with 40g/1½ oz of the sugar, but no liquid, until pulpy. Cool slightly.
2. Pre-heat oven to 190°C
3. Butter and line the base of a roasting tray with parchment.
4. In a large pan, heat the remaining sugar with the butter and syrup until dissolved, but do not boil, whisk in the fig paste and stir in the oats, cobnuts, salt and ginger.
5. Before it cools, line the base (of the parchment-lined roasting tray) with three-quarters of the flapjack mixture
6. Pour the apple pulp over the flapjack mixture and spread evenly. Cover with the remaining mixture, pressing it down lightly.
7. Bake for 35 minutes. Remove from the oven, leave to cool for 10 minutes before scoring into portions.
8. Cool thoroughly before turning out.
9. Store in an airtight container. Will keep for up to 1 week.

Ease of cooking: ★☆☆ Simple to do. Any type of cooking apple can be used.
Preparation & cooking time: 1 hour

Tina's Tip

If you are a fan of crystallized ginger, finely chop or purée some stem ginger and use it to replace the fig paste.
Allens Farm Kent Cobnuts sell organic cobnuts by mail order (www.cobnuts.co.uk). Order when they are in season – from October. Hazelnuts (much more widely available) used as a substitute provide an equally good flapjack!

Caramelised Apple Tart

delicious upside-down dessert

As soon as the orchard apples are ready in the autumn, this sweet is definitely at the very top of my dessert list. Rich and warming, the luscious caramel topped with melt-in-the-mouth pastry combines fantastically with cinnamon ice cream. Savour slowly with a nice glass of Calvados.

Serves 6 individual portions

Ingredients

Quantity of sweet pastry (p239)
3 good clean fresh large Bramley apples
300g/10oz in weight and 3⅝"/90–110mm in diameter

For the caramel

510g/18oz soft brown sugar
125g/4½oz butter
1 tsp ground star anise or one whole pod
2–3 cinnamon sticks
145ml/5 fl oz water

Method

To make the caramel

1. Place all ingredients in a wide heavy-based stainless steel pan. Bring to the boil stirring continuously to dissolve the sugar.
2. Simmer to infuse the spices 5–10 min.
3. Strain into another pan to remove spices. Boil to evaporate the water until a caramel consistency is reached (you can also use a sugar thermometer and cook the caramel to 160°C–175°C).
4. Place approx. 90g/3oz into each of 6 small bowls and set aside in a warm oven to keep soft.

To prepare the apples

1. Cut apples in half, remove the core, peel and slice evenly (see photo overleaf).
2. Fan the sliced apples as shown then push them into the softened caramel.
3. Place the six bowls on to a tray and then cook, uncovered in an oven at 150°C for 30 minutes.
4. Leave to cool.

To prepare the pastry

1. Roll out the pastry approx. 8mm thick and then cut into 6 discs and 110mm wide (approx. 70–80g/2½–3oz in weight) using a 4½"/10½ cm cutter.
2. Place pastry discs on top of the apples and bake for a further 30 min at 160°C until pastry is cooked through.
3. Rest for at least a couple of hours.
4. When ready to serve heat for 12 minutes at 150°C, then run a small knife around the edge of the bowl to loosen the apples and caramel.
5. Carefully tip out of bowl upside down onto plates, trim with a round cutter if desired and serve with ice cream.

Ease of cooking: ★★☆
Handle the caramel carefully: it is hot
Preparation & cooking time: 2 hours

Tina's Tip

Don't be alarmed if the apples look too large for the bowl. They will shrink considerably when cooked.

Best to make the tarts a day before if you can – they somehow hold together a little better when you come to turn them out. This recipe can be made in a single pie dish if preferred.

Poached Pears in Elderflower Syrup

versatile, simple dessert or breakfast

This is a good standby dessert best served chilled straight from the fridge. These pears are also delicious with thick creamy Greek yoghurt for breakfast.

Serves 4

Ingredients

4 large pears, ripe but not soft
570ml/1 pint elderflower syrup (p156)

Tina's Tip

This is a great way to preserve pears. When just cooked, pot into sterilized jars and seal whilst still warm. These will last at least 1 year kept in a cool dark place.

Method

1. Halve, core and peel the pears
2. Place in a stainless steel or ceramic saucepan or casserole.
3. Cover with the syrup.
4. Bring to the boil, turn down the heat and simmer for 15 minutes.
5. Turn off the heat and leave to cool (the pears will continue to cook for a while as the liquor cools).
6. Chill (preferably overnight) and serve with ice cream or crème fraîche.

Ease of cooking: ★☆☆
Preparation & cooking time: 40 minutes

Elderflower Syrup

summer in a bottle

They say that summer begins when the elder comes into flower, and ends when the berries are ripe. The large white clusters of elderflower blooms can be found in flower from as early as late April until the end of July (depending on where you live). It is best to collect the flowers well away from roads and other possible forms of pollution. This delightfully fragrant flower has a heady scent, which provides endless possibilities for a bountiful harvest with many uses, of which elderflower syrup happens to be just one. Diluted with some sparkling water it makes a very refreshing summer drink and is especially energizing if you need a boost when doing sports. Mix with a little hot water for a tonic to help cure sore throats and colds. Why not try mixing a little of the syrup with Champagne to make a kir royale with a difference.

Makes a generous 2 litres

Ingredients

35 freshly picked, clean elderflowers, stalks removed, approx. 100g/3½oz
1kg/2lb 3oz sugar
2 organic lemons, washed, grated, squeezed, rinds cut up
60g/2oz citric acid
1 litre/1¾ pints cold, bottled still water or previously boiled tap water

Method

1. Put all the ingredients into a stainless steel pan in a cool place for two days. Stir occasionally.
2. Strain through a fine strainer or muslin to remove the elderflowers and lemon pieces and then pour the syrup into sterilized bottles.
3. Keep refrigerated.
4. Dilute to drink.

Tina's Tip

Citric acid is a natural preservative. It is available (from chemists and home brew outlets) in crystalline form and is extracted mainly from lemons and limes. It is also useful for sprinkling over avocados or apples to prevent browning.

Avoid washing or wetting the flowers, as this will spoil the fragrance.

Once you have bottled your elderflower syrup, be sure to store in a cool place. If they happen to be somewhere warm, fermentation can occur, and you may well be seriously taken by surprise (with the sound of an unplanned firework display) when the bottles start to explode!

Ease of cooking: ★ ☆ ☆
An easy pantry ingredient to prepare, this syrup also makes a welcome gift.
Preparation & bottling time: 2 days

Baked Pears

easy late summer dessert

When the majestic evening sun is about to set on a halcyon summer's evening, and you have decided to invite the neighbours around for a spur-of-the-moment 'al fresco' meal, rustle up this sweet in twenty minutes, from start to finish, to reinforce your 'super-neighbour' status.

Serves 4

Ingredients

4 large pears, ripe but not soft
1 large washed organic lemon, grated and juiced.
100g/3½oz walnuts
300g/10½oz soft light brown sugar
60g/2oz butter

Method

1. Pre-heat the oven to 200°C. Peel, halve and core the pears.
2. Place them in a well-buttered oven tray, flat side uppermost.
3. Paint with the freshly squeezed lemon juice.
4. Combine the nuts, sugar, grated rind and butter in a blender and process lightly.
5. Sprinkle the mix over the pears.
6. Bake for 15–20 minutes until the mixture is bubbling and caramelising.
7. Serve.

Tina's Tip

Lightly toast the walnuts if you have the time. The butter can be replaced by walnut oil for a nuttier flavour. Cinnamon or ground ginger can be added to the brown sugar for a hint of spice.

Ease of cooking: ★☆☆ Super simple
Preparation & cooking time: 30 minutes

Rhubarb – Fruit or Vegetable?

Although commonly used as a fruit, rhubarb is actually a vegetable related to plants such as sorrel and buckwheat. In the United States it was considered a vegetable until the 1940s. Then it was reclassified as a fruit when US customs officials decided it should be classified according to the way it was eaten.

Rhubarb boasts an incredible versatility, and can be used to make jam, chutney, crumbles, cobblers, pies, cakes, sorbets, ice creams, jellies, bread, fools, confit and even a sauce to accompany oily fish.

So, there is no excuse not to have a rhubarb crown or two growing in your garden if you have the space. It appears each year, is rarely bothered by pests, is frost-hardy (a frost actually improves the flavour), has an excellent yield and a long fruiting season (May to August). However, if you are as fond of this vegetable as I am, you might be tempted to encourage some early growth by forcing it – use old chimney pots, up-turned buckets or even old tyres, which you can build up and fill with straw and then keep covered with a lid to keep the warmth in. The plants will then flourish, providing you with delicious tender stalks at a point when there is little else cropping in the garden.

Forced rhubarb is infinitely more delicate than its hardy un-protected counterpart and is even more succulent. If you do not grow your own rhubarb, the way to tell if the stems are forced is to look at its incredible colour: a particularly eye-pleasing vibrant crimson as opposed to ruby red and green stems.

Rhubarb & Elderflower Sorbet

surprise intercourse

Elderflowers are in flower predominantly during May by which time the rhubarb is well-established and growing fast, and the two together are delightful. This sorbet makes an exceptional palate cleanser for a surprise 'intercourse' at a dinner party, or, if you enjoy the combination, why not try making this into a slush-granita to enjoy as a refreshing drink?

Serves 4

Ease of cooking: ★☆☆ Easy
Preparation & freezing time: 5–10 hours

Ingredients

750ml/25 fl oz/3 cups water
110g/4½oz/½ cup sugar
30g/1oz/10 freshly-picked, clean elderflowers, stalks removed
Freshly squeezed juice of 1 lemon
6 stems of rhubarb, washed, cooked and sieved

Method

1. Combine the elderflowers and sugar in a food processor and pulverize for about 1 minute.
2. Bring the water to the boil, remove the pan from the heat and add the sugar/elderflower mixture, stirring to dissolve the sugar.
3. Cover with a lid and leave to cool for half an hour.
4. Remove the flowers through a sieve, pressing the flowers to get out any remaining liquid.
5. Add the sieved rhubarb and lemon juice. Chill in the refrigerator, then freeze in a sorbet or ice cream mixer.

Tina's Tip

One lightly beaten egg white, added to the sorbet as it is churning, helps it to stay soft enough to be able to scoop straight from the freezer. Alternatively, take out of the freezer 15 minutes before serving to soften.

If you don't want to make a sorbet, then try making a syrup from the elderflowers and use it to poach the rhubarb. Chill the resulting compote and enjoy with thick Greek yoghurt, cream or ice cream.

Rhubarb, Ginger & Oatmeal Crumble

advance preparation for an unforgettable pud

Rhubarb, ginger and cardamom enjoy each other's company enormously. This zinging combination is absolutely fantastic, and the added beauty of this recipe is that the crumble can be made several days in advance, will also keep well after cooking and tastes fabulous cold. Certainly one for discerning 'foodies', this recipe gives the taste buds a complete workout, leaving them feeling totally exhausted, yet overwhelmingly at peace.

Serves 6–8

Ingredients

For the rhubarb
900g/2lb rhubarb, washed and cut into
1" diagonal dice
60g/2oz/¼ cup sugar
60g/2oz freshly grated root ginger
Butter for greasing

For the crumble
160g/6oz soft brown sugar
120g/4oz self-raising flour
5g/1tsp ground ginger
100g/3½oz oats
150g/5oz butter, chilled
5g/1tsp freshly ground cardamom

Method

For the rhubarb

1. Butter an 8" oven-proof dish.
2. Combine the rhubarb, sugar and grated ginger.
3. Fill the dish with the mixture. Pack tightly.

For the crumble

1. Place the chilled butter, sugar, ground ginger, cardamom and flour in a food processor.
2. Blitz until it resembles a fine crumb.
3. Add the oats and blitz again on pulse, just enough to chop the oats roughly.

To assemble

1. Pre-heat the oven to 180°C.
2. Cover the rhubarb with the crumble mix.
3. Press down firmly for a crispy crust.
4. Bake for 1 hour until the topping is golden brown and the rhubarb is cooked.

Ease of cooking: ★ ☆ ☆
Preparation & cooking time: 1½ hours

Tina's Tip

To peel the ginger root easily, soak in a bowl of cold water for 15 minutes and then scrape off the peel. Serve the crumble with ginger or cardamom ice cream (see p212) to mirror the flavour of the fresh ginger (cardamom is the seed pod of the ginger plant).

Plum Cobbler

popular, easy dessert

The scent and texture of plums is a good indication of ripeness. They should feel soft to the touch and smell sweet and plummy. If you are fortunate enough to have a plum tree, and you preserve them, you can enjoy them all through the winter months.

A 'cobbler' (as in cobble together) can be likened to a 'crumble'. The topping is like shortbread dough, which soaks up all the delicious fruit juices during cooking making it moist underneath, yet crisp on top. Many different types of fruit can be used in this dessert, such as gooseberry, blackcurrant, blackberry and apple. This recipe is very reliable, will appeal to the masses, and also makes an interesting alternative served cold, for breakfast.

Serves 6

Ingredients for the fruit

24 large ripe plums, stoned
240g/8oz/1 cup soft brown sugar
½ cup cold water
2 tbsp cornflour
2 tbsp fresh lemon juice
½ tsp ground cinnamon
½ tsp freshly grated nutmeg
butter for greasing

... and for the cobbler

220g/9oz/2 cups plain flour
3 tsp baking powder
Pinch salt
100g/3tbsp caster sugar
90g/3oz/6 tbsp butter
180ml/7 fl oz/¾ cup of milk
2 tbsp caster sugar, for sprinkling

Method for the fruit

1. Place the plums in a saucepan with the sugar, water, and ground cinnamon.

2. Bring to the boil and simmer gently until the plums are tender and the water has reduced by half.
3. Mix the cornflour with the lemon juice and add to the plums.
4. Cook for another 5 minutes until the sauce has thickened.
5. Transfer the fruit to a buttered baking dish and set aside.

For the topping

1. Pre-heat oven to 200°C.
2. Sift together the dry ingredients.
3. Rub in the butter.
4. Add the milk and mix to a soft paste.

To assemble

1. Drop the shortbread mix by spoonfuls onto the fruit; sprinkle with caster sugar.
3. Bake for 30 minutes or until the topping has risen and is golden brown.
4. Serve hot or cold with cream, creamy yoghurt or ice cream.

Ease of cooking: ★☆☆ Easy
Preparation & cooking time: 1 hour

Summer Fruit Meringue & Lavender Ice Cream

impressive dessert

Visually stunning, this dessert owes its success not only to the mouthwatering flavours but also to the combination of textures: soft and juicy, cool and creamy, light and crunchy, this meringue simply stimulates every sense – and it melts in the mouth!

Serves 4

Ingredients

140ml/¼ pint of egg white
110g/4oz caster sugar
170g/6oz raspberries
170g/6oz loganberries
170g/6oz red & blackcurrants
Maple syrup to sweeten fruit (optional)
Qty of lavender ice cream (p212)
Small tub crème fraîche
Qty toffee sauce (p209)
¼ cup hazelnuts, lightly crushed

To make the meringue

1. Pre-heat the oven to 120°C.
2. Whisk the egg whites for 8–10 minutes until stiff.
3. Add half of the sugar and whisk for a further 1 minute.
4. Fold in the rest of the sugar.
5. Pipe or spoon the mix into four nests on a tray lined with parchment, making a slight indent in each one with the back of a spoon.
6. Bake for 2 hours.

To assemble

1. In a bowl, combine the fruit and a few drops of maple syrup.
2. Place a meringue nest on a little blob of crème fraîche on each plate (this prevents the meringue from sliding around).
3. Spoon a little more crème fraîche into each meringue nest and top with a scoop of lavender ice cream.
4. Arrange the fruit around the base of the meringue. Ladle some toffee sauce over the ice cream and sprinkle with a few hazelnuts. Garnish with mint, dust with icing sugar, and finish with a pansy.

Ease of cooking: ★ ☆ ☆
Preparation & cooking time: 2½ hours

Tina's Tip

The slightest hint of grease on your utensils will prevent the egg whites from whisking up properly, so wash them with hot soapy water before you start. Any fruit can be used with the meringue – if using strawberries, lightly crush a few ripe berries to release the juices in a bowl before adding the rest.

Stem ginger syrup, sugar or honey can be substituted for the maple syrup. For a lighter sauce, serve mango or raspberry coulis.

The meringues can be made in advance. They store well in an airtight container, so why not make a few extra as the oven is on anyway?

Raspberry Trifle

wow-factor dinner party flourish

My mother was really quite accomplished at making trifle – a dish she normally prepared for a treat or a party. Large enough quantities were always made to have some left over. I can remember that as a small girl, I used to look forward to getting up before the rest of the family to raid the fridge and have a big bowl of cold trifle for breakfast – it went down exceptionally well on an empty stomach.

This recipe certainly gives the wow factor at a dinner party. If you consider dessert the grand finale, this does not disappoint.

Serves 8

Ingredients

4 punnets raspberries (150g each)
½ litre/18 fl oz raspberry brandy
750g/1lb 10oz sponge cake
1 litre raspberry coulis (*see opposite*)
Gelatine to set 1 litre/1.75 pints liquid
1 litre double cream
Grated dark chocolate
110g/4oz caster sugar
Quantity egg custard (p240)

Method

1. Dissolve the gelatine in 3 tbsp water, then add the coulis a little at a time until well mixed.
2. Ladle some of the coulis into the bottom of one large or 8 individual dishes. Place some raspberries on top, followed by a layer of sponge.
3. Drizzle the sponge with some of the raspberry brandy and then spoon over a layer of custard.
4. Repeat layers of coulis, raspberries, sponge, and custard until it has all been used up (don't forget the raspberry brandy).
5. Lightly whip the cream and either pipe or spread on top of the trifle.
6. Garnish with a few extra berries, some dark grated chocolate and a fresh sprig of mint.

Ease of cooking: ★★☆
Preparation & cooking time: 1 hour
Chilling time: 2 hours or overnight

Raspberry Coulis

To make raspberry coulis, add 10% caster sugar to a quantity of fresh, very ripe raspberries, blitz, strain and refrigerate.

Brandy Snap Lace Baskets

easier than it looks

These baskets look so professional they are almost daunting, but don't be put off. Once you have made this recipe for the first time, you will be making it frequently. There is a great sense of satisfaction in creating something unique, as you can never mould the same shape twice.

Fill the baskets with summer berries with ice cream or sorbet. The crunch of the snap, the moist yummy fruit and the delectable ice cream is to die for.

Serves 8

Ingredients

250g/9oz butter
250g/9oz sugar
250g/9oz golden syrup
170g/6oz plain flour
1 tbsp lemon juice
10g/1 tbsp ground ginger

Method

1. Pre-heat oven to 160°C
2. Place butter, sugar & golden syrup into a pan and heat gently for 4 min until bubbling and sugar well dissolved.
3. Transfer to a cold bowl, add lemon juice, and stir to cool slightly.
4. Add the flour and ginger. Mix well.
5. Put a heaped tablespoon onto greased parchment on a metal tray and bake for approx. 10 minutes.
6. Each tablespoon of the mix will spread about 20cm diameter, so keep them well apart to allow for that.
7. Leave to cool slightly.
8. Shape by draping over glasses. When set, store in airtight containers.

Ease of cooking: ★★☆
Preparation & cooking time: 1 hour

Tina's Tip

The brandy snaps will keep quite well in an airtight container and so can be made ahead of time. If the snaps set too quickly, return to oven for another minute to re-soften.

Gorgeous Gooseberry Granita

light summer dessert for a hot day

Tangy gooseberries provide the perfect base for this summery granita. A coarser version of sorbet, this semi-frozen dessert, of Sicilian origin, has a more crystalline appearance than a regular sorbet. The texture can vary considerably according to the ingredients and how it is frozen: a fine puree of fruit, sugar and water will result in a smooth finish if produced in an ice cream machine, whereas the same ingredients stirred in a bowl in the freezer will have larger, chunkier crystals (as it freezes more slowly).

This recipe, using ripe gooseberries, is particularly refreshing on a hot day when a little respite is needed perhaps from weeding the garden.

Serves 2

Ease of cooking: ★☆☆ Easy
Preparation & freezing time: 2–2½ hours

Ingredients

300ml/11 fl oz water
150g/5oz sugar
Zest and juice of 2 limes or 1 large lemon
500g/18oz ripe gooseberries

Method

1. Place all but the gooseberries into a stainless steel pan and heat gently to dissolve the sugar.
2. Boil fairly rapidly for 3 minutes, then remove from the heat and allow to cool.
3. Liquidise the gooseberries with the syrup until smooth, sieve to remove the pips.
4. Chill and churn if you have a machine, or place in the freezer in a container and periodically stir until the right texture has been reached.
5. Serve immediately.

The Pantry

The Pantry

The idea of the pantry evolved in England during the early 1800s. It began as the small 'Butler's pantry' between the kitchen and dining room. This was where the china and silver were stored and meals were plated and served (often by a butler or household staff). In the beginning, pantries were found only in great estate homes, but were later incorporated into moderate middle class dwellings. A radical change in kitchen design (around the late 1800s) brought the pantry into the kitchen itself and meant that most new kitchens included this new facility.

In the 1950s, following the 2nd World War, there was a sudden increase in the availability of prepared foods. Fridges and freezers became commonplace household appliances and there was no longer any need to preserve the summer and autumn harvest to last through the winter months. The pantry became all but obsolete, maybe with the exception of some farmhouse kitchens.

Today, however, there is a strong resurgence of 'growing your own'. With that comes the welcome gluts at harvest time, and so the need for preservation. The pantry is filling up once again.

Preserves will keep almost indefinitely, providing the utensils have been properly sterilized. To do this you will need to wash the jars, lids and any rubber seals thoroughly. The jars should then be immersed in simmering water for 8–10 minutes, or alternatively be placed in an oven pre-heated to 100°C for 10–15 minutes. The lids and seals are best soaked in a sterilising solution (such as Milton) for the recommended time, and then rinsed with warm water and dried with a clean cloth. Pot the chutney whilst still warm as this will help to create a vacuum. Ensure the lids fit tightly.

By making your own preserves, you will be able to 'capture' the seasons and savour the flavours of freshly picked fruits and vegetables all year round.

Spicy Bramley Apple Chutney

From my really carefree childhood days, when all I had to worry about was taking care of my pony and helping my mother put food on the table, I have very fond memories of autumn Sundays when my grandparents came over for Sunday lunch. It was a whole day affair. My father would collect his ageing parents from Harrow, about 20 miles from where we lived. He would set off at around ten in the morning, visit a pub or two on the way, and deliver them home to my mother at about noon. Lunch was customarily served at 2pm or slightly later (depending on when chucking-out time at the local pub happened to be). My grandmother was very sweet-natured and always offered to help prepare the meal of the day. In the summer this meant stringing beans or shelling peas, and in the autumn it was invariably peeling windfall apples for chutney, purée, pies, and the like. One of the fondest memories I have of those Sundays is the whole family (except Dad) mucking in together to prepare enough chutney to last a season. As children, we were happy to help out, as we adored this chutney. It was an accompaniment to pigs' hearts, liver, burgers, bread and cheese and much more.

Makes approx. 5 x 1lb jars

Ingredients

2300/5lb Bramley apples, cut into ½"
pieces
450g/1lb Muscovado sugar
900g/2lb onions
1½ litres/2 pints/13 fl oz malt vinegar
30g/1oz black mustard seeds
2½ cm cube of ginger, grated
1 tsp cayenne or a finely chopped chilli

Method

1. Put all ingredients into a large preserving pan and bring to the boil, stirring frequently.
2. Turn down heat and cook until it has a jam-like consistency.
3. Cool and pot in the usual way.

Ease of cooking: ★★☆
Preparation & cooking time: 1½–2 hours

Marjorie's Green Tomato Chutney

Many recipes are passed down from one family generation to the next. Such is the case with this green tomato chutney. Marjorie, my late mother-in-law, lived on her own and was a wizard at growing tomatoes in her small greenhouse. Invariably she produced more than she could eat, and at the end of the season this is what she chose to do with the un-ripened green tomatoes. When I first tried the recipe, I liked it so much that I telephoned a couple of local growers to see if they could spare me some green tomatoes.

Makes 12 x 454g/1lb jars

Ingredients

3405g/7½lb green tomatoes, sliced
2010ml/2½ pints malt vinegar
140g/5oz coarse sea salt
2 tsp each of cloves, allspice & white peppercorns
90g/3oz fresh root ginger
560g/1¼lb dark brown sugar
1130g/2½lb onions finely sliced
1¼ tsp cayenne pepper

Method

1. Sprinkle the sliced tomatoes with the salt and leave for 24 hours to draw out the juices.
2. Pour off the salted liquor and discard, and then place the tomatoes in a preserving pan.
3. Bruise the ginger, combine with the cloves, allspice and peppercorns and tie into muslin.
4. Add these to the tomatoes.
5. Add the cayenne pepper and sugar together with the onions and vinegar and simmer gently until the correct (sloppy jam-like) consistency has been achieved.
6. Pot hot into sterilized jars.
7. Cool and label.

Ease of cooking: ★ ★ ☆
If this is your first preserving experience, this recipe will help you grasp the basics fairly quickly.
Preparation cooking & potting time: 2 hours
Salting time: 24 hours

Tina's Tip

Adding this delectable preserve is a fantastic way to liven such meals as shepherds pie, cauliflower cheese, meat stews, toad in the hole etc.

Mediterranean Chutney

This mouth-watering and beautifully vibrant chutney adds a kick to barbecued meats and fish, as well as vegetables such as potato, pumpkin and fried marrow.

Makes approx. 5 x 454g/1lb jars

Ingredients

900g/2lb red onions, finely chopped
680g/1½lb peeled, seeded & chopped tomatoes
340g/12oz diced aubergine
450g/1lb diced courgettes
340g/12oz diced mixed peppers
2tsp chopped garlic
1 tbsp sea salt
1 tbsp ground paprika
1 tsp chilli powder or cayenne pepper
900g/2lb sugar
570ml/1pt malt vinegar
1½ tbsp dried herbes de Provence (thyme, rosemary, marjoram, basil, and bay leaf), or ½ cup fresh chopped herbs

Method

1. Put the vegetables, garlic and half of the vinegar into a pan and simmer for 20 minutes to reduce some of the liquid.
2. Then add the salt, spices, herbs, sugar, and the rest of the vinegar.
3. Gently simmer for 1½ hours. The chutney needs to reduce, but not to the extent that it becomes too dry.
4. Pot into warm sterilized jars.

Ease of cooking: ★ ★ ☆
Stick to making a single batch of this recipe, to ensure good texture and colour
Preparation, cooking & potting time: 2½–3 hours

Marrow, Bean & Onion Chutney

As a person almost as keen on gardening as cooking, each year I grow a fabulous variety of pole beans in deep trenches filled with manure, using robust canes to support the beans and withstand the strong winds. The pole beans (Blue Lake Climbing French are my favourite variety) are good croppers and, providing they are frequently watered, grow long and straight, which saves a great deal of time when cutting into diamonds, as in the recipe below. The marrows I use are 'long trailing white' but if no marrows are on hand, overgrown courgettes will fit the bill. This recipe has a good depth of flavour and is a nice compliment to parfaits & pâtés, and sautéed chicken livers.

Makes approx. 15 x 454g/1lb jars

Ingredients

2500g/5½lb marrow, peeled, de-seeded and diced
1240g/2¾lb onion, sliced
1700g/3¾lb young, string-less beans, cut into diamonds
1600g/3½lb chopped dates
1600g/3½lb sultanas
3200ml/5 pints 10 fl oz malt vinegar
900g/30oz soft dark brown sugar
100g/½ cup fenugreek seed
100g/½ cup mustard seed
100g/½ cup grated ginger root
1 tbsp dried minced chillies
½ cup ground cumin or 30g cumin seed
½ cup ground coriander
2 tsp ground allspice

Method

1. Place the marrow, beans, onions, dates, sultanas, and all of the spices together with 2272ml/4 pints of the vinegar in a large clean stainless steel pan.

2. Cook on a very low heat for 2½ hours, stirring occasionally.
3. Dissolve the sugar in the remaining vinegar and add to the pan.
4. Leave uncovered and simmer until correct consistency is reached.
5. Pot into sterilized jars and label.

Ease of cooking: ★★☆
Read the recipe carefully – if the sugar is added too early, the chutney can burn.
Preparation, cooking & potting time: 3½–4 hours

Tina's Tip

Check that the dates you purchase have not been rolled in any sort of starch, such as flour. If they have, it is essential to remove it, otherwise it will thicken the chutney into a pickled soup – which is not the result you are aiming for. White wine vinegar can be used, but has a higher acidity than the malt variety, so you will need to use 2750ml vinegar plus 450ml water.

Mustard & Honey Dressing

This is a useful store cupboard ingredient and is especially suited to cured fish and meats such as gravad mackerel, pork terrine and bacon-based dishes. It also complements seafood such as seared scallops & squid.

Makes one litre/1¾ pints

Ingredients

250g/9oz Dijon mustard
150ml/5 fl oz honey
150ml/5 fl oz white wine vinegar/lime juice or a mixture
500ml/18 fl oz vegetable oil
Freshly ground black pepper
¼ teaspoon minced fresh garlic
1 teaspoons garlic salt
Freshly ground black pepper
Herb of your choice

Method

Combine all ingredients and taste. Correct seasoning.
If texture is too thick to drizzle, add a few drops of boiling water to slacken.

Ease of cooking: ★ ☆ ☆
Preparation time: 15 minutes

Tina's Tip

Use the very best quality mustard you can afford – it really makes a difference, especially as many cheaper mustards contain thickeners such as flour, which compromises the flavour.
For use with meats, add thyme & chives.
For fish, use dill, chervil or tarragon.

Catherine's Sicilian Dressing

This is my mother's recipe, whose family was Sicilian. From as far back as I can remember, there was always an old honey jar filled with this dressing in the kitchen spice drawer. This dressing was a daily staple ingredient and was an admirable partner to the omnipresent bowl of salad served with dinner in the evenings; sometimes with avocado, usually with tomato, and, on a day when there were a few pennies left from the housekeeping, as a treat a little Roquefort cheese would also be added.

Makes a scant litre/1¾ pints

Ingredients

¼ cup Dijon mustard
1 tsp freshly ground black pepper
2 egg yolks
2 tsp paprika
200ml/7 fl oz lemon juice
570ml/1 pint vegetable oil
2 cloves garlic, peeled and finely chopped
Freshly chopped herbs: marjoram, oregano, thyme, tarragon, chives, dill etc. to taste

Method

1. Combine all the ingredients into a bowl and whisk.
2. Taste to check the seasoning, add salt & more pepper if needed.

Ease of cooking: ★☆☆
Preparation time: 15 minutes
Stores well in the fridge

Tina's Tip

Lime juice or white wine vinegar can replace the lemon juice.

Redcurrant Jelly

If you have some redcurrant bushes in your garden, be well advised to cover them with some netting. These delicious berries are highly prized by our two legged flying friends, who have a knack of getting them just before I do. Take care to pick the fruit in the dry weather because if it is wet, it will alter the concentration of pectin within the fruit and effect the jelly's setting capabilities. This jelly is a great accompaniment to game (both furred and feathered) and lamb.

Ingredients

Redcurrants
To every 570ml/1 pint of extracted juice allow:
340g/12oz sugar

Method

1. Remove some of the stalks from the redcurrants by gently using a fork to prise the fruit off the stem (it is not necessary to remove every last bit, as these will be left in the jelly bag).
2. Put the fruit into a jar and place the jar in a saucepan of boiling water over the heat (or use a stainless steel double boiler) and let it simmer gently until the juice has been extracted from the currants.
3. Strain them through a jelly bag or muslin, taking care not to squeeze them too much, as a clear jelly is wanted. If the skin and pulp from the fruit is pressed through with the juice, it can make the jelly muddy.
4. Measure the juice and the sugar.
5. Put into a preserving pan and place over the heat.
6. Stir the jelly constantly, carefully removing any scum as it rises.
7. When it has boiled for 20 to 30 minutes, do a plate test (or gel test) to see if the jelly has reached setting. Put a spoonful of the jelly on a plate and leave to cool. If you push your finger through the jelly, and the skin wrinkles, you're done! If not, boil longer.
8. Take the jelly off the heat, pour into sterilised jars. Cover with airtight lids.
9. Label and store in a dry place.

Ease of cooking: ★ ☆ ☆
Take care not to over-reduce, as it will affect the flavour of the fruit
Preparation, cooking & potting time: 1 hour 45 minutes

Tina's Tip

When testing if the jelly is set, have some plates ready in the freezer; if they are cold, it will cool the jelly immediately and speed up the setting time.

Pickled Eggs

I had always dreamt of having my own chickens, and plenty of them. When finally that dream came true, I started with a sturdy and docile breed called Black Rock. I purchased them from a chap named Ben Wetherden, who made his living rearing organic chickens and was located very conveniently just down the bottom of the hill, only about 2 miles away. From him I purchased about 150 point-of-lay pullets which we installed into our newly acquired chicken house.

Black Rocks lay an average of 280 eggs in their first year, so when they did start to produce eggs, we typically had 115 of them to collect every day! Even though I have plenty of use for eggs in my kitchen, from breakfast dishes to my lemon tart dessert, I was collecting them much faster than I could use them. Once I had filled the freezer with liquidised egg (I rinsed out plastic milk bottles and filled them with the eggs) and could fit no more, I was stumped as to what to do with the continuing glut. One day while out shopping, I spotted some attractive preserving jars on sale, had a brainwave and decided (with purposeful resolve) to pickle all those extra eggs.

These pickled eggs taste fabulous and are a glorious accompaniment to salads, cold meat, and fish and chips, or sliced for a roll or sandwich.

Ingredients

24 fresh eggs

For the spiced vinegar

6 cups cider vinegar
2 tbsp peppercorns
1 tbsp whole allspice
½ tbsp mace
½ tbsp coriander seeds
½ tbsp cardamom seeds
½ tbsp cloves
10 small hot red chilli peppers
3 tbsp sugar

Method

1. Place the eggs in cold water to cover, bring to the boil and simmer for 15 minutes. Plunge the eggs in cold water, leave to cool, remove the shells and pack into sterilized jars.

2. Combine the vinegar, sugar and spices in a saucepan.
3. Bring to boil, reduce the heat and simmer for 5 minutes. Pour the hot liquid over hardboiled eggs.
4. Place lid on jar and store in refrigerator when cooled. Use within a month.

Ease of cooking: ★ ★ ☆
Use fresh eggs and don't over-cook them. For ease of peeling, once chilled, pop the eggs back into boiling water for 1 minute and shell hot, starting from the round end where the air cell is situated.
Preparation & cooking time: 35 minutes

Blackcurrant Jam

Seriously simple. Seriously good. Make this jam in July when the fruit is at its ripest. The density of flavour you can achieve by making your own is far better than anything you can buy.

Makes 5 x 454g/1lb jars

Ingredients

1kg/2lb 3 oz blackcurrants
1.5kg/3lb sugar

Method

1. Place the currants in a large bowl and lightly crush with a potato masher or prick with a fork.
2. Put sugar over the currants, cover the bowl with cling film and refrigerate overnight to draw the juices (this is better than cooking the fruit with water first – as some recipes might call for – as it reduces the cooking time and therefore leaves the jam with a better flavour).
3. Empty the bowl into a large pan and bring slowly to the boil, carefully dissolving the sugar.
4. Boil for 3–4 minutes.
5. Cool for 30 minutes, stir to distribute the fruit evenly and then pot into sterilized jars.

Ease of cooking: ★☆☆ Very easy
Preparation & cooking time: 45 minutes

Tina's Tip

If you grow your own blackcurrants and don't have time to turn them all into jam, pick the currants when ripe and then freeze them to make jam at a later date. The freezing will burst the fruit, so there will be no need to crush or prick. At the end of the season, the slightly under ripe currants are best used for jelly – or can be combined with other fruits such as apple.

Cranberry & Orange Relish

Easy and delightful to make, and a little sharper than the non-homemade variety, this relish is good with pork as well as turkey, chicken and ham pie. Make good use of the abundance of fresh cranberries that flood the shelves around Christmas time.

Makes 2 x 1lb jars

Ingredients

570ml/1 pint fresh orange juice
285g/10oz raisins
700g/24oz fresh cranberries

Method

1. Simmer the raisins in the orange juice for approx. 15 min. or until most of the liquid has been absorbed.
2. Liquidise, return to pan then add the cranberries.
3. Cook gently until they burst – about 15 minutes.
4. Cool and pot into sterilized jars.

Ease of cooking: ★ ☆ ☆
Very easy to make, so snap up the fresh cranberries when they are on sale
Preparation & cooking time: 20 minutes

Tina's Tip

For an additional dimension, try adding a herb such as sage or thyme just prior to potting. Dried cranberries can be used. Simmer 1 kilo with the orange juice, blitz half of them, return them to the pan, mix and pot

Pumpkin Chutney

This chutney is delightfully colourful. Mix with avocado, spring onions & boiled potato for an instant salad or lob into a banana sandwich!

Makes 2 jars

Ingredients

400g/14oz/2 heaped cups pumpkin, peeled and diced
2 small apples, peeled and diced
120ml/4 fl oz/½ cup cider vinegar
60ml/2 fl oz/¼ cup water
¼ tsp turmeric powder
½ tsp red chilli powder
2 tbsp sugar
Salt to taste

Method

1. Place all the ingredients together in a pan. Bring to the boil and then simmer until soft.
2. Take off the heat and crush very lightly with a potato masher.
3. Cool, pot and label.

Ease of cooking: ★ ☆ ☆
Cooking time: 20 minutes

Tina's Tip

Be sure to make plenty of this. Serve it up at a party and everyone will want a jar. You can add a generous spoon of chopped coriander before serving.

Tomato & Chilli Chutney

This is a particularly piquant and colourful chutney. It is a great accompaniment to roasted vegetables such as aubergine and pumpkin. A little of this in a jacket potato with cream cheese and chives is divine. It is also good with most meats, especially barbequed chicken.

Makes 6 x 454g/1lb jars

Ingredients

2kg/4lb 6oz diced, peeled & seeded tomatoes
400g/14oz diced white onion
8 cloves of crushed garlic
400g/14oz diced peppers
4 tsp grated fresh ginger
1150ml/2 pints cider vinegar
900g/2lb sugar
1 tbsp coarse salt
320g/11oz sultanas
4 tsp chilli powder
¼ tsp ground cloves
¼ tsp ground cinnamon

Method

1. Put first seven ingredients into a pan and cook for 20 min and then add the remaining ingredients.
2. Simmer 1 to 1½ hour until a sloppy jam-like consistency has been reached.
3. Pot in the usual way.

Ease of cooking: ★☆☆
This can be made as hot as you want it, just add the chilli accordingly.
Preparation & cooking time: 2 hours

Rhubarb & Ginger Chutney

This is a fantastic way to preserve rhubarb. It is almost sweet and sour and is a truly grand accompaniment to oily fish such as mackerel or tuna, as well as grilled cheese.

Makes 2 x 450g/1lb jars

Ingredients

1kg/2lb 3oz rhubarb, washed and cut into 2cm lengths
350g/12oz onion, peeled and chopped
300ml/11 fl oz cider vinegar
300g/11oz soft brown sugar
70g/2½oz freshly grated root ginger
1 tbsp ground ginger
1 tsp ground white pepper
200g/7oz dried apricots cut into 1cm dice

Method

1. Place all the ingredients in a preserving pan and simmer gently until cooked and chutney is thick.
2. Pot into sterilized jars while still hot and seal with lids.

Ease of cooking: ★ ★ ☆
Preparation & cooking time: 1½ hours

Tina's Tip

Try to find nice plump apricots, as they will contribute well to the overall texture.

Piccalilli

A great texture, combined with robust, up-front flavours, makes this pungent relish a perfect accompaniment to cheese, terrines, chicken and ham. It is a nice way to preserve cauliflower and bears no resemblance to eating this vegetable with cheese sauce.

Makes approx. 4 x 450g/1lb jars

Ingredients

650ml/23 fl oz white wine vinegar
1 tbsp coriander seeds
500g/18oz cauliflower, neatly cut into even-sized florets
3 large onions, peeled and chopped
¼ cup English mustard powder
¼ cup potato starch or cornflour
1 tbsp turmeric
1 tbsp ground ginger
150ml/5 fl oz cider vinegar
150g/5oz peeled marrow or courgette, diced ½ cucumber, cut lengthways, seeds removed and cut into 1 cm pieces
3 large garlic cloves, peeled and sliced
200g/7oz golden caster sugar

Method

1. In a preserving pan, bring the white wine vinegar to the boil with the coriander seed.
2. Add the cauliflower and onion and simmer for 2–3 minutes until lightly cooked but still crunchy.
3. Add the marrow or courgette, cucumber, garlic and sugar to the pan and cook for a further 2–3 minutes, stirring to dissolve the sugar.
4. Pour the contents of the pan into a colander (set over a large bowl to collect the vinegar).
5. Transfer the vinegar back to the preserving pan.
6. In a small bowl, make a paste with the mustard, potato starch or cornflour, ginger, turmeric and cider vinegar. Add to the pan and simmer gently until the mixture has thickened.
7. Take off the heat; add the drained vegetables and pot immediately into sterilized jars.

Ease of cooking: ★☆☆ Deceptively easy
Preparation & cooking time: 45 minutes

Rowanberry & Juniper Jelly

The hardy rowan tree can grow at elevations of up to 1,000 feet, hence its other name, the mountain ash. There are plenty of rowan trees planted on the Coombeshead Estate and harvest time in the autumn means these stunning red berries can be easily turned into a clear, vibrant burnt orange jelly (full of vitamins A and C), which is slightly tart-but-sweet and pairs especially well with venison, lamb, cold pork or ham, chicken or pheasant terrine and cheese & crackers. Rowanberries generally taste better after a frost, but if you have some lovely ripe berries (and can get to them before the birds), pick them and then freeze overnight. This will burst the berries and there will be no need to crush them.

Makes 6 x 454g/1 lb jars

Ingredients

2.7g/6lb rowanberries, washed, stalks removed, crushed
570ml/1 pt water
570ml/1 pt white wine vinegar
¼ cup juniper berries, crushed
340g/12oz granulated sugar

Method

1. Put the rowanberries into a large pan with the water and half the juniper berries.
2. Bring to the boil, turn down the heat and simmer for 40–50 minutes.
3. Add the vinegar. Mix well. Boil for 5 minutes.
4. Pour or ladle into a jelly bag and leave to strain for at least 2 hours.
5. Measure the juice and return to pan. Add 12 oz warmed sugar to 568ml/1pt liquid. Stir to dissolve the sugar.
6. Boil rapidly until setting point is reached.
7. Add the remaining juniper berries. Cool, pot and store.

Ease of cooking: ★ ☆ ☆
Preparation time: 15 minutes
Straining time: 2 hours
Sterilising, cooking & potting time: 1½ hours

Tina's Tip

Apples can be substituted for the rowanberries and sage or mint can be substituted for the juniper berries.

Pickled Beetroot

Given the correct soil conditions, beetroot is very easy to grow. It stores well if clamped over the winter months and will keep even longer if pickled. Full of flavour and with a range of stunning colours, from deep crimson to golden yellow, a few jars of this wonderfully vibrant vegetable will brighten up the dullest picnic, al fresco meal or mid-week supper.

Makes 3 x 1 litre jars

Ingredients

2 kg/4½ lb fresh beetroot, washed, skins left intact
Spiced vinegar to cover (see p181, as used for pickled eggs)

Method

1. To prepare the beetroot, twist off the leaves (do not cut or the beetroot will bleed) and place in a pan with clean cold water.
2. Bring to the boil and simmer until cooked (for small young freshly-pulled beetroot this may only take 10 minutes – for large older roots, much longer cooking may be necessary). Alternatively, wrap in foil and bake in a moderate oven until a skewer can be pushed gently through the beetroot.
3. Cool and then remove the skin by rubbing with your fingers.
4. Pot whole or slice into 5ml/¼" slices (depending on the size) and place into a sterilized preserving jar.
5. Cover with the spiced vinegar, seal with a lid, label and store.

Ease of cooking: ★☆☆
If your beetroot are different sizes, grade before cooking.
Preparation & cooking time: 30–40 minutes

Spiced Tomato Ketchup

This vibrant sauce is a little more racy than regular ketchup and has a more full-bodied flavour because of the use of fresh ingredients. You probably know what to do - use it to spice up barbequed meat, sandwiches, meatloaf and sausages. Once bottled, this sauce should keep for up to 1 year.

Makes 4 pints

Ingredients

4.5kg/10 lbs ripe tomatoes, chopped
900g/2 lbs tomato concentrate
1 kg/6 medium onions, finely chopped
4 cloves garlic, finely chopped
480ml/17 fl oz/2 cups cider vinegar
1 tsp peppercorns
1 tsp whole allspice berries
1 tsp whole cloves
1 tsp dry mustard powder
1 tbsp paprika
½ tsp cayenne pepper
½ cup light brown sugar
1tsp salt

Method

For the vinegar

1. Prepare the spiced vinegar by placing the cider vinegar into a pan and adding all the spices.
2. Simmer for about half an hour with the lid on, to steep the spices in the vinegar.
3. Strain and then pour into a large pan.

For the ketchup

1. Add the garlic, onions, chopped tomatoes and tomato concentrate to the spiced vinegar and simmer for about 1 hour, or until the onion has softened.

2. Put the mixture into a food processor and blitz until smooth.
3. Return to the pan; add the sugar, mustard, cayenne, paprika and salt.
4. Cook, stirring occasionally, until the correct consistency has been reached.
5. Taste. At this point you can add more vinegar, sugar, mustard, cayenne if you wish.
6. Taste and adjust again.
7. Allow ketchup to cool, then ladle into bottles or jars.
8. Cover and refrigerate.

Ease of cooking: ★★☆
Take care not to over-reduce, as the sauce will thicken slightly as it matures in the bottle
Preparation & cooking time: 5 hours

Tina's Tip

For a bit of texture and extra flavour, add a few onion, cumin or fennel seeds at Stage 3. Ripe tomatoes are essential.

Beetroot & Onion Chutney

This really fresh-tasting chutney is exceptionally easy to make. Delicious served with grilled goat's cheese or cold meats.

Makes approx. 3½ kg (7-8 1lb jars)

Ingredients

1½kg/3¼lb cooked fresh beetroot cut into 1cm dice
900g/2lb onions, peeled and finely sliced
680g/1½lb (after peeling and coring) cooking apples, peeled and roughly chopped
225g/8oz soft brown sugar
1 teaspoon ground ginger
1 pint malt vinegar
1 tablespoon of salt

Method

1. Mix all the ingredients together in a large heavy-bottomed saucepan.
2. Stir over a medium heat until the sugar has dissolved.
3. Simmer until the mixture has thickened (40-45 minutes) stirring occasionally.
4. Pot into sterilized jars while still hot and cover with lids.

Ease of cooking: ★☆☆
Preparation & cooking time: 1½ hours
Stores well in a cool dry place for at least one year.

Avocado Vinaigrette

Firstly, I would like to say a word about avocado oil. Avocados are regarded as the most nutritionally complete fruit in the world – a superfruit – and extra-virgin avocado oil is one of nature's healthiest oils, proven to lower cholesterol absorption. Pressed from the flesh of fresh avocados, avocado oil is 100% natural and completely unrefined with absolutely nothing added. It contains no cholesterol, low levels of saturated fats, and is packed full of micronutrients, vitamins and antioxidants. Health benefits including the prevention of macular degeneration, cataracts, prostate cancer and heart disease. It is at the top of my list of culinary oils.

On the cooking front, its light, soft, nutty flavour enhances the natural flavours of other ingredients rather than overpowering them. It is also far less 'greasy' than other oils, which is another reason I use it for salads. I use some of this dressing almost daily on a large bowl of mixed salad.

Ingredients

120ml/4 fl. oz extra virgin avocado oil
60ml/2 fl. oz white wine vinegar
Freshly ground sea salt
Freshly ground white pepper

Method

Place all ingredients in a bowl and whisk to combine.

Ease of cooking: ★ ☆ ☆
A great way to eat yourself healthy!

Tina's Tip

Avocado oil is generally sold in dark green 250ml bottles. This is to prevent light from destroying the nutrients in the oil. Keep any empty bottles and use for any left-over dressing.

With the addition of capers and chives this vinaigrette beautifully complements pork terrine (see page 30)

Red Wine Vinaigrette

This is made in exactly the same way as avocado vinaigrette (above) except that the red wine vinegar is substituted for the white and olive oil takes place of the avocado oil.

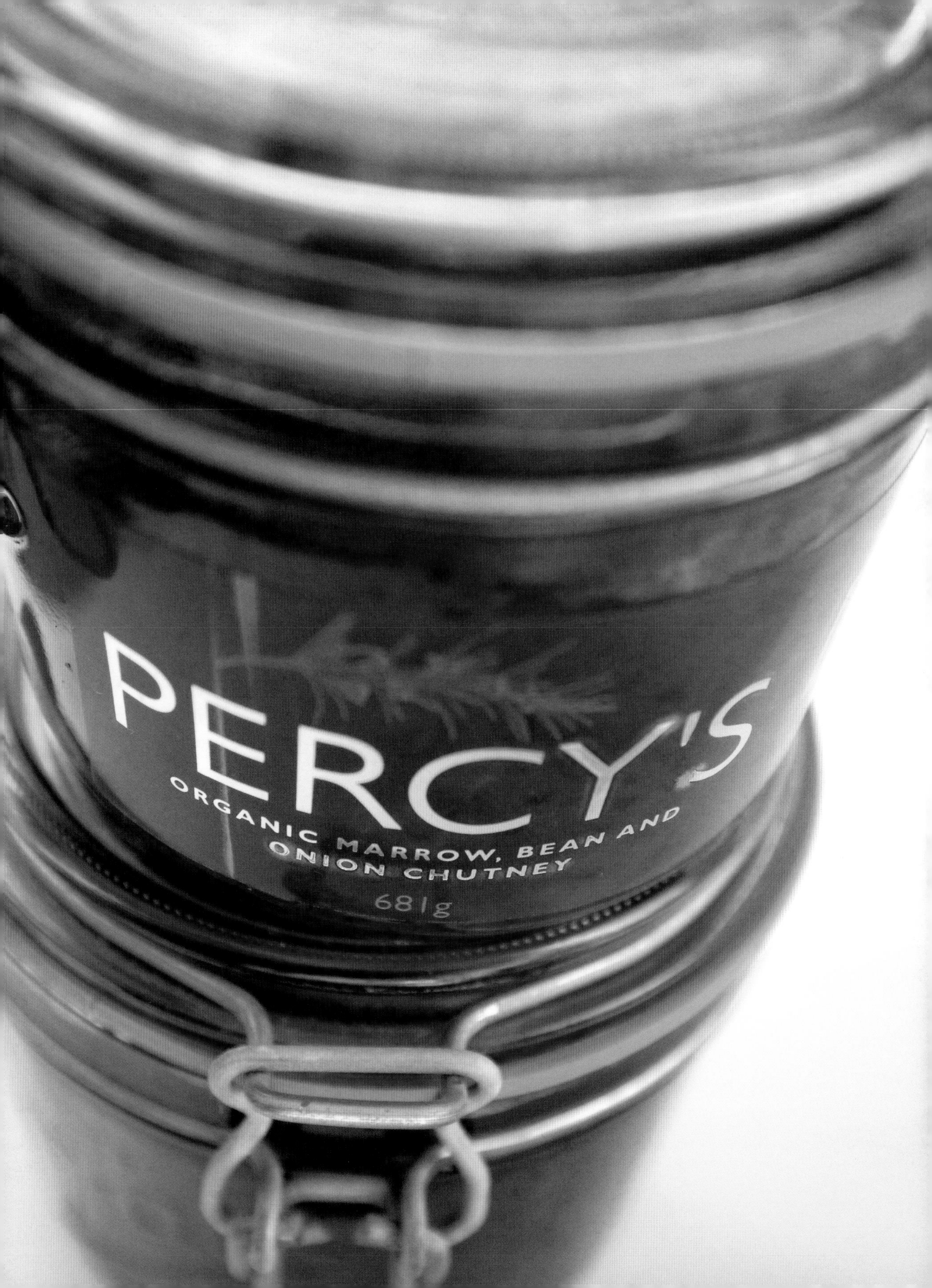
PERCY'S
ORGANIC MARROW, BEAN AND
ONION CHUTNEY
681g

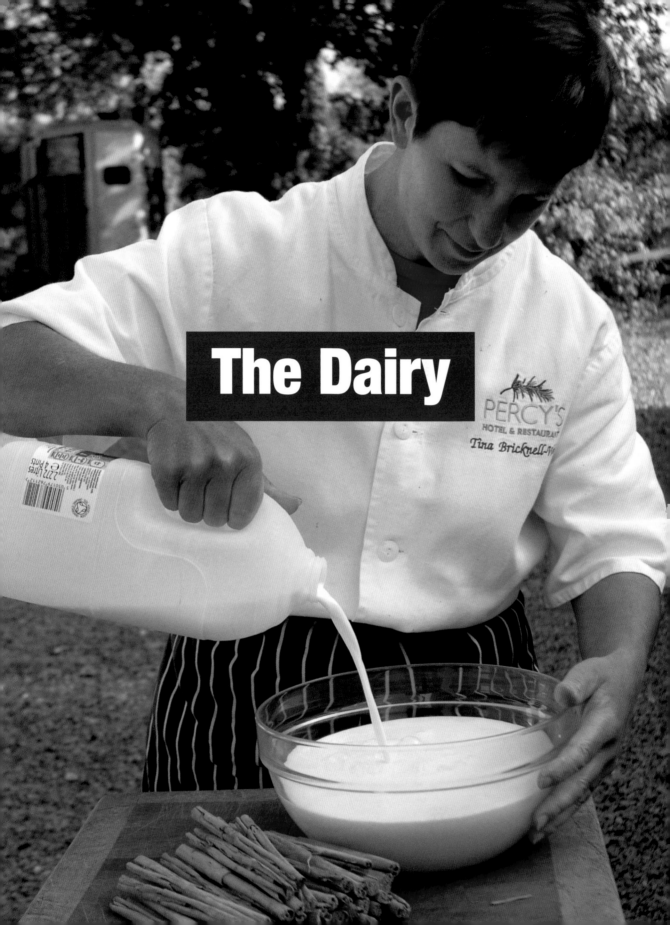

The Dairy

The Dairy

I have chosen to include a chapter entitled 'Dairy' as milk and milk-related products are found in so many dishes that feature on a daily basis.

We pour milk onto cereal, we spread butter on toast. We use cream for pouring into coffee or over desserts. We eat ice cream. Crème frâiche or soured cream is in soups or sauces, puddings and fruit, clotted cream is spooned onto scones, condensed and evaporated milks are in fudge and other sweetmeats.

Then there are fresh cheeses such as fromage frais, quark, curd, cream, ricotta & cottage; hard cheeses such as Cheddar and Caerphilly; soft and semi-soft cheeses such as Brie, Goldilocks, Finn and Keltic Gold; and blue cheeses such as Stilton, Beenleigh Blue and Cornish Blue. All these are utilized for cooking, baking, sweet-making or cheeseboard displays. Dairy plays no small role in the English diet.

The cat with the cream: when I think of milk and cereal, my thoughts turn to my brother Gordon. When I was a child, we had milk in glass bottles, with about three inches of thick yellow cream on the top. Gordon was very fond of the 'top of the milk' – to the extent that he would make sure to be down for breakfast before anyone else . By the time the rest of us appeared, all the milk bottles had been tapped, the cream decanted and Gordon was sitting at the breakfast table munching cornflakes with a wide grin on his face.

As you continue to read, you might ask why eggs are included in the Dairy chapter. I have asked myself that very same question. It seems second nature to group 'eggs' and 'dairy' – but why? What exactly do they have in common? One basis for the confusion might be that before refrigerators were invented, eggs, milk and cheese were kept together in a dairy, a cool room for dairy products. My assistant chef felt that the connection might be that both eggs and milk contain colostrums for the unborn/newly born foetus. My husband Tony however felt that the milkmaid probably had to look after the chickens as part of her duties.

Eggs for Breakfast

On a farm, one of the first chores of the day is to let out the geese, ducks and chickens, feed them all, and then take any eggs that may have been laid to the kitchen. Chickens lay pretty much all of the year round, although the natural yield reduces dramatically in the winter with the cold wet weather and diminished daylight hours.

Geese and ducks, on the other hand, generally start to lay in February or March and finish sometime in June. Each year around the beginning of February, I rummage around in the straw for the first goose egg. Discovering that first egg always excites me almost as much as the first hidden chocolate Easter egg I ever found as a child.

Eggs from free-ranging geese and ducks generally have a more pronounced earthy flavour than chicken eggs. The yolks from these free-ranging, grazing birds contain xanthophyll (a natural yellow/orange pigment present in green plants and yellow corn), which gives the yolks their bright ochre colour.

Tina's Tip

To test the freshness of your eggs, crack one onto a large white dinner plate. The further the egg white spreads, the older the egg.

How to Poach an Egg

The simplest way to enjoy an egg is to poach it and for this, you need a pan two-thirds full of cold water, with a couple of teaspoons of vinegar or lemon juice added (this helps to 'set' the white). Bring the water to the boil, then turn down and leave to simmer.

Stir the water vigorously in a circular motion to create a vortex and gently slide the egg into the centre of that vortex. Poach for 2–4 minutes, depending on the size, age and temperature of the egg. With a little wobble still left in the egg, remove from the water with a slotted spoon, and place on a clean, dry tea towel or cloth to remove any excess moisture. Rest a minute or two and then serve sprinkled with a little salt and pepper.

Poached Hens' Eggs with Fresh Asparagus and Hollandaise Sauce

A simple yet satisfying dish, very easy to rustle together, highly nutritious – and delicious.

Serves 2

Ingredients

2 hens eggs
1 bunch asparagus
Sea salt
225g/8oz of butter, melted, kept warm
1 tablespoon of white wine vinegar
Freshly ground black pepper
1 egg yolk

Method

Quantity of Hollandaise sauce (p218)

To cook the asparagus and the eggs

1. Top the pan of water up and bring to the boil. Add a pinch of salt and cook the asparagus for one minute.
2. Drain and divide between two warm plates.
3. Poach two hens' eggs (p197) and arrange on top of the asparagus. Spoon the sauce over and serve immediately. Good with crusty bread such as Ciabatta (p232) to mop up the rich buttery sauce.

Ease of cooking: ★☆☆
Preparation & cooking time: 15 minutes

Poached Goose Egg & Broccoli Leaves

On our farm, the arrival of our first goose egg usually coincides with the end of the sprouting broccoli season, just as the heads are flowering. The leaves, however, are still quite delicious and their flavour when coupled with the sweet nutty garlic and the oozing earthy yolk of the goose egg, is deliciously intense.

Serves 2

Ingredients

2 goose eggs
Sea salt
Black pepper
½ tablespoon garlic purée (or very finely chopped garlic)
30g/1oz butter
340g/12oz broccoli leaves, de-ribbed and washed
1 tsp of white wine vinegar

Method

1. Bring a pan of water to the boil.
2. Poach two goose eggs (p197), but cook slightly longer than a hen's egg: about 5 minutes.
3. Take out of the water and leave to rest until needed.
4. In a large heavy-bottomed pan heat the butter, add the garlic purée and fry gently until the garlic is golden in colour. Add the broccoli leaves and stir rapidly over a high heat until just wilted.
5. Draw the pan off the heat and rest for 5–8 minutes (the greens will continue to cook at this stage).
6. Place the goose eggs back in the simmering water to re-heat.

7. Heap the cooked greens onto two warmed plates, pop the goose eggs on top, sprinkle with salt and pepper and enjoy.

Ease of cooking: ★ ☆ ☆
Preparation & cooking time: 15 minutes

Tina's Tip

Winter greens can be used instead of broccoli leaves. The recommended resting time for the goose egg helps to avoid it from becoming 'rubbery'.

The Perfect Omelette

Crack three eggs into a bowl, season, add a few drops of water then whisk until the white is thoroughly mixed with the yolk. In an omelette pan, heat a tbsp of olive or avocado oil until almost smoking. Draw off the heat and pour the egg mix into the pan.

Shake the pan gently whilst stirring the egg mix with the heel of the fork to prevent it sticking. When half-set, scatter over a filling of your choice. Then tilt the pan away from you to allow half of the omelette to rest on the rim of the pan. With the fork, carefully encourage the top half of the omelette over onto the bottom half to cover the filling. Leave in the pan (off the heat) to continue cooking for 1–2 minutes then serve.

Tina's Tip

Fillings such as ham and Parmesan with lovage or parsley, tomato and goat's cheese with basil, sautéed chicken livers with thyme, or bacon, tarragon and blue cheese all make a fast and easy impromptu meal at any time of the day.

For a fluffier omelette, add a tsp of water to the eggs before whisking.

Clotted Cream

Originating from the West Country (where the rich soil, mild climate and the right breed of cattle all combine to produce a high butterfat cream), this most famous of all creams achieves its thick clotted texture by being kept at a constant temperature in a water bath of 62°C for 24 hours and then being allowed to cool slowly. The 'clot' on top acts as a seal and keeps the runnier cream beneath nice and fresh.

With its high fat content, clotted cream has a consistency similar to soft butter and can be used as a replacement for butter in such things as toffees.

My favourite way of eating clotted cream is to blend it with Calvados and a little sugar to serve with caramelised apple tart (p153). This is a great recipe to make if you have a dairy herd in your back yard or live next to one. The creation of this cream almost equals the joy of eating it.

Makes 250ml/1 cup

Ingredients

480ml/17 fl oz/2 cups double cream

Method

1. Place the cream in a metal or ceramic bowl and place over a pan of barely simmering water.
2. Cook very slowly for about 24 hours or until it has reduced by about half (it should almost be the consistency of butter, with a golden 'crust' on the top).
3. Remove the bowl from the heat.
4. Cover and let stand for 2 hours, and then refrigerate for at least 12 hours.
5. Keep unused portions refrigerated, tightly covered, for up to 4 days.

Tina's Tip

It is best to serve clotted cream at room temperature, and remember to serve some of the 'crust' as well as the runnier cream underneath to get the benefit of both the farmyard aromas and the 'mouth feel' of the different textures together as you get a bit of the 'clot' with the cream.

Really thick clotted cream is fairly stiff and very spreadable and I feel is best used for scones or even spread on homemade fruit bread with jam.

Tina's Breakfast Muesli

Running a busy hotel and restaurant is a chaotic affair, and it often leaves little time for preparations. On numerous occasions, a guest has ordered muesli only for me to find that it had run out (or, to be more precise, that my husband had eaten the last of it!). Always wanting to please, I would stand in my dry store clutching the breakfast order and spend a few moments scanning the shelves for inspiration.

The porridge oats formed a good solid basis, with a few crumbled Weetabix for added texture. Then I would throw in some fruitcake ingredients: nuts, raisins, sultanas, dates, and the many seeds used in the mixed grain bread: sesame, sunflower, hemp, pumpkin, linseed. Next, from my 'ingredients bought to play with' shelf, I found things such as goji berries and dried cranberries, which also wound up in the mix.

Combining all of these ingredients always came up trumps, especially when topped with a few home-dried bananas and some fresh raspberries or blueberries.

Makes 1300g/10 portions

Ingredients

1kg/2lb 3oz rolled oats
200g/7oz quinoa flakes
200g/7oz crunchy (mix together oat or wheat flakes, cane sugar, quinoa flakes, vegetable oil, glucose syrup, sultanas, dessicated coconut, honey, ground almonds, sunflower seeds, natural vanilla aroma) spread on a tray and baked in a moderate oven til crispy
1 tsp ground ginger
70g/2½oz pumpkin seed
70g/2½oz sunflower seed
60g/2oz linseed
100g/3½oz toasted coconut
70g/2½oz toasted cashew nuts
70g/2½oz toasted hazelnuts
70g/2½oz goji berries
100g/3½oz dried cranberries
100g/3½oz dried blueberries
90g/3oz dried sliced bananas
90g/3oz chopped dates

Method

Combine all ingredients. Mix well. Store in an airtight container until needed.

Ease of cooking: ★☆☆
Preparation time: 20 minutes

Tina's Tip

Sugar or dried milk can also be added for a little extra sweetness.

Crème fraîche

Crème fraîche is a thickened cream made by adding lactic acid bacteria culture to cream, giving it a slightly tangy flavour more akin to sour cream. It has between 18 and 36% fat, and a smooth, thick texture, similar to cream cheese (single cream is 18-21%, whipping 35-38% and double 45-48% fat).

Originally developed by artisan producers in the Brittany and Normandy regions of France, each brand of crème fraîche has its own distinct characteristics (both texture and flavour) and is greatly appreciated in much the same way savvy connoisseurs enjoy different types of yoghurt.

I prefer to use crème fraîche instead of fresh cream because it can be boiled, reduced and thickened, without the risk of curdling. It can also be whipped like double cream and has a much longer shelf life than other creams as it has been heated during production.

Crème fraîche is very easy to make at home. Below is a recipe and whilst it takes some time to make, it's certainly worth the effort.

Makes 300ml

Ingredients

240ml/8 fl oz pasteurised double/whipping cream
2 tbsp buttermilk

Method

1. Place the cream into a saucepan.
2. Heat to 37°C (blood temperature).
3. Pour into a glass bowl, add the buttermilk and mix well.
4. Cover, and leave to stand at room temperature (about 21°C) for 8 to 24 hours, or until thickened.
5. Stir well, cover with cling-film, refrigerate and use within 10 days.

Ease of cooking: ★ ☆ ☆
The most difficult thing is the waiting time
Preparation time: 8¼–24 hours

Tina's Tip

Crème fraîche makes a great topping for fresh fruits, puddings and other desserts, such as cheesecake. It also makes an excellent addition to meat dishes such as stroganoff and goulash or soups because it is less likely to curdle when heated, than ordinary cream. Smoked salmon pairs well with a little crème fraîche and caviar.

A simple substitute for buttermilk:

1. Place a tablespoon of white wine vinegar or lemon juice in a liquid measuring cup.
2. Add enough milk to bring the liquid up to the one-cup line.
Let stand for five minutes, then use as much as your recipe calls for.

Chocolate, Prune, Hazelnut & Armagnac Cake

This is a piece of cake to make. Surprisingly easy, deliciously moist.

Serves 6

Ease of cooking: ★☆☆
Preparation & cooking time: 2 hours

Ingredients

125g/4½oz softened butter
170g/6oz caster sugar
125g/4½oz ground hazelnuts
140g/5oz bitter chocolate (74% cocoa)
3 medium/165g whole eggs
1 tsp vanilla essence
20g/2 tbsp self-raising flour
20ml Armagnac
300g/10½oz soaked, well-drained cut up pitted prunes

Method

1. Set the oven to 140°C.
2. Place the chocolate into a bowl and set over a pan of simmering water to melt.
3. Cream the butter and sugar together in a mixing bowl until light and fluffy.
4. Add the eggs one at a time, mixing after each addition until all of them have been well incorporated.
5. Fold in the flour, nuts, vanilla and Armagnac.
6. Add the warmed chocolate carefully and combine thoroughly.
7. Add the prunes to the chocolate mix and fold in gently.
8. Pour into a well-greased cake tin.
9. Bake in the oven for 1–1½ hours.

Tina's Tip

To turn this cake into a dessert, warm slightly, then serve with ice cream and/or crème fraîche. Try substituting rosewater for vanilla essence. If you like the flavour of rosewater, the combination with Armagnac will blow you away.

Lemon Tart

This is always a real hit. It needs a bit of practice to get spot on, but once mastered, this dessert will be a permanent fixture in your dinner party repertoire.

Makes 10 portions

Ingredients

1 x 10" pastry case, baked blind (cover base with parchment and fill with baking beans to hold the sides in place during cooking)

Lemon Tart Filling

7 medium whole eggs
6 medium egg yolks
285g/10oz caster sugar
285ml/10 fl oz lemon juice (1 medium lemon yields 1 tbsp zest and 2 tbsp/30g juice)
285ml/10 fl oz double cream
Zest of 2 lemons

Method

1. Pre-heat oven to 140°C.
2. In a food processor whiz the eggs and sugar to mix.
3. Add the cream and lemon juice then pass through a fine strainer.
4. Add the lemon zest.
5. Pour into the baked tart case and bake for approx. 20 min. at 140°C.
6. Turn off heat and leave in oven a further 5–10 minutes or until set.
7. Cool in a warm place away from any draught to prevent cracking.

Ease of cooking: ★ ★ ☆
Preparation & cooking time:
45 minutes–1 hour
Freezes well but needs to be reheated at 190°C for 12 minutes from frozen.

Tina's Tip

To make in advance, mix some egg yolk with a little water and paint the cooked pastry case prior to baking with the filling. This gives it a coating which prevents the pastry from becoming soggy from the topping. If your tart should overcook and split, and is beyond presentation, whisk some egg whites with sugar, place on top of the tart and into a hot oven for 10 minutes and call it lemon meringue pie!

Banana & Ginger Parfait

Bananas are a fantastic and almost complete food. They are a rich source of vitamin A, vitamin B6, vitamin C, potassium and manganese, and contain enough natural sugar to make them exceedingly palatable. This light-yet-rich parfait can be served straight from the freezer with sliced fresh banana, topped with whisky and toffee sauce.

Serves 6

Ingredients

80g/4 egg yolks
110g/4oz caster sugar
60g/2 tbsp water
140g/5oz banana purée
170ml/6 fl oz whipping cream
Concentrated lemon or lime juice to taste
1 tsp ground ginger
2 tbsp chopped crystallized ginger

Method

1. Boil the water and sugar together until syrupy.
2. Whisk the syrup onto the yolks over a bain marie (pan with hot water below) until light and frothy.
3. Remove the bowl and whisk until cold.
4. Fold in the banana purée.
5. Whip the cream with the ground ginger to a medium peak and fold in.
6. Add the crystallized ginger and lemon juice to taste.
7. Pour into small conical moulds.
8. Freeze for 2–3 hours.
9. When required, tap out of the mould and on to a plate and serve.

Ease of cooking: ★★☆
This parfait can also be made in a bread tin and then served in slices. To cut evenly, heat a thin knife in hot water.
Preparation & cooking time: 3–4 hours

Tina's Tip

Bananas past their sell-by date come into their own for this recipe. The sugars concentrate and the flavour intensifies. No point in using unripe bananas for this dessert.

Toffee Sauce

No home should be without this irresistible recipe. This is definitely a comfort sauce, which is suitable for many applications; meringue, apple sponge pudding, sticky toffee pudding, baked pears and much, much more.

Makes 1½ litres/2 pts 13 fl. oz

Ingredients

225g/8oz soft brown sugar or jaggery
225g/8oz golden syrup
450g/1lb butter
570ml/1 pint double cream
1 tsp vanilla essence

Method

1. Combine all ingredients in a glass or ceramic bowl and place over a pan of simmering water, heating until the butter melts and the sugar dissolves, then stir until thick and glossy. Alternatively, microwave on low for about 10 minutes and then whisk well. Add a few drops of water if it splits to compensate for the water evaporation in the microwave.

Ease of cooking: ★ ☆ ☆
Simple to make, good either hot or cold.
Preparation & cooking time: 40 minutes

Tina's Tip

This is a great standby sauce, will keep in the fridge and also freezes well.
Whisky can be substituted for the vanilla.

Ice Creams

There is something incredibly therapeutic, wholesome and rewarding about making your own ice cream. Firstly, you know that it will not contain any of the 'nasties' found in many commercial ice creams. Secondly, there is a lot of room for experimentation, as your basic custard can act as a neutral base for your individual taste and imagination.

For example, if you want to add some chocolate to your regular vanilla ice cream recipe, reduce the sugar a little and add some cooled (but not set) melted dark chocolate just as the ice cream is finishing on its last few turns. These days, ice cream makers are really easy to get a hold of and are pretty inexpensive – so have a go.

Cardamom & Lime Ice Cream

Makes 1½ litres

Ingredients
570ml/1 pint whole milk
285ml/½ pint Greek yoghurt
430ml/¾ pint double cream
170g/6oz caster sugar
8 egg yolks
¼ cup lime juice
2 tbsp cardamom seeds
½ tbsp glycerine (optional: makes it scoopable straight from the freezer)

Method

1. Put cardamom seeds into the milk. Place in a heavy-bottomed saucepan together with the milk.
2. Heat to scalding point (just below boiling when the milk forms a skin which starts to wrinkle).
3. Remove from the heat and allow to cool.
4. Refrigerate overnight to allow the flavour to infuse.
5. Next morning, warm the milk and cardamom gently, ensuring the milk does not boil.
6. Whisk the egg yolks and sugar together in a large bowl.
7. Strain and pour the warmed milk slowly onto the egg yolks and sugar, stirring all the time.
8. Place the mixture into a clean thick-bottomed saucepan and stir over a low heat until the custard coats the back of a wooden spoon.
9. Cool, add the double cream and the yoghurt and then strain through muslin or a fine sieve, twice.
10. Add the lime juice.
11. Chill. Then churn in an ice cream maker.
12. If you do not have an ice cream maker then place in a suitable deep freeze container and freeze for about 30 minutes and then stir. Repeat twice more until the ice cream sets.

Ease of making: ★★☆
Take care not to scramble the custard.
Preparation time: 40 minutes

Tina's Tip

Take care not to let the custard boil – if it does it will scramble. Blitzing the mix in a blender can, to a certain degree, rectify this, but the resulting custard will not be as smooth.

Straining custard through muslin gives a better result than through a sieve. If you strain it through muslin several times the resulting texture is exceptional.

Once you have strained the seeds, rinse them under a tap; place on a roasting tray and into a warm oven. When dried, pulverise in a coffee grinder and store in an airtight jar for later use in biscuits and cakes.

Tina's Tip

The glycerine is optional. It prevents the ice cream from becoming solid and is therefore easier to scoop. A few drops of cardamom oil (check suitability for culinary use) can be used to replace the seeds or to strengthen the flavour once the seeds have been removed.

Lavender Ice Cream

Makes 1½ litres/2 pints 13 fl. oz

Ingredients

8 medium egg yolks
570ml/1 pint whole milk
570ml/1 pint double cream
170g/6oz sugar
1 tbsp glycerine (see above)
12–15 lavender stems (cut about 8cm long, young shoots only, picked just before flower head develops) or ¼ cup dried lavender flowers

Method

Use the same method as for the Cardamom & Lime Ice Cream, leaving out the lime juice and substituting lavender (chopped into 1 cm pieces, using either a knife of scissors) for the cardamom.

Ease of making: ★☆☆
Don't stint on the lavender: the flavour needs to be bold.
Making and freezing time: 2–3 hours

Cinnamon Ice Cream

Serves 8

Ingredients

8 egg yolks
170g/6oz sugar
570ml/1 pint milk
430ml/¾ pint double cream
100g/3½oz cinnamon sticks

Method

Use the same method as for other ice creams, substituting cinnamon sticks for the cardamom or lavender.

Ease of preparation: ★☆☆
Cassia bark, similar to cinnamon (although with a more rustic flavour), can be used as a substitute.
Making and freezing time: 2–3 hours

Cardamom, White Chocolate & Lime Panna Cotta

Light and refreshing and easy to make, this unusual little pudding is well-received when you are looking to serve something just a little out of the ordinary.

Serves 12

Ingredients

570ml/1 pint whole organic milk
800ml/27 fl oz double cream
365g/13oz caster sugar
½ cup cardamom seeds
225g/8oz white chocolate
Zest and juice of three limes
6 sheets of leaf gelatine

Method

1. Soak the gelatine leaves in a bowl of cold water.
2. Place the milk, cream, sugar and cardamom seeds into a saucepan.
3. Heat gently to scalding point (just before boiling when the milk skins over and starts to wrinkle).
4. Remove from the heat and rest for 1 hour.
5. Heat the mix once again to just below boiling point.
6. Remove from the heat.
7. Remove the gelatine leaves from the water and then add one at a time stirring until thoroughly dissolved.
8. Add the white chocolate and stir until melted.
9. Strain the mix into a clean bowl, add the lime zest and juice and pour into moulds.
10. Chill for 2–4 hours. Serve with fresh mango or summer berries and/or fruit coulis.

Ease of cooking: ★☆☆

Blue Cheese Sauce

If you can get your hands on it, Beenleigh Blue Cheese is my favourite for this recipe. It is very well made and has a wonderful balance of tangy saltiness and acidity. The rough, crusty, natural rind is slightly sticky and has some patches of blue, grey and white moulds.

Made from ewe's milk, Beenleigh Blue Cheese is moist, yet crumbly, with the blue appearing as bold blue-green streaks through the white interior. The flavour has a burnt caramel sweetness, characteristic of fine sheep's milk. It melts on the palate, disclosing its strong, spicy character. The cheese takes about six months to ripen and is available from August to January. Alternatives are Harbourne Blue (see picture), made from goat's milk, or cheeses similar to Roquefort, such as Stilton, Oxford Blue or a lovely Buffalo Blue.

This combination of ingredients is quite spectacular and can be used to accompany pasta, potatoes or rice and will even compliment pork and chicken and makes fabulous baked eggs. For this, pour some sauce into a greased ramekin, crack an egg on top, and spoon more cheese sauce over before baking for 15 minutes in a hot oven. This sauce is also good with fresh spinach tagliatelle, spaghetti or macaroni. I love to serve this to large groups of people who can help themselves to seconds (which they invariably do).

Serves 25

Ingredients

1360g/3lb button mushrooms
1360g/3lb finely chopped onions
1 tbsp garlic purée or 3 finely chopped cloves of garlic
900g/2 lb Beenleigh Blue cheese or alternative
570ml/1 pint white wine
850ml/1½ pints single cream
2 tbsp cornflour or potato starch
Freshly ground black pepper, herbs (tarragon, chives, parsley, thyme)

Method

1. Sweat the onions and garlic until they are opaque. Add the mushrooms and cook for 6–8 minutes.
2. Add the white wine then boil to reduce the liquid by about a third.
3. Add the cream, bring to the boil, and then thicken with the cornflour or potato starch mixed with a little water.
4. Add the cheese.
5. Taste and correct the seasoning if necessary.
6. Add the freshly chopped herbs just before serving.

Ease of cooking: ★ ☆ ☆
Simple to prepare but do not boil once the cheese has been added.
Preparation & cooking time: 30 minutes

Tina's Tip

This sauce freezes well, but will also keep for a couple of weeks if stored in the fridge in clean jars with tight-fitting lids. If making to store, do not add the herbs.

Yoghurt, Sultana & Almond Mint Dressing

This tangy, fruity, crunchy, creamy dressing is full of texture and tastes extremely good with barbequed meats and vegetables eg lamb chump chops, roasted aubergine, peppers, courgettes and chicken.

Makes 2 x 1lb jars

Ingredients

60ml/2 tbsp lemon juice
110g/4oz/½ cup sultanas
30ml/2 tbsp honey, warmed
500ml/18 fl oz natural yoghurt
100g/3½oz/¼ cup toasted flaked almonds
30g/2 tbsp crushed garlic
¼ cup chopped fresh mint
Freshly ground black pepper

Method

1. Combine the sultanas with the lemon juice and plump up in the microwave by heating in a glass bowl covered with cling film on low for two to five minutes until most of the lemon juice has been absorbed (alternatively soak overnight).
2. Add the yoghurt, honey, garlic, almonds & black pepper and store in the fridge.
3. Chop the mint and add to the yoghurt mix just before serving.

Ease of cooking: ★☆☆
Preparation time: 20 minutes

Tina's Tip

Try this sauce to accompany lamb burgers (p22), but omit the mint and use sweet marjoram instead.

Rich Egg Custard Mix

Use this for baking quiches, making frittata/Spanish omelette or scrambled eggs with smoked salmon. If you have your own chickens and a glut of eggs, make ahead of time and freeze.

Makes 600ml

Ingredients

8 medium eggs
145ml/5 fl oz double cream
½ tsp sea salt
Freshly ground black pepper

Method

Whisk all the ingredients together and chill until ready to use.

Ease of cooking: ★☆☆
Preparation time: 5 minutes

Tina's Tip

If you are using this for quiche or scrambled eggs, experiment with a few teaspoons of cream cheese stirred in at the last minute, perhaps with some chopped thyme or tarragon, or smoked salmon. For a custard tart mix, delete the salt and pepper, add sugar to taste and add a pinch of nutmeg.

Hollandaise Sauce

Hollandaise means 'from Holland'. It is thought that Hollandaise Sauce was originally called Sauce Isigny after a town in Normandy, Isigny-sur-Mer, which was famous for its Normandy butter. During World War I, butter production came to a halt in France and had to be imported from Holland, which resulted in the name being changed to Hollandaise Sauce to indicate where the butter came from.

This sauce is traditionally served with meats such as beef, egg dishes such as Eggs Benedict, and vegetables such as steamed asparagus, although I love to make it to accompany stir-fried broccoli leaves & goose eggs (p199).

Serves 4

Ingredients

250g butter, melted
2 egg yolks
2 tsp vinegar or 1 tbsp lemon juice
Hot water

Method

1. Mix the yolks with the vinegar or lemon juice in a glass or ceramic bowl.
2. Place over a saucepan with a small amount of simmering water and whisk continuously until the ribbon stage is obtained (this is when it is light, fluffy but slightly thickened or when some of the sauce is dropped back into the bowl and leaves a trail behind that is visible for a short while before merging back into the mixture).
3. Remove from the heat and cool slightly.
4. Gradually whisk in melted butter until thoroughly combined.
5. Taste and correct the seasoning.
6. Hollandaise must be kept at just above room temperature.

Ease of cooking: ★ ★ ☆
Preparation & cooking time: 15 minutes

Bérnaise Sauce

To make Bérnaise Sauce use tarragon vinegar to replace the white wine vinegar and add 2 tablespoons of chopped tarragon to the finished sauce. If you have ever made mayonnaise, then you will find this easy, as the process is very similar although Hollandaise is a warm butter emulsion as opposed to a cold, oil-based one.

The main trick in making this sauce is to heat the egg yolks enough to achieve the correct consistency (drops off the spoon), but not to the extent that the yolk proteins coagulate into little solid curds and the sauce separates (resembling scrambled egg).

There is a risk of the sauce splitting if the butter is too hot or is added too quickly or if the mix becomes too thick and is not slackened with water before adding the rest of the butter. If the Hollandaise should split, place a teaspoon of boiling water in a clean bowl and gradually whisk in the curdled sauce. If this fails put a fresh yolk in a bowl with a teaspoon of hot water and re-make a sabayon (stage 2) and then gradually whisk in the curdled sauce. Bon chance!

Béchamel

This white sauce is made from flour, flavoured milk and butter. It is found all over the world in many different guises. Béchamel sauce is the base to many sauces such as cheese (a component of lasagne and mousakka) caper, onion and mustard (see tip overleaf).

Ingredients

570ml/1 pint milk
1 small onion, peeled and halved
4 bay leaves
6 cloves
Blade of mace

For the roux:
60g/2oz butter
60g/2oz plain flour
Salt and white pepper

Method

Pin the bay leaves to the onion halves with the cloves. Place the onion and the mace in the milk and infuse over a gently heat for 8–12 minutes. Strain.

Melt the butter (do not allow to sizzle) in a pan and stir in the flour and mix. Remove from the heat and stir in the milk little by little, stirring to prevent lumps forming. Return to the stove, bring to the boil then turn down the heat and simmer until the sauce thickens. Season with salt and white pepper.

Tina's tips on sauces

Bacon, pork or beef fat can replace the butter – for example, if cooking roast pork with cauliflower cheese, cook the béchamel with pork or bacon fat.

For cheese sauce add 175g/6oz Parmesan cheese. To make caper sauce, add 3 tbsp very small capers and 1 tbsp of the caper vinegar to the Béchamel. For a really good onion sauce crush some herbs such as rosemary, thyme or marjoram (to release the essential oils) and infuse with the milk, then sweat a finely chopped onion in the butter, before adding the flour. Half of the milk can be replaced by good quality chicken stock.

Mustard sauce is as the onion sauce but with the addition of 1 tbsp English mustard powder mixed with 1 tbsp white wine vinegar. White pepper is not essential but I find it more aesthetically pleasing in a white sauce, as I do not like to see black flecks.

The Bread Oven

The Bread Oven

Making bread is not only a very satisfying task, but it is also a nurturing, soul-enhancing experience. In my opinion, handling yeast dough is much more fun than any other type of cooking. You are dealing with something alive.

Kneading the dough to a smooth elasticity and watching it spring to life and rise to a puffy lightness, taking the beautiful nutty loaves out of the oven and breathing in that heavenly warm aroma of freshly baked bread is almost as rewarding as watching the faces of those lucky enough to enjoy the fruits of your labours.

Experimenting with the multitude of different flours and grains available is a journey that can last a lifetime. Just a note: fresh yeast is readily available from most health food shops – if you don't have one near you, try the local bakery as I do – that way, I know it is as fresh as it can get, as they have very regular deliveries.

Sage, Apricot & Sunflower Seed Bread

Fresh sage and soft fruity apricots make this dough aromatic with a hint of sweetness. The combination of seed, grain and fruit evokes a sense of late summer harvest and rich autumnal colours. Good with unsalted butter or soft cheese, especially a creamy goat's or a brie.

Makes 3 x 370g/13oz oval loaves

Ingredients

540g/19oz strong white flour
15g/½oz fresh yeast
80ml/3 fl oz egg whites
300ml/11 fl oz water
40g/⅓ cup fresh sage, chopped or 2 tbsp dried
70g/2½oz dried chopped apricots
40g/1½oz toasted sunflower seeds
15g/½oz salt

Method

1. Sieve flour into a mixing bowl.
2. Add the yeast mixed with a little of the water at 30°C.
3. Add the rest of the water. Whisk egg whites lightly and add.
4. Knead by hand or with a dough hook for 10 minutes.
5. Leave to rise for 35 minutes or until doubled in bulk. Knock back.
6. Add apricots, sunflower seeds and either chop the sage or blitz it in a food processor with the salt, then add to the dough and mix for a further 10 minutes.
7. Shape into 3 x 370g oval loaves, place on to a greased baking tray and leave to prove for 40 minutes or until doubled in bulk.
8. Bake at 175°C for 35 minutes.
9. Cool on a wire rack.

Ease of cooking: ★★☆
Chop the sage at the last moment to capture the essential oil.
Preparation, rising and cooking time: 2 hours

Tina's Tip

To freeze, cook for 20 minutes to par-bake. When needed, thaw and bake at 180°C for 15 minutes for a 'freshly-baked' loaf. For best results, always ensure that all your ingredients are at room temperature.

Sesame Breakfast Bread

Many years ago, when I was working in my fathers' betting shops, a little old lady called Annie Marks used to place a small bet each day (I think at the time she was in her early nineties). Often she would hand me a loaf of bread. It was called a 'milk loaf' and tasted nice and sweet due to the lactose (milk sugar) in the bread and was particularly good for breakfast toast.

Milk makes bread that is more nourishing, has a more velvety grain and creamy white crumb, a browner crust, and keeps longer than that made with water. The following recipe is one I developed years later with Annie in mind.

Makes 2 x 900g/2lb loaves
or 4 x 450g/1lb loaves

Ingredients

900g/2lb strong white flour
30g/1oz fresh yeast
5 egg whites
200ml/7 fl oz milk, warmed to 30°C
300ml/11 fl oz water, warmed to 30°C
½ cup sesame seed
30g/1oz salt
Sesame oil for greasing the tins

Method

1. Sieve the flour into a mixing bowl.
2. Mix the yeast with a little of the water to dissolve.
3. Add to the flour together with the rest of the milk and water.
4. Lightly whisk the egg whites and add.
5. Knead for 10 minutes.
6. Cover with a damp cloth and allow the dough to rise for 35 minutes or until doubled in bulk (35–40 minutes).
7. Grease bread tins with the sesame oil.
8. Knock back. Add the salt and the sesame seed.
9. Divide into 2 x 900g/2lb loaves or 4 x 450g/1 lb loaves.
10. Leave to rise until doubled in bulk (35–40 minutes).
11. Place in an oven pre-heated to 180°C and bake for 35 minutes.
12. Turn out onto a wire rack and leave to cool.

Ease of cooking: ★★☆
If you make bread on a regular basis, do not wash the tins with soap, as this will cause the dough to stick to the sides even after greasing.
Preparation & cooking time: 1½ hours
Freezes well.

Tina's Tip

Greasing the tins with sesame oil is not obligatory (ordinary vegetable oil or butter will do), but it does give the crust a lovely flavour and the nutty aroma of sesame fills the room when a slice or two are put in the toaster.

Pumpkin & Sesame Seed Bread

This is a favourite of mine in the autumn when the pumpkins are ripe and sweet. If you don't usually save your seed, then try this recipe. Not only does it give the bread a sweet, nutty aroma but the golden strands of the pith are particularly attractive running through the bread at random.

Follow the recipe for the Sesame Break-fast Bread (*opposite page*), but after the first rising add 2 cups of fresh, wet, plump pumpkin seeds together with the stringy pith which surrounds the seeds, and an extra pinch of salt. Mix well and then finish as for sesame bread.

Suitable for toast for that extra special 'sunshine breakfast'.

Tina's Tip

When scooping out the fresh seed from pumpkins, be sure to have bread-making on the agenda that day as the pith around the seeds needs to be used as fresh as possible to capture the colour and arrest any possible deterioration.

Any left over can be baked on a greased tray for an hour at 120°C until crisp and served with a dry sherry.

Brown Breakfast Bread with Mixed Grain

Full of fibre and nutritional seeds, this wholesome and ambrosial recipe is especially good with butter and homemade jam, at any time of the day. Potato water adds a characteristic flavour and moisture to the bread, the dough becomes marginally heavier and yields a slightly coarser grain.

Makes 2 x 900g/2lb loaves

Ingredients

900g/2lb strong brown flour
450g/1lb rye flour
60g/2oz wheat germ
750ml/26 fl oz water, warmed to 30°C
45g/1½oz fresh yeast
20g/¾oz salt
60g/2oz sunflower seed
¼ cup hemp seed
¼ cup linseed
¼ cup sesame seed

Method

1. Soak the seeds in ⅔ of the water.
2. Sieve both the flours into a mixing bowl. Add the wheat germ.
3. Mix the yeast to a sloppy paste with the rest of the water, then add to the flour.
4. Mix on a low speed (or knead by hand in a large bowl) for 10 minutes. Cover with a damp cloth. Prove for 45 minutes or until the mix has doubled in bulk.
5. Knock back the dough. Add the salt and the rest of the ingredients and mix for a further 10 minutes.
6. Divide into two 900g/2lb loaves if baking in tins, or divide into four 400g/1lb loaves if shaping. Knead into shape.
7. Place on greased trays or in tins and prove until doubled in bulk. Bake 20 minutes in an oven that is pre-heated to 180°C, and then reduce the heat to 150°C for a further 20 minutes.
8. Turn out onto wire rack to cool.

Ease of cooking: ★★☆ Experiment with different seed combinations.
Preparation & cooking time: 2 hours

Tina's Tip

Make a large batch of this bread, cool, slice and freeze. This way, individual slices can be taken straight from the freezer and popped in the toaster – instant tasty toast! Add a little extra water to the dough if dry.

Wholemeal Raisin & Sultana Loaf

Arriving home after school, there was always banana milkshake and fruit loaf on the table to tide us kids over until suppertime. My mother was always baking and the recipe for this sweet dough never failed her. A couple of buttered slices of this delicious loaf are packed with calcium and vitamin D, making it a nutritious snack, especially for growing children (of any age!)

Makes 2 x 900g/2lb loaves

Ingredients

2 cups lukewarm milk
½ cup sugar
2 tsp salt
2 tbsp fresh yeast
4 eggs
¼ cup butter, margarine or oil
9 cups sifted wholemeal flour
½ cup seedless raisins
½ cup sultanas

Method

1. Place the milk, sugar & salt into a bowl and crumble in the yeast.
2. Stir until the yeast is dissolved and then stir in the softened butter and the eggs.
3. Add the flour and the fruit and mix thoroughly.
4. Dust a work surface with some flour, turn out the mix and then shape into two loaves.
5. Leave to rise for 1 hour (or until doubled in bulk), and then bake in an oven pre-heated to 175°C for 45–50 minutes, or until well browned.

Ease of cooking: ★★☆ Pure delight.
Preparation, rising & cooking time: 2¼ hours

Tina's Tip

The softer and stickier you are able to keep the dough (use just enough flour to prevent the dough from sticking to your hands or the work surface) the more you will improve both the eating and storing quality of the loaf. The moisture in the fruit also helps this loaf to be an excellent keeper.

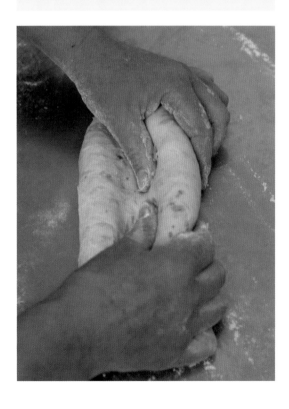

Irish Soda Bread

This is probably the easiest of all breads to make. It is certainly a good one to start with – a great confidence-booster for the otherwise intimidated cook. The benefits of soda bread are that it is rapidly mixed, needs no rising time, is consigned straight to the oven and cooked in roughly half the time of yeasted bread, and can be eaten immediately. The downside, however, is that once made, the loaf can stale quickly, and so it is best only to make enough for one day.

Soda bread evolved in Ireland following the introduction of bicarbonate of soda in 1840. This was a time when 'hard wheat' proved exceptionally difficult to grow because of a fungus that attacked the crops. As soon as soda became available, it replaced traditional yeast and was used in conjunction with buttermilk and soft flour to make a 'quick bread,' which was aptly called soda bread. The buttermilk is an important ingredient as it is the lactic acid in the milk that reacts with the soda as soon as they meet, producing a gas which makes the bread rise. It is therefore important that the bread be put together quickly to harness that gas. It is best to bake Irish Soda Bread in a cast iron pot covered with a lid (or a buttered cast iron 'Dutch oven' dish), although a ceramic casserole or baking rings can also be used.

Unlike yeasted breads, where the external factors such as temperature, altitude and humidity can affect results, breads made with a chemical leavener (baking powder and cream of tartar can also be used) are generally uniform and reliable. Foods such as banana bread (page 234), biscuits, muffins, pancakes, scones, Yorkshire puddings/Popovers (page 236) and griddlecakes are also considered quick breads.

Makes 2 x 500g/18oz loaves

Ingredients

270g/9½oz wholemeal flour
270g/9½oz plain flour
¾ tsp salt
1½ tsp caster sugar
1½ tsp bicarbonate of soda
420ml/15 fl oz buttermilk or sour milk

Method

1. Pre-heat oven to 185°C.
2. Sieve the flours together with the sugar, salt, and soda into a large bowl.
3. Make a well in the centre, add the buttermilk and draw the flour gradually into the liquid to form a slack dough.
4. Knead lightly on a floured surface, divide into 2 loaves and put directly into a hot oven to cook for 30 minutes.
5. Cool on a wire rack. Eat the same day.

Ease of cooking: ★ ☆ ☆
Preparation & cooking time: 50 minutes

Tina's Tip

As this bread is best made in small quantities, it can be made to suit a particular meal. Try adding some rosemary if accompanying a lamb stew or lovage for a light lunch with home-cured ham and pickle.

Walnut & Oatmeal Baguette

Try this one for a brunch or light lunch, when the spread might include cold meats and cheese or eggs baked in cheese sauce. This bread is also good with hearty soups, such as spiced pumpkin & ginger (page 74).

Makes 3 baguettes

Ingredients

300ml/10½ fl oz/1¼ cups water at 30°C
60g/2oz fresh yeast
30ml/2 tbsp olive oil
225g/1½ cups strong white bread flour
225g/1½ cups strong wholemeal bread flour
60g/2oz/½ cup coarse jumbo oats
(porridge oats will do)
125g/4½oz/1 cup walnut pieces, lightly toasted
45g/1½oz honey
1½ tsp coarse sea salt

Method

1. Pre-heat oven to 180°C. Mix the yeast to a paste with a little of the water.
2. Place the flours, walnuts and oats in a mixing bowl; add the yeast and the rest of the water.
3. Add the honey and the sea salt.
4. Mix for 10 minutes, making sure the mix comes away from the side of the bowl. If it sticks, add a little more flour or oatmeal.
5. Turn the dough onto a floured surface. Divide into three, shape into baguettes, place onto a greased tray and leave in a warm place for 45 minutes to 1 hour or until doubled in size.

6. Bake for ½–¾ hour.
7. Cool on a wire rack.

Ease of cooking: ★★☆
Pecans, cashews or hazelnuts can be used as an alternative to walnuts.
Preparation & cooking time: 1 hour 45 minutes
Freezes well

Background to Sourdough Bread

Sourdough is a type of bread that is baked using naturally occurring wild yeasts and given a long, slow rising period so that it develops a characteristic sour flavour. Sourdough was the first sort of leavening available to bakers. It originated in Ancient Egyptian times and was used until the Middle Ages, when it was superseded by barm (a yeast produced by beer brewing), which in turn was replaced by commercially-cultured yeast.

To make sourdough bread, first a 'starter' or 'mother sponge' needs to be made. This is done simply by mixing together equal quantities of fresh flour and water and leaving it loosely covered at room temperature in order to capture the atmospheric yeasts.

The best way to create a stable culture is to use un-chlorinated water and unbleached, un-bromated organic and bran-containing flours, as they provide the highest level of live organisms. Adding some unwashed organic grapes or a couple of sticks of unwashed organic rhubarb (for the wild yeasts on their skins) increases the leavening power of the bacteria, as does using the leftover water from boiling organic potatoes, which provides additional starch.

However, if you are lucky enough to have a friend who can give you some of their already-made starter, you will save time and get a 'head start'. Each hand-made batch has slightly different characteristics, which are determined by several factors, including the type of flour and the yeast, the humidity and temperature, the altitude, and even the types of bare wood present in the kitchen.

Creating a sourdough and then keeping it alive is quite a nurturing process (if you or your children ever owned a Tamagotchi you will love this!). The 'starter' or 'mother sponge' can be left at room temperature and fed daily (see below) or kept in the fridge and fed at less regular intervals – about once a week – which is probably more practical if you are not a baker. This is not a process for the 'short-cut' cook, as creating a 'starter' from scratch can take as long as two weeks. Once you have your starter though, remember the sequence: divide, feed, prove, use to bake, or refrigerate.

The result, however, is truly satisfying, and you can rest assured that although there may be similar loaves available, there won't be anyone who can replicate the starter you have created.

Now that you have gone to all this trouble, it had better be worth it! It is definitely a very good 'all-rounder', suitable for breakfast toast, sandwiches, for dunking in soups or sliced thinly with smoked salmon pâté (page 60). The bread itself keeps reasonably well and the starter will keep indefinitely, providing it is well looked after! My favourite way of eating sourdough bread is with cheese, especially with the addition of a little cumin seed in the dough.

How to make a Sourdough Starter

Mix equal parts flour and water (not too much, as it keeps growing) in a large wide bowl to the consistency of a sloppy batter. Cover with a damp tea towel and leave at room temperature for 24 hours. Then add more flour and water until you have doubled the quantity. Repeat this process for several days until the mix starts to bubble and smell yeasty. At this point, you have a 'live' starter, ready to rumble. You can either start baking or you can put the starter into a wide ceramic bowl, loosely covered, and then in the fridge to store it. To use the starter in a recipe: let the starter sit on the counter and come to room temperature. Remove the amount you need for baking, and then stir in equal amounts of flour and water until the texture of a sloppy apple sauce has been reached. Leave at room temperature for a few hours before returning to the fridge.

The reason for dividing and replenishing (feeding) the starter (even when you don't need any for baking), is that when it is fermenting, the starter produces certain acids that inhibit growth, and as this is a dough leavener, we do not want that to happen!

Sourdough Bread

Makes 2 or 3 loaves

Ingredients

500g/18oz white flour
400g/14oz wholemeal flour
100g/3½oz rye flour
300g/10½oz sourdough starter
2½ tsp salt
400ml/14 fl oz spring water

Method

1. Combine all ingredients in a mixing bowl and knead for 10 minutes.
2. Leave to rise, covered with a damp cloth for 6 hours. Knock back lightly.
3. Mould and place onto a greased baking tray or into bread tins and leave to rise for a further 2–2½ hours.
4. Pre-heat the oven to 185°C.
5. Slash the loaves (with a thin sharp knife), bake for 20 minutes, then turn the heat down to 170°C for a further 20 minutes.
6. Turn out onto a wire rack to cool.

Ease of cooking: ★★☆
Looked after properly, the sourdough can last indefinitely and also makes an everlasting gift!
Preparation & cooking time: 9½–10 hours

Tina's Tips

Making a starter with un-chlorinated water and organic flour is imperative, as any chlorine in the water inhibits the starter.
Sourdough starter can be used to replace the Biga (see page 232). Try rosemary and olives as alternatives to oregano and tomato.

Ciabatta with Oregano, Coarse Sea Salt and Sun Dried Tomato

The beauty of this loaf, apart from its wide slipper-like appearance, is its texture. The dough is formed with large, irregular holes, which remain soft and porous when baked, yet, when made well, Ciabatta bread combines its moist crumb with a golden-brown, crisp and crunchy crust. A champion 'sauce-mopper,' this bread is equally good with stews, chunky soups, and a fresh basil, tomato and feta cheese salad with avocado oil vinaigrette (p193). A torn off chunk of Ciabatta is ideal when you reach the bottom of the bowl and need something to soak up the residual dressing and small pieces of cheese & basil.

As Ciabatta is made with slack dough, a machine is beneficial for mixing, as kneading by hand can turn into quite a messy affair. There are two stages to making Ciabatta, not too dissimilar to sourdough. A starter (Biga) needs to be made first.

Biga (Starter)

Makes enough for 3 loaves

Ingredients

¼ tsp instant yeast
145ml /5 fl oz½ cup/water
225g/8oz/1½ cups un-bleached white bread flour

Method

Combine all the ingredients in a wide bowl. Cover with a damp cloth and set aside for 12 hours or overnight. When it is ready, the mix should be light and puffy.

Ciabatta Bread

Makes 3 loaves

Ingredients

1 tsp instant yeast
1½ tsp coarse flaked sea salt (Maldon is good)
240ml/8 fl oz water
1 tbsp/15ml olive oil
300g/11oz/2 cups un-bleached strong white bread flour
1 cup fresh or ⅓ cup dried oregano
1 cup sun-dried tomatoes, drained and halved

Method

1. Place the prepared and risen Biga into an electric mixing bowl. Add the yeast, water, oil, salt and flour and slowly knead with a dough hook or paddle for several minutes. When all the ingredients are

combined, increase the speed and knead for a good 7 minutes, until the dough is sticky and slack. Add the tomato and oregano and mix for a further 3–5 minutes to combine.

2. Transfer the dough to a greased bowl and leave to rise for 2–3 hours, covered with a damp cloth, gently pushing the dough back with your fingers every 35 minutes or so.

3. Tip the dough out onto an oiled surface, divide into equal amounts and then shape into a flattish loaf.

4. Transfer to a non-stick or greased baking sheet, cover with a large piece of plastic (a clean bin bag is quite useful) and leave to rise for several hours, until light and puffy. The rising time will depend on the room temperature and humidity and can vary from summer to winter.

5. When almost ready, pre-heat the oven to 220°C, place a small roasting tray filled with water on the bottom rack (to create steam to help it rise), place the loaves in the oven and bake for approx. ½ hour or until nicely browned. Turn oven off.

6. Cool on a wire rack. Dust with flour.

Ease of cooking: ★ ★ ★
Ciabatta is best eaten on the day it is made.

Preparation & cooking time:
16–24 hours
Freezes well. After thawing, re-crisp in oven.

Oatmeal, Ginger & Banana Bread

Ripe bananas are always in short supply in my kitchen – there are so many uses for them, and one of my favourites is this bread. It is a cross between soda bread and a cake and the infusion of ginger gives it a nice kick. The oatmeal makes it hearty with a slight chewy texture, while the bananas and buttermilk makes it sweet and moist. This bread is fast to prepare, quick to devour, and great to freeze for unexpected guests.

Makes 1 large 900g/2 lb loaf

Ingredients

2 cups mashed bananas (3-4 large bananas)
2 tbsp lemon juice
1/3 cup buttermilk
1/3 cup butter
1/2 cup honey
2 eggs
3 cups rolled jumbo oats
2 tsp baking powder
2 tbsp chopped crystallized ginger
2 tbsp coarsely chopped hazelnuts
1 tbsp ground ginger
1/2 tsp bicarbonate of soda
1/2 tsp salt

Tina's Tip

Sultanas can be used to replace the crystallised ginger. This is an ideal tea loaf: it keeps well and tastes great with or without clotted cream or butter. It is always popular with children.

Method

1. Pre-heat oven to 175°C.
2. Grease a 2lb loaf tin.
3. Mash the bananas with the lemon juice, set aside.
4. Blitz half of the oats until they resemble fine flour.
5. Mix together the ground ginger, blitzed oat flour, salt, bicarbonate of soda and baking soda.
6. Combine the buttermilk with the remaining oats.
7. Cream the butter & honey until light and fluffy.
8. Add the eggs, one at a time, beating well after each addition.
9. Add the chopped nuts, mashed banana and lemon juice, followed by the buttermilk, remaining oats and crystallised ginger.
10. Fold in the ingredients listed in method point 5.
11. Spoon the batter into the greased loaf tin.
12. Place in oven and bake for 1 hour and 10 minutes, or until a toothpick or tester inserted in the centre comes out clean.

Ease of cooking: ★ ☆ ☆
Preparation & cooking time: 1½ hours

Popovers

Inherited from my mother, this 'quick bread' recipe never fails. The slack batter, made with simple ingredients, is poured into a very hot cup and there it undergoes a metamorphosis whereupon it is transformed into a light, puffy form, increasing its volume five or six-fold in a very dramatic way. This American version of Yorkshire pudding, perfect with a Sunday roast or Toad in the Hole alike, is both delightfully delicious and so easy to make. It really has a 'wow factor' when presented at the dining table.

Many years ago, whilst at university, my brother Gregory had a part-time job waiting in a restaurant in Camden Lock. Every time I make this recipe, I remember him telling me how he was forced by management to serve leftover Yorkshire puddings filled with cream and covered with chocolate sauce for dessert, when the Profiteroles had sold out!

Serves 6–9

Ingredients

145g/5oz/1 cup sifted plain flour
½ tsp salt
240ml/8 fl oz/1 cup milk
2 eggs
Butter, dripping or oil for greasing the moulds

Method

1. Pre-heat oven to 230°C.
2. Combine all the ingredients and beat until smooth.
3. Pour into pre-heated deep cups, which have been liberally greased with a couple of teaspoons of extra fat poured into the base.
4. Place in the oven.
5. Bake for 35–45 minutes, or until well-risen and golden brown.

Ease of cooking: ★ ☆ ☆
Never fails to please.
Preparation and cooking time: 1 hour

Tina's Tip

If you are making popovers to accompany a joint such as beef, collect some dripping from the joint as it is cooking, place 1–1½ tbsp in each cup and then heat before pouring in the batter.

Why not make a pudding such as apple popovers with toffee sauce? (p209). Butter the mould then line with some sliced apple mixed with a little sugar and cinnamon, pour the batter over the top and cook as above. Serve with toffee sauce, custard, cinnamon ice cream (p212), or crème fraîche.

Dog Biscuits

We could all do with being treated now and then, and the same is true for our best, albeit hairy, friends. Set aside half a day, make these in bulk and then enjoy the anticipating eyes and wagging tail of your four-legged pet for weeks to come. This is a recipe I have conjured up using the 'pluck' from the lamb carcasses slaughtered from our organic flock. The 'pluck' is a term used to describe the edible innards of an animal and include the lights (lungs), heart, spleen, liver and kidneys. Most butchers can procure pluck for you, but may need a little notice.

Makes 60 biscuits

Ingredients

2kg/4lb 6oz rolled oats
4kg/8lb 12oz pluck

Method

1. Mince the pluck through a medium mincer plate.
2. Mix with the oats and leave for several hours or overnight to allow the oats to absorb the offal juices, thereby plumping up the mixture.
3. Turn oven on to 100°C, grease about 6 large roasting trays, then roll the mixture between both hands in to balls, place on the trays and flatten with a knife or the palm of your hand, until about 1 cm thick.
4. Place in the oven and cook slowly until the mixture has cooked through and dried completely (this process can take from 6 hours to overnight).
5. When dry and crisp, take out of the oven to cool and place in an airtight container until needed.

Ease of cooking: ★☆☆ Ruff ruff, howl
Preparation & cooking time: 7 hours

Vegetable Bread with Mixed Grain

This idea of putting vegetables into bread materialised initially during the Napoleonic wars when there was a shortage of grain. Potato, cooked and mashed was added to bread in an effort to make the limited supplies of flour go further. Adding potato to the dough achieved three things: it acted as an additional leavening agent, gave the dough more 'bulk' and it also kept the finished loaf moist.

Ingredients

900g/2lb strong brown flour
450g/1lb rye flour
340g/12oz vegetable purée (potato, broad bean, butter bean, pumpkin etc.)
750ml/26 fl oz water warmed to 28°C
45g/1½oz fresh yeast
30g/1oz cumin seed
30g/1oz coriander seed
30g/1oz salt
40g/1½oz hemp seed
40g/1½oz linseed
40g/1½oz sesame seed
115g/4oz kibbled (chopped, dried) onion

Method

1. Sieve the flour into a mixing bowl.
2. Mix the yeast to a sloppy paste with a little of the warmed water.
3. Add the vegetable, yeast and rest of water to the flour. Mix 10 minutes.
4. Cover with a damp oven cloth.
5. Prove for 45 min. or until mix doubled in bulk.
6. Preheat oven to 180°C.
7. Knock back, add rest of ingredients and mix for a further 10 min.
8. Divide into 3 x 2 lb loaves. Knead into shape.
9. Place on greased trays, prove until doubled in bulk.
10. Cook for 45 min.
11. Turn out onto wire rack to cool.

Ease of cooking: ★★☆
Preparation & cooking time: 2 hours
Freezes well.

Tina's Tip

The vegetable content keeps this bread moist for far longer than shop-bought bread. If loaves should become slightly dry, sprinkle with cold water, wrap in a tea towel and then place in a hot oven for 10 minutes to refresh.

Appendix

Sweet Pastry

Ingredients

110g icing sugar, sieved
220g butter, softened
2 egg yolks
75g cornflour
250g plain flour
Pinch of sea salt

Method

1. Mix icing sugar & softened butter in mixing bowl with paddle.
2. Gradually add egg white, yolks and lemon zest.
Sift the flours and the salt together and fold in.

Shortcrust Pastry

Ingredients

450g/1lb plain flour
250g/9oz butter
1 egg made up to 170ml/6 fl oz with cold water
Pinch of salt

Method

1. Sift the flour and salt together.
2. Cut the butter in to small pieces and rub it lightly into the flour using your fingertips.
3. Add the egg and water and mix to a stiff paste.
4. Use as required.

Tina's Tip

For speed, chill the butter, place in a food processor with the flour and salt and whiz until the mix resembles fine breadcrumbs. Pour into a bowl; add the egg and water and mix.

Chicken Stock

1–2 kg/2–4 lb chicken carcasses
3 carrots, peeled and roughly chopped
1 head celery or ½ celeriac, chopped
3 onions, halved
bunch thyme
6 sprigs rosemary
1 tbsp black peppercorns
8 dried bay leaves

Place the chicken bones in a large pan and cover with cold water.
Bring to the boil then turn down to simmer for 20 minutes, skimming any scum that rises to the surface.
Add the rest of the ingredients and cook for 2½–3 hours, skimming from time to time.
Strain the stock through a fine sieve or muslin.
Cool, refrigerate overnight then remove any fat that has risen to the surface.
Will keep for three days in the fridge or can be frozen.

Fresh Egg Custard

Ingredients

40g/¼ cup cornflour
120g/½ cup caster sugar
4 egg yolks (90g)
750g/1¼ pints whole milk
Vanilla essence rum, kirsch or whisky to flavour

Method

1. Combine the eggs, sugar and corn flour in a bowl and with a little of the cold milk.
2. Heat the remainder of the milk to scalding point and pour on to mix stirring all the time.
3. Place the bowl in microwave and heat on high for 2 minutes. Stir, heat again and repeat until custard is nice and thick. Alternatively cook in a pan on the stove, stirring constantly.
4. Add flavouring, stir and serve.

Tina's Tip

A few crushed cloves of garlic and some juniper berries can be added to the ingredients for extra flavour. A stronger flavour can be achieved by boiling the stock to reduce by half.
For duck stock: simply replace the chicken bones with duck bones.

Index

THE KNITTING BOOK

THE WOOLPACK

IN ASSOCIATION WITH

 YORKSHIRE TELEVISION & *Richard Poppleton*

BOXTREE LTD

FIRST PUBLISHED IN GREAT BRITAIN IN 1989
BY BOXTREE LIMITED
PUBLISHED IN ASSOCIATION WITH
YORKSHIRE TELEVISION LIMITED

TEXT © RICHARD POPPLETON & SONS LIMITED 1989
PHOTOGRAPHS © YORKSHIRE TELEVISION LIMITED 1989
ARTWORKS © BOXTREE LIMITED 1989

ALL RIGHTS RESERVED. NO PART OF THIS PUBLICATION MAY BE
REPRODUCED, STORED IN A RETRIEVAL SYSTEM, OR TRANSMITTED IN ANY
FORM OR BY ANY MEANS, ELECTRONIC, MECHANICAL OR OTHERWISE,
WITHOUT THE PRIOR PERMISSION IN WRITING OF THE COPYRIGHT OWNERS.

PHOTOGRAPHY BY ALAN HARBOUR
TYPESET BY FLORENCETYPE LTD, KEWSTOKE, AVON
PRINTED IN ITALY BY
OFSA, MILAN

FOR BOXTREE LIMITED
36 TAVISTOCK STREET
LONDON
WC2 7PB

British Library Cataloguing in Publication Data
Emmerdale Farm : The Knitting Book
1. Knitting. British designs—patterns
746.43'2041'0941
ISBN 1-85283-270-3

Abbreviations

alt	alternate	**psso**	pass slip stitch(es) over
cm	centimetre(s)	**rem**	remain(s) (ing)
cont	continue	**rep**	repeat (ing)
dec	decrease	**RS**	right side
foll	follow(s) (ing)	**sl**	slip
g	gramme(s)	**st st**	stocking stitch
in	inch(es)	**st(s)**	stitches
inc	increase(e) (ing)	**tbl**	through back of loop(s)
K	knit	**tog**	together
P	purl	**WS**	wrong side

Contents

Preface

This book shows you how to knit 22 lovely designs, ranging from large, chunky sweaters to keep you snuggly wrapped in chilly weather, to the smart black number with is unusual flower motifs, which I model on the opposite page – tea at the vicarage in this or, at the very least, a bite at the Woolpack!

Most of us who knit get almost as much pleasure from browsing through a good pattern book as we do from completing a chosen garment and, if you are an Emmerdale Farm fan as well, this book will give you twice the enjoyment. All your favourite characters pop out from the pages, wearing a lovely assortment of jackets and sweaters. Annie and Seth, Amos and Matt, Kathy looking trendy in a boxy jacket with garter stitch edges. Sam's gorgeous sheepdog sweater was a great hit with young Benjamin Whitehead who plays him. He refused to be parted from it!

During the past nine years, as a member of the cast of Emmerdale Farm, I have grown to love the Yorkshire countryside with its sweeping dales, dry stone walls and grazing sheep. I have also come to understand and appreciate the process of making yarn, from its first stages as wool straight off the sheep's back, through its many processes, until it appears in shop windows in tempting colours and textures – ready for the creative knitter. This knowledge has made me appreciate and enjoy knitting even more.

So, now the choice is yours. I am sure that you will feel inspired to tackle many of the patterns in this book, and that you will enjoy both knitting the garments and seeing yourself and your family wearing them.

Jean Rogers

NOTE: IT IS IMPORTANT TO WORK TO THE STATED TENSION IN ORDER TO OBTAIN THE CORRECT MEASUREMENT. THE YARN RECOMMENDED IN THE PATTERNS SHOULD BE USED WHEREVER POSSIBLE AND WE CANNOT ACCEPT RESPONSIBILITY FOR AN IMPERFECT GARMENT IF ANY OTHER THAN THE RECOMMENDED YARN IS USED. IF YOU ARE USING A SUBSTITUTE YARN, USE THE GENERAL YARN WEIGHT AS A GUIDELINE.

WITH THANKS TO OUR KNITWEAR DESIGNERS:
JOY GAMMON
ANN SWETMAN
DEBBIE SCOTT
SUSAN WILKINSON

Red roses

This chic design, worn by Dolly Skilbeck (Jean Rogers), is ideal for cool evenings when you want something 'extra special' to wear. The red roses add an original eye-catching touch to the garment.

MEASUREMENTS

To fit sizes

76	81	86	91	97	102	107	112	cm
30	32	34	36	38	40	42	44	in

Actual measurement

86	91	97	102	107	112	117	122	cm
34	36	38	40	42	44	46	48	in

Length

61	61	64	64	66	66	69	69	cm
24	24	25	25	26	26	27	27	in

Sleeve length

44	44	44	44	46	46	46	46	cm
17½	17½	17½	17½	18	18	18	18	in

MATERIALS

Emmerdale Double Knitting

Black (037)

A	7	7	8	8	9	9	10	10	50g balls

Scarlet (034)

B	1	1	1	1	1	1	1	1	50g ball

Bottle (027)

C	1	1	1	1	1	1	1	1	50g ball

NEEDLES

1 pair 3¼mm (No 10) needles
1 pair 4mm (No 8) needles

TENSION

24 sts to 10cm (4in) on 4mm (No 8) needles

ABBREVIATIONS See page 2

BACK

With 3¼mm (No 10) needles and A cast on
103(109:115:121:127:133:139:145) sts.
1st Row K1, *P1, K1, rep from * to end.
2nd Row P1, *K1, P1, rep from * to end.
Rep 1st and 2nd rows 11 times more.
Change to 4mm (No 8) needles and proceed in st st
until work measures 61(61:64:64:66:66:69:69)cm
(24(24:25:25:26:26:27:27)in) ending with RS facing
for next row.

Shape Shoulders

Cast off 7(8:9:9:10:11:11:12) sts at beg of next 2
rows.
Cast off 8(8:9:10:10:11:11:12) sts at beg of next 2
rows.
Cast off 8(9:9:10:10:11:12:12) sts at beg of next 2
rows.
Cast off 8(9:9:10:11:11:12:13) sts at beg of next 2
rows.

Leave rem 41(41:43:43:45:45:47:47) sts on a thread

FRONT

With 3¼mm (No 10) needles and A cast on
103(109:115:121:127:133:139:145) sts.
1st Row K1, *P1, K1, rep from * to end.
2nd Row P1, *K1, P1, rep from * to end.
Rep 1st and 2nd rows 11 times more.
Change to 4mm (No 8) needles and proceed in st st
until work measures 53(53:56:56:58:58:61:61)cm
(21(21:22:22:23:23:24:24)in) ending with RS facing
for next row.

Shape Neck

Next Row K44(47:50:53:55:58:61:64) sts only, turn.
Working on these 44(47:50:53:55:58:61:64) sts only
proceed as follows:
Work 13(13:14:14:14:14:15:15) rows dec one st at
neck edge only in every row.
31(34:36:39:41:44:46:49) sts.
Cont in patt until work measures same as back to
shape shoulder ending with RS facing for next row.

Shape Shoulder

Next Row Cast off 7(8:9:9:10:11:11:12) sts, patt to
end.
Next Row Patt to end.
Next Row Cast off 8(8:9:10:10:11:11:12) sts, patt to
end.
Next Row Patt to end.
Next Row Cast off 8(9:9:10:10:11:12:12) sts, patt to
end.
Next Row Patt to end.
Next Row Cast off rem 8(9:9:10:11:11:12:13) sts.
With RS facing slip first 15(15:15:15:17:17:17:17) sts
onto a thread rejoin yarn to rem sts and patt to end.
Work 13(13:14:14:14:14:15:15) rows dec one st at
neck edge only in every row.
31(34:36:39:41:44:46:49) sts.
Cont in patt until work measures same as back to
shape shoulder ending with WS facing for next row.

Shape Shoulder

Next Row Cast off 7(8:9:9:10:11:11:12) sts, patt to
end.
Next Row Patt to end.
Next Row Cast off 8(8:9:10:10:11:11:12) sts, patt to

end.

Next Row Patt to end.

Next Row Cast off 8(9:9:10:10:11:12:12) sts, patt to end.

Next Row Patt to end.

Next Row Cast off rem 8(9:9:10:11:11:12:13) sts.

SLEEVES

With 3¼mm (No 10) needles and A cast on 47(47:49:49:51:51:53:53) sts.

1st Row K1, *P1, K1, rep from * to end.

2nd Row P1, *K1, P1, rep from * to end.

Rep 1st and 2nd rows 10 times more inc one st at each end of last row. 49(49:51:51:53:53:55:55) sts.

Change to 4mm (No 8) needles and proceed in st st inc one st at each end of 3rd and every foll 4th row to 97(97:99:99:101:101:103:103) sts.

Cont in patt until work measures 44(44:44:44:46:46:46:46)cm (17½(17½:17½:17½:18:18:18:18)in ending with RS facing for next row. Cast off.

NECKBAND

Sew up right shoulder seam. With RS of work facing 3¼mm (No 10) needles and A pick up and K 25 sts down left side of neck, K 15(15:15:15:17:17:17:17) sts from front neck, pick up and K 26 sts up right side of neck, K 41(41:43:43:45:45:47:47) sts from back neck 107(107:109:109:113:113:115:115) sts.

Next Row Knit to end.

Next Row Knit to end.

Next Row Knit to end.

Work 8 rows in st st.

Cast off.

ROSES

With 4mm (No 8) needles and B cast on 60 sts.

1st Row K2 tog, knit to end.

2nd Row Purl to last 2 sts, P2 tog tbl.

Rep 1st and 2nd rows once.

Next Row K2 tog, cast off 15 sts, knit to end, 40 sts.

Next Row Purl to last 2 sts, P2 tog tbl.

Next Row K2 tog, cast off rem 38 sts.

PETALS (work 2)

With 4mm (No 8) needles and B, cast on 20 sts.

Work 2 rows in st st.

Work 4 rows inc one st at each end of every row, 28 sts.

Work 4 rows dec one st at each end of every row, 20 sts.

Work 2 rows in st st.

Cast off.

LEAVES

With 4mm (No 8) needles and C cast on 9 sts, work 6 rows in st st.

Next Row K2 tog, K5, K2 tog.

Next Row Purl to end.

Next Row K2 tog, K3, K2 tog.

Next Row Purl to end.

Next Row K2 tog, K1, K2 tog.

Next Row Purl to end.

Next Row Sl 1, K2 tog, psso, fasten off.

MAKING UP

Sew up shoulder and neckband seam, fold neckband in half on to wrong side and slip stitch in position, sew up side and sleeve seams.

Sew up roses as follows roll up centre of roses and sew in position, fold petals in half and sew round centre of rose.

Sew on roses and leaves as shown with a chain stitch and C embroider stalks.

Flowers and shells

The design of this feminine jacket, modelled by Kathy Merrick (Malandra Burrows) was based upon rows of natural objects such as shells and flowers. Its soft colours and unusual texture make it suitable for wearing over pastel evening clothes, as well as with more casual outfits.

MEASUREMENTS

To fit sizes		
86–91	97–102	107–112 cm
34–36	38–40	42–44 in
Actual measurement		
102	112	117 cm
40	44	46 in
Length		
51	51	51 cm
20	20	20 in
Sleeve length		
44	44	44 cm
17½	17½	17½ in

MATERIALS

Emmerdale Double Knitting

Turquoise (052)	5	5	6	50g balls
Candy Pink (050)	3	4	4	50g balls
Pampas Yellow (004)	1	1	1	50g ball
Willow Green (018)	1	1	1	50g ball
Horizon Blue (051)	1	1	1	50g ball

NEEDLES

1 pair 4mm (No 8) needles
1 pair 3¼mm (No 10) needles
long circular 4mm (No 8) needle

TENSION

24 sts and 32 rows = 10cm (4in) in st st on 4mm (No 8) needles over Fair Isle pattern

ABBREVIATIONS

See page 2

BACK

Using 3¼mm (No 10) needles and main colour (turquoise), cast on 121(133:145) sts and work 2½cm (1in) in garter st (every row K).
Change to 4mm (No 8) needles and work in colour and pattern sequence:–

BELL PATTERN

Do not count sts for garment when making this pattern as they vary. You may prefer to work on a long circular needle used in both directions not in the round as there are a very large number of sts.
Work 3 rows in main colour in st st starting with a K row. Change to pink and work 1 further st st row, then work bells in pink:–

1st Row P5,* turn, cast on 8, turn P4 *, rep from * to * to end.
2nd Row (K4, P8) to last 5, K5.
3rd Row P5, (K8, P4) to end.
4th Row (K4, P8) to last 5, K5.
5th Row P5,* K2 tog tbl, K4, K2 tog, P4 * rep from * to * to end.
6th Row (K4, P6) to last 5, K5.
7th Row P5,* K2 tog tbl, K2, K2 tog, P4 *, rep from * to * to end.
8th Row (K4, P4) to last 5, K5.
9th Row P5,* K2 tog tbl, K2 tog, P4 *, rep from * to * to end.
10th Row (K4, P2) to last 5, K5.
11th Row P5, (K2 tog, P4) to end.
12th Row (K4, P1) to last 5, K5.
13th Row P4, (K2 tog, P3) to last 6, K2 tog, P4.
Change to main colour and work 3 rows in st st starting and ending with a P row.
Starting with a P row, work 4 rows of reversed st st.

SHELL PATTERN

Starting with a K row work 2 rows of st st.
Next Row Cont in st st starting with the st marked * on the shell pattern chart, work across the 12 sts of row 1 of this chart 10(11:12) times in all with X as yellow and working rem sts in main colour until 1 st rem, K1 in main colour.
Using this as an establishing row, work the 11 further rows of the chart on each rep, so completing the shell pattern.

SHELL PATTERN

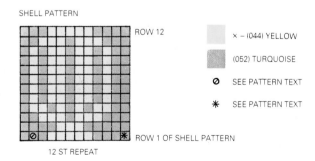

ROW 12

× – (044) YELLOW
(052) TURQUOISE
⊘ SEE PATTERN TEXT
✳ SEE PATTERN TEXT

ROW 1 OF SHELL PATTERN

12 ST REPEAT

Work 2 further st st rows.
Starting with a P row, work 4 rows of reversed st st.

FLOWER PATTERN

Starting with a K row, work 2 rows of st st.
Next Row Cont in st st starting with the st marked ‡
on the flower pattern chart, work across the rem 6 sts
of row 1 of the chart, then across all 12 sts, 9(10:11)
times, then across the first 7 sts once more, with X as
green and working all rem sts in main colour.
Using this as an establishing row, work 5 further rows
of the chart with green as the contrast, then the rem 6
rows of the chart with O as blue and all rem sts in main
colour, so completing the flower pattern.
Work 2 further st st rows.
Starting with a P row, work 4 rows of rev st st **
Rep from ** to ** until work measures approx 51cm
(20in) ending with a P row which would have been
immediately before a reverse st st band.
Next Row Cast off 42(47:52), K until 42(47:52) sts
rem, place the 37(39:41) sts just worked onto a holder.
Cast off to end.

FLOWER PATTERN

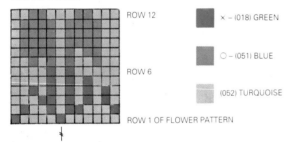

ROW 12

ROW 6

ROW 1 OF FLOWER PATTERN

‡

× – (018) GREEN

O – (051) BLUE

(052) TURQUOISE

LEFT FRONT

Using 3¼mm (No 10) needles and main colour, cast
on 67(67:79) sts and work 2½cm (1in) in garter st.
Change to 4mm (No 8) needles and work in colour and
pattern sequence:– ***
Next Row K.
Next Row K6, P to end.
**** Cont to keep these edge sts always in K, and
always in main colour on every row throughout rem of
work, thus creating a garter st front edge band, work in
pattern and colour sequence in the same way as given
for the back on the rem 61(61:73) sts until work is 8cm
(3in) shorter than the back to shoulder, ending at the
neck edge.
NB The garter st edge band should be worked in main
colour on the pink bell pattern rows also.
Shape neck Cont to keep pattern correct throughout,

patt 15(10:17) sts and place them on a holder, patt to
end.
Dec 1 st at neck edge only on next 5 rows, then on
every alt row until 42(47:52) sts rem.
Work straight until front matches back to shoulders, so
ending with a P row.
Cast off.

RIGHT FRONT

Work as given for left front as far as ***.
Next Row K.
Next row P to last 6, K6.
Work as for left front from **** to end.

SLEEVES

For all sizes. Using 3¼mm (No 10) needles and main
colour, cast on 52 sts and work 4cm (1½in) in K1, P1
rib, inc by 8 sts evenly over last row. (60 sts).
Change to 4mm (No 8) needles and work in colour and
pattern sequence in the same way as given for the
back, at the same time, working all incs into the
pattern (see note below) inc 1 st each end of the 5th,
then every foll 3rd row until there are 120 sts, then
working straight to a total length of approx 44cm
(17½in) ending with a 4 reversed st st row stripe.
NB The 27th pattern row on which the shell pattern
begins will have 76 sts and the shell pattern should be
begun with the st marked Ø on the chart in order to
arrange the shells symmetrically across. The flowers
should then be arranged centrally above the spaces
between the shells.
Cast off loosely.

NECKBAND

Do not press.
Join shoulder seams. Using 3¼mm (No 10) needles
and main colour, with right side facing, commencing at
top of right front neck, slip the first 6 sts from the
holder onto the needle without knitting them, then knit
the rem 9(4:11) sts from the holder, pick up and
K 23 sts up the right front neck slope, the 37(39:41) sts
from the back neck holder, 23 sts down the left front
neck slope and knit all 15(10:17) sts from the left neck
holder. (113:105:121 sts).
Work 2½cm (1in) in garter st. (Every row K).
Cast off.

MAKING UP

Join all rem seams matching pattern and shaping and
ensuring that armholes are 25cm (10in) deep after
making up.

Lacy looks

Modelled by Sandie Merrick (Jane Hutcheson) this loose and comfortable sweater looks great when teamed with blue jeans or casual trousers. The attractive lace design is surprisingly easy to knit.

MEASUREMENTS

To fit sizes

86–91	97–102	cm
34–36	38–40	in

Actual measurement

106	116	cm
42	46	in

Length

62	64	cm
24	25	in

Sleeve length

41	42	cm
16	16½	in

MATERIALS

Poppleton Nicole

Roseate (109)	9	10	50g balls

NEEDLES

1 pair 4½mm (No 7) needles
1 pair 5½mm (No 5) needles

TENSION

16 sts and 21 rows = 10cm (4in) over pattern

ABBREVIATIONS

m1 = make 1 st by picking up loop lying before next st and knitting into the back of it
yf = yarn forward over needle to make a st

BACK

With 4½mm (No 7) needles, cast on 75(85) sts and work in K1, P1 rib for 8cm, (3¼in) ending with WS facing.

Inc row Rib 6(6), * m1, rib 7(8), rep from * to last 6(7) sts, m1, rib 6(7), 85(95) sts.

Change to 5½mm (No 5) needles and work in pattern as follows:

1st Row K4(2), P7, * K3, yf, sl 1, K1, psso, K2, P7, rep from * to last 4(2) sts, K4(2).

2nd, 4th, 6th, 8th and 10th Rows P4(2), K7, * P7, K7, rep from * to last 4(2) sts, P4(2).

3rd Row K4(2), P7, * K1, K2 tog, yf, K1, yf, sl 1, K1, psso, K1, P7, rep from * to last 4(2) sts, K4(2).

5th Row K4(2), P7, * K2 tog, yf, K3, yf, sl 1, K1, psso, P7, rep from * to last 4(2) sts, K4(2).

7th Row K4(2), P7, * K2, yf, sl 1, K2 tog, psso, yf, K2, P7, rep from * to last 4(2) sts, K4(2).

9th Row As 1st row.

11th Row P4(2), K3, yf. sl 1, K1, psso, K2, * P7, K3, yf, sl 1, K1, psso, K2, rep from * to last 4(2) sts, P4(2).

12th, 14th, 16th and 18th Rows K4(2), P7, * K7, P7, rep from * to last 4(2) sts, K4(2).

13th Row P4(2), K1, K2 tog, yf, K1, yf, sl 1, K1, psso, K1, * P7, K1, K2 tog, yf, K1, yf, sl 1, K1, psso, K1, rep from * to last 4(2) sts, P4(2).

15th Row P4(2), K2 tog, yf, K3, yf, sl 1, K1, psso, * P7, K2 tog, yf, K3, yf, sl 1, K1, psso, rep from * to last 4(2) sts, P4(2).

17th Row P4(2), K2, yf, sl 1, K2 tog, psso, yf, K2, * P7, K2, yf, sl 1, K2 tog, psso, yf, K2, rep from * to last 4(2) sts, P4(2).

19th Row As 11th row.

20th Row As 18th row.

These 20 rows form the pattern. Cont in pattern until work measures 40(41)cm (16(16½)in) ending with RS facing.

Shape Armholes

Keeping pattern correct, cast off 5(6) sts at beg of next 2 rows, then dec 1 st at each end of next 3 rows and foll 2 alt rows, 65(73) sts. Cont straight until work measures 62(64)cm (24(25)in) ending with RS facing.

Shape Shoulders

Cast off 15(18) sts at beg of next 2 rows. Leave rem 35(37) sts on holder.

FRONT

Work as for back until work measures 54(56)cm (21(22)in) ending with RS facing.

Shape Neck

Pattern across 24(27) sts and turn. Working on this side only, dec 1 st at neck edge on next 5 rows and every foll alt row until 15(18) sts rem. Cont straight until work measures same as Back to shoulder ending with RS facing.

Shape Shoulder

Cast off 15(18) sts.

Return to rem sts and sl 17(19) sts onto holder. Rejoin yarn and complete to match first side.

SLEEVES

With 4½mm (No 7) needles, cast on 33(43) sts and

work in K1, P1 rib for 8cm (3¼in), ending with WS facing.

Inc Row Rib 3(3), * m1, rib 3(4), rep from * to last 3(4) sts, m1, rib 3(4), 43(53) sts.

Change to 5½mm (No 5) needles and work in pattern as for Back. AT THE SAME TIME, and keeping pattern correct, inc 1 st at each end of 5th row and every foll 4th row, adding new sts into pattern, until there are 71(81) sts. Cont straight until work measures 41(42)cm (16½(17)in) ending with RS facing.

Shape Top

Cast off 5(6) sts at beg of next 2 rows, then dec 1 st at each end of next 3 rows and foll 11(10) alt rows. Now dec 1 st at each end of every row until 19(21) sts rem. Cast off, marking first, centre and last st with coloured threads.

NECKBAND

Sew right shoulder seam. With 4½mm (No 7) needles and RS facing, pick up and knit 19 sts down left front neck, 17(19) sts from centre front, 19 sts up right front neck and 35(37) sts from Back, inc 1 st in centre, 91(95) sts. Work in K1, P1 rib for 3cm (1¼in). Cast off ribwise.

MAKING UP

Sew left shoulder and neckband seam. Make pleat in top of sleeves by placing first and last coloured markers to centre marker on wrong side. Oversew with a couple of stitches to hold in place. Sew in sleeves, placing centre of top of sleeves to shoulder seam and easing fullness to top of sleeve. Sew side and sleeve seams. Press according to instructions on ball band.

Collared jacket

Modelled by Matt Skilbeck (Frederick Pyne), this casual knitted jacket is perfect for slipping over a shirt when the weather turns cooler. The unusual button fastenings and soft, ribbed collar add distinctive design features to this very useful garment.

MEASUREMENTS

To fit sizes

97	102	107	112	cm
38	40	42	44	in

Actual measurement

112	117	122	127	cm
44	46	48	50	in

Length

69	70	70	71	cm
27	27½	27½	28	in

Sleeve length

46	47	47	48	cm
18	18½	18½	19	in

MATERIALS

Granary Chunky Tweed

Woodland (734) 20	21	23	24	50g balls

5 fasteners

NEEDLES

1 pair 5½mm (No 5) needles
1 pair 6mm (No 4) needles
1 pair 6½mm (No 3) needles
Cable needle

TENSION

16 sts and 18 rows = 10cm (4in), measured over pattern on 6½mm (No 3) needles

ABBREVIATIONS

Sl: slip purlwise
C3L: slip next st onto cable needle, leave at front of work, k2 then knit st from cable needle
C3R: slip next 2 sts onto cable needle, leave at back of work, knit one then k2 from cable needle

BACK

With 5½mm (No 5) needles, cast on 67(71:75:79) sts.
1st Row (RS) K1, *P1, K1, rep from * to end.
2nd Row P1, *K1, P1, rep from * to end.
Rep these 2 rows until work measures 6cm (2½in), ending with a RS row.
Inc row Rib 1(3:5:7), inc in next st, (rib 2, inc in next st) 21 times, rib 2(4:6:8). 89(93:97:101) sts.
Change to 6½mm (No 3) needles and pattern.
1st Row K1, *sl 1, K3, rep from * to end.
2nd Row *P3, sl 1, rep from * to last st, P1.
3rd Row K1, *C3L, K1, rep from * to end.
4th Row Purl.

5th Row K5, *sl 1, K3, rep from * to end.
6th Row *P3, sl 1, rep from * to last 5 sts, P5.
7th Row K3, *C3R, K1, rep from * to last 2 sts, K2.
8th Row Purl.
These 8 rows form pattern.
Cont in patt until Back measures 66(67:67:69)cm [26(26½:26½:27)in] from beg, ending with a RS row.
Shape Neck
Next Row Patt 35(36:37:38), cast off next 19(21:23:25) sts, patt to end.
Working on first set of sts and keeping cont of patt, dec 1 st at neck edge on next 3 rows.
Work 1 row then cast off remaining 32(33:34:35) sts loosely.
Rejoin yarn to remaining 35(36:37:38) sts and complete to match first side of neck.

POCKET LININGS (make 2)
With 6mm (No 4) needles, cast on 19 sts and work 20 rows in st st, starting with a K row.
Leave sts on a spare needle.

LEFT FRONT
** With 5½mm (No 5) needles, cast on 31(35:35:39) sts and work 6cm (2½in) in rib as given for Back, ending with a RS row.
Inc row: Rib 0(2:2:4), inc in next st, (rib 2, inc in next st) 10 times, rib 0(2:2:4). 42(46:46:50) sts.
Change to 6½mm (No 3) needles and patt, placing this as follows: **
1st Row K1, *sl 1, K3, rep from * to last st, K1.
2nd Row P1, *P3, sl 1, rep from * to last st, P1.
3rd Row K1, *C3L, K1, rep from * to last st, K1.
4th Row Purl.
5th Row K5, *sl 1, K3, rep from * to last st, K1.
6th Row P1, *P3, sl 1, rep from * to last 5 sts, P5.
7th Row K3, *C3R, K1, rep from * to last 3 sts, K3.
8th Row Purl.
Work a further 12 rows in patt as set.
Place Pocket
Next Row Patt 11(13:13:15), slip next 19 sts onto a stitch holder, patt across sts of first Pocket Lining, patt to end.

Cont in patt across all sts until Front measures 33cm (13in) from beg, marking front edge of last row with a coloured thread and ending with a WS row.

Shape Front Edge

Keeping cont of patt, dec 1 st at front edge on next and every following 6th(5th:5th:4th) row until 32(33:34:35) sts remain.

Work straight until Front matches Back to shoulder. Cast off loosely.

RIGHT FRONT

Follow instructions for Left Front from ** to **.

1st Row K2, *sl 1, K3, rep from * to end.

2nd Row *P3, sl 1, rep from * to last 2 sts, P2.

3rd Row K2, *C3L, K1, rep from * to end.

4th Row Purl.

5th Row K6, *sl 1, K3, rep from * to end.

6th Row *P3, sl 1, rep from * to last 6 sts, P6.

7th Row K4, *C3R, K1, rep from * to last 2 sts, K2.

8th Row Purl.

Work a further 12 rows in patt as set.

Place Pocket

Next Row Patt 12(14:14:16), slip next 19 sts onto a stitch holder, patt across sts of second Pocket Lining, patt to end.

Complete to match Left Front, reversing shaping.

SLEEVES

With 5½mm (No 5) needles, cast on 33(35:37:39) sts and work 8cm (3in) in rib as given for Back, ending with a RS row.

Inc row: Rib 1(0:3:2), inc in next st, (rib 1, inc in next st) 15(17:15:17) times, rib 1(0:3:2). 49(53:53:57) sts. Change to 6½mm (No 3) needles and work in patt as given for Back, inc and working into patt 1 st at each end of 3rd and every following 4th row until there are 67(71:71:77) sts on the needle then 1 st at each end of every following 3rd row until there are 85(89:89:93) sts on the needle.

Work straight until Sleeve measures 46(47:47:48)cm [18(18½:18½:19)in] from beg, ending with a WS row. Cast off loosely.

POCKET TOPS

With RS of work facing and using 6mm (No 4) needles, rejoin yarn to sts of first Pocket Top and work as follows:

1st Row K2, *P1, K1, rep from * to last st, K1.

2nd Row K1, *P1, K1, rep from * to end.

Rep these 2 rows twice more then cast off neatly in rib.

FRONT BANDS AND COLLAR

Join shoulder seams.

Right Front Band With RS of work facing and using 6mm (No 4) needles, pick up and K 53 sts evenly up Right Front from cast on edge to start of front shaping, 64(65:66:69) sts from start of front shaping to shoulder and 16(17:18:19) sts from shoulder to centre back. 133(135:137:141) sts.

1st Row K1, *P1, K1, rep from * to end.

2nd Row K2, *P1, K1, rep from * to last st, P1.

Shape Collar

***

1st Row Rib 16(17:18:19) sts and turn.

2nd and every alt row Sl 1, rib to end.

3rd Row Rib 24(25:26:27) sts and turn.

5th Row Rib 32(33:34:35) sts and turn.

Cont working 8 sts extra in this way on every alt row until the row Rib 80(81:82:83) sts and turn has been completed.

Next Row Sl 1, rib to end. ***

Cont in rib as set across all sts for 5(5:6:6)cm [2(2:2½:2½)in]. Cast off neatly in rib.

Left Front Band With RS of work facing and using 6mm (No 4) needles, pick up and K 16(17:18:19) sts from centre back to shoulder, 64(65:66:69) sts evenly from shoulder to start of front shaping and 53 sts from start of front shaping to cast on edge. 133(135:137:141) sts.

1st Row K1, *P1, K1, rep from * to end.

2nd Row P1, *K1, P1, rep from * to last 2 sts, K2.

3rd Row As 1st row.

Shape Collar

Work as for Right Front Band from *** to ***. Complete as for Right Front Band.

MAKING UP

Place marker threads 27(28:28:29)cm [10½(11:11:11½)in] either side of shoulder seams to mark armholes. Set in sleeves between markers. Join side and sleeve seams. Sew Pocket Linings in place to WS of work then sew ends of Pocket Tops neatly in place. Join centre back seam of collar, reversing seam for turn down section. Sew fasteners to inner edge of Right Front Band, the first to come 3cm (1in) above lower edge, the last to come level with start of front shaping and the remainder spaced evenly between. Make loops on outer edge of Left Front Band to correspond with fasteners.

Mohair slipover

This soft, fluffy sweater, worn by Rachel Hughes (Glenda McKay) is very quick and easy to knit. It looks good when teamed with a blouse, as shown here, but can also be worn on its own complemented with lots of jewellery, for a glamorous evening look.

MEASUREMENTS

To fit sizes		
86–91	97–102	107–112 cm
34–36	38–40	42–44 in
Actual measurement		
102	112	122 cm
40	44	48 in
Length		
58	58	58 cm
23	23	23 in

MATERIALS
Nicole Mohair

Dragonfly Red (112)	**5**	**6**	**7**	50g balls

NEEDLES
1 pair 5½mm (No 5) needles
1 pair 4½mm (No 7) needles

TENSION
16 sts and 21 rows = 10cm (4in) in st st .
on 5½mm (No 5) needles

ABBREVIATIONS
See page 2

BACK
Using 4½mm (No 7) needles, cast on 73(81:89) sts and work:
1st Row K2, (P1, K1) to last st, K1.
2nd Row K1, (P1, K1) to end.
Rep these 2 rows until rib measures 10cm (4in) ending with row 2, and inc by 8 sts evenly across this row. (81:89:97) sts.
Change to 5½mm (No 5) needles and st st starting with a K row. Work straight to a total measurement of 33cm (13in) ending with a P row.
Mark both ends of this row. *
Cont in st st to a total measurement of 58cm (23in) ending with a P row.
Next Row Cast off 29(32:35) sts, K until 29(32:35) sts rem, place the 23(25:27) sts just worked onto a holder, cast off to end.

FRONT
Work as for back as far as *.
Cont in st st.
Shape Neck
Next Row K40(44,48), turn, P2 tog tbl, P to end.

** Dec 1 st at neck edge only on every foll 4th row until 29(32:35) sts rem.
Work straight until front matches back to shoulder, ending with a P row.
Cast off. **
Place centre front st on a safety pin.
Rejoin yarn to inside edge of rem sts and K to end.
Next Row P to last 2, P2 tog.
Rep from ** to **.

NECKBAND
Do not press.
Join left shoulder seam. Using 4½mm (No 7) needles, with RS facing, pick up and K the 23(25:27) sts from the back neck holder, working 2 tog in the middle, 42(44:46) sts evenly down the left neck slope, the 1 st at the pin at centre neck leaving the pin as a marker, and 42(44:46) sts evenly up the right neck slope. (107:113:119 sts)
Next Row (K1, P1) to 2 sts before marked st, K2 tog, P1, K2 tog, (P1, K1) to end.
Next Row K1, rib to 2 sts before marked st, P2 tog, K1, P2 tog, rib to last st, K1.
Next Row K1, rib to 2 sts before marked st, K2 tog, P1, K2 tog, rib to last st, K1.
Rep the last 2 rows until 8 rib rows have been worked in all.
Cast off in rib, dec in the same way as before on this row also.

ARMBANDS
Work both alike.
Join rem shoulder seam.
Using 4½mm (No 7) needles and with RS facing, pick up evenly and K 40 sts up the right side edge from one marked point on the side to the shoulder seam, then pick up and K 39 sts evenly down the side edge from the shoulder seam to the other marked point. (79 sts)
Starting with row 2, work 6 rows in rib as given for the back welt.
Cast off in rib.

MAKING UP
Join rem seams matching shapings.

16

Textured squares

This straightforward, classic design, worn by Joe Sugden (Frazer Hines) will be appreciated by most men. The unusual textured pattern adds an attractive feature to this otherwise very traditional garment.

MEASUREMENTS

To fit sizes

91	97	102	107	112	117	122	cm
36	38	40	42	44	46	48	in

Actual measurement

102	107	112	117	122	127	132	cm
40	42	44	46	48	50	52	in

Length

66	69	71	71	71	74	74	cm
26	27	28	28	28	29	29	in

Sleeve length

48	48	48	48	50	50	50	cm
19	19	19	19	19½	19½	19½	in

MATERIALS

Emmerdale Double Knitting

Slate Blue (060) 8	9	9	10	10	11	12	50g balls

NEEDLES

1 pair 3¼mm (No 10) needles
1 pair 4mm (No 8) needles

TENSION

12 sts to 2in (5cm) on 4mm (No 8) needles
over st st

ABBREVIATIONS

See page 2

BACK

With 3¼mm (No 10) needles cast on 121(127:133:139:145:151:157) sts.
1st Row K1, * P1, K1, rep from * to end.
2nd Row P1. * K1, P1, rep from * to end.
Rep 1st and 2nd rows 10 times more.
Change to 4mm (No 8) needles and proceed in patt as follows:
1st Row Knit to end.
2nd row Purl to end.
3rd Row Knit to end.
4th Row P26(29:32:35:38:41:44)(P1, K3, P3, K3, P3, K2, P3, K2, P3, K3, P3, K3, P4) twice, P23(26:29:32:35:38:41).
5th Row K23(26:29:32:35:38:41), (K3, P3) 12 times, K26(29:32:35:38:41:44).
6th Row P26(29:32:35:38:41:44), (K2, P3, K3, P3, K3, P5, K3, P3, K3, P3, K2, P3) twice, P23(26:29:32:35:38:41).

7th Row K23(26:29:32:35:38:41), (K3, P1. K3, P3, K3, P3, K7, P3, K3, P3, K3, P1) twice, P26(29:32:35:38:41:44).
8th Row P26(29:32:35:38:41:44), (P3, K3, P3, K3, P9, K3, P3, K3, P6) twice, P23(26:29:32:35:38:41).
9th Row K23(26:29:32:35:38:41), (K5, P3, K3, P3, K3, P1, K3, P1, K3, P3, K3, P3, K2) twice, K26(29:32:35:38:41:44).
Rep 4th to 9th row twice.
22nd Row As 4th Row.
23rd Row As 5th Row.
24th row Purl to end.
25th Row Knit to end.
26th Row Purl to end.
27th Row As 5th Row.
28th Row As 4th Row.
29th Row As 9th Row.
30th Row As 8th Row.
31st Row As 7th Row.
32nd Row As 6th Row.
Rep 27th to 32nd row twice.
45th Row As 5th Row.
46th Row As 6th Row.
From 1st to 46th row forms patt **
Cont in patt until work measures 66(69:71:71:71:74:74)cm (26(27:28:28:28:29:29)in) ending with RS facing for next row.

Shape Shoulder

Cast off 9(10:10:11:11:12:13) sts at beg of next 2 rows.
Cast off 9(10:10:11:12:12:13) sts at beg of next 2 rows.
Cast off 9(10:11:11:12:13:13) sts at beg of next 2 rows.
Cast off 10(10:11:12:12:13:13) sts at beg of next 2 rows.
Leave rem 47(47:49:49:51:51:53) sts on a thread.

FRONT

Work as for back to **
Cont in patt until work measures 56(58:61:61:61:64:64)cm 22(23:24:24:24:25:25)in ending with RS facing for next row.

Shape Neck

18

Next Row Patt 52(55:57:60:62:65:67) sts turn.
Working on these 52(55:57:60:62:65:67) sts only proceed as follows:
Work 15 rows dec one st at neck edge only in every row. 37(40:42:45:47:50:52) sts.
Cont in patt until work measures same as back to shape shoulder ending with right side facing for next row.

Shape Shoulder
Next Row Cast off 9(10:10:11:11:12:13) sts patt to end.
Next Row Patt to end.
Next Row Cast off 9(10:10:11:12:12:13) sts patt to end.
Next Row Patt to end.
Next row Cast off 9(10:11:11:12:13:13) sts patt to end.
Next Row Patt to end.
Next Row Cast off rem 10(10:11:12:12:13:13) sts.
With RS of work facing slip first
17(17:19:19:21:21:23) sts on to a thread, rejoin yarn to rem sts and patt to end.

Work 15 rows dec one st at neck edge only in every row. 37(40:42:45:47:50:52) sts.
Cont in patt until work measures same as back to shape shoulder ending with wrong side facing for next row.

Shape Shoulder
Next Row Cast off 9(10:10:11:11:12:13) sts, patt to end.
Next Row Patt to end.
Next Row Cast off 9(10:10:11:12:12:13) sts patt to end.
Next Row Patt to end.
Next Row Cast off 9(10:11:11:12:13:13) sts patt to end.
Next Row Patt to end.
Next Row Cast off remaining 10(10:11:12:12:13:13) sts.

SLEEVES

With 3¼mm (No 10) needles cast on 65(65:67:67:69:69:71) sts.
1st Row K1, * P1, K1, rep from * to end.
2nd Row P1, * K1, P1, rep from * to end.
Rep 1st and 2nd rows 10 times more inc one st at each end of last row 67(67:69:69:71:71:73) sts.
Change to 4mm (No 8) needles and proceed in st st inc one st at each end of 3rd and every foll 4th row to 105(105:107:107:109:109:111) sts.
Cont in st st until work measures 48(48:48:48:50:50:50)cm (19(19:19:19:19½:19½:19½)in) ending with RS for next row. Cast off.

NECKBAND

With RS of work facing 3¼mm (No 10) needles pick up and knit 27 sts down left side of neck, K17(17:19:19:21:21:23) sts at front neck pick up and knit 28 sts up right side of neck, K47(47:49:49:51:51:53) sts from back neck, 119(119:123:123:127:127:131) sts.
1st Row P1, * K1, P1, rep from * to end.
2nd Row K1, * P1, K1, rep from * to end.
Rep 1st and 2nd rows 10 times more.
Cast off.

MAKING UP

Sew up shoulder and neckband seams and fold neckband in half on to wrong side and stitch in position.
Sew sleeves in position, sew up side and sleeve seams.

Winter flakes

This woolly winter outfit, worn by Sam Skilbeck (Benjamin Whitehead), is guaranteed to keep children warm in winter. The set would make a much appreciated present for youngsters.

MEASUREMENTS

To fit sizes

56	61	66	71	76	81	86	cm
22	24	26	28	30	32	34	in

Actual width across back at underarm

66	71	76	81	86	91	97	cm
26	28	30	32	34	36	38	in

Length

34	37	41	46	52	55	57	cm
13½	14½	16	18	20½	21½	22½	in

Sleeve length

19	27	30	34	38	43	43	cm
7½	10½	12	13½	15	17	17	in

MATERIALS
Emmerdale Double Knitting

PULLOVER

Denim (019) A	4	4	5	5	5	6	6	50g balls
Jersey Cream (011) B	2	2	2	2	2	3	3	50g balls

SCARF:

Denim (019) A	2	2	2	2	2	2	2	50g balls
Jersey Cream (011) B	1	1	1	1	1	1	1	50g balls

HAT:

Denim (019) A	1	1	1	1	1	1	1	50g balls
Jersey Cream (011) B	1	1	1	1	1	1	1	50g balls

NEEDLES
1 pair 3¼mm (No 10) needles
1 pair 4mm (No 8) needles

TENSION
24 sts to 10cm (4in) on 4mm (No 8) needles over st st

ABBREVIATIONS
See page 2

PULLOVER

BACK
With 3¼mm (No 10) needles and A cast on 79(85:91:97:103:109:115) sts.
1st Row K1, * P1, K1, rep from * to end.
2nd Row P1, * K1, P1, rep from * to end.
Rep 1st and 2nd rows 8 times more.
Change to 4 mm (No 8) needles and st st and proceed as follows:
Work from 1st to 20th row of chart A joining in and breaking off colours as required and working size required as indicated.
The odd rows are knit and the even rows are purl.
From 15th to 20th row forms patt **
Cont in patt until work measures 34(37:41:46:52:55:57)cm (13½(14½:16:18:20½:21½:22½)in) ending with RS facing for next row.

Shape Shoulders
Cast off 8(9:9:10:11:12:12) sts at beg of next 2 rows.
Cast off 9(9:10:11:11:12:13) sts at beg of next 2 rows.
Cast off 9(10:10:11:12:12:13) sts at beg of next 2 rows.
Leave rem 27(29:33:33:35:37:39) sts on a thread.

FRONT
Work as for Back to **.
Cont in patt until work measures 28(30:34:38:44:47:48)cm (11(12:13½:15:17½:18½:19in) ending with RS facing for next row.

Shape Neck
Next Row Patt 34(37:40:42:45:48:51) sts turn.
Working on these 34(37:40:42:45:48:51) sts only proceed as follows:
Work 8(9:11:10:11:12:13) rows dec one st at neck edge only in every row. 26(28:29:32:34:36:38) sts.
Cont in patt on rem sts until work measures same as back to shape shoulder ending with RS facing for next row.

Shape Shoulder
Next Row Cast off 8(9:9:10:11:12:12) sts, patt to end.
Next Row Patt to end.
Next Row Cast off 9(9:10:11:11:12:13) sts patt to end.
Next Row Patt to end.
Next Row Cast off rem 9(10:10:11:12:12:13) sts.
With RS of work facing slip first 11(11:11:13:13:13:13) sts onto a thread rejoin yarn to rem sts and patt to end.
Work 8(9:11:10:11:12:13) rows dec one st at neck edge only in every row. 26(28:29:32:34:36:38) sts.

Cont in patt on rem sts until work measures same as back to shape shoulder ending with WS facing for next row.

Shape Shoulder

Next Row Cast off 8(9:9:10:11:12:12) sts, patt to end.

Next Row Patt to end.

Next Row Cast off 9(9:10:11:11:12:13) sts, patt to end.

Next Row Patt to end.

Next Row Cast off rem 9(10:10:11:12:12:13) sts.

SLEEVES

With 3¼mm (No 10) needles and A cast on 39(41:43:45:47:49:51) sts.

1st Row K1, * P1, K1, rep from * to end.

2nd Row P1, * K1, P1, rep from * to end.

Rep 1st and 2nd rows 8 times more inc one st at each end of last row. 41(43:45:47:49:51:53) sts.

Change to 4mm (No 8) needles and st st and proceed as follows:

Work from 1st to 20th row of chart B joining in and breaking off colours as required and working size

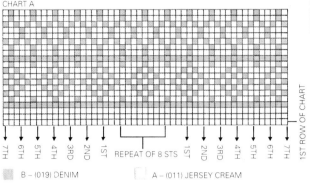

CHART A

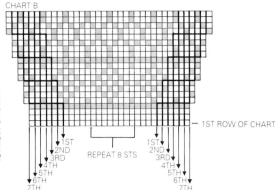

CHART B

■ B – (019) DENIM   □ A – (011) JERSEY CREAM

required as indicated.

The odd rows are knit and the even rows are purl.

From 15th to 20th row forms patt.

Cont in patt inc one st at each end of next and every foll 4th row to 67(73:79:85:91:97:99) sts, working inc sts in patt.

Cont in patt until work measures 23(27:30:34:38:43:43)cm or 9(10½:12:13½:15:17:17)in ending with RS facing for next row.

Cast off.

NECK BAND

Sew up right shoulder seam.

With RS of work facing 3¼mm (No 10) needles and A pick up and knit 15(15:15:18:18:18:18) sts down left side of neck, knit 11(11:11:13:13:13:13) sts from front neck, pick up and knit 16(16:16:19:19:19:19) sts up right side of neck, knit 27(29:33:33:35:37;39) sts from back neck.

1st Row P1, * K1, P1, rep from * to end.

2nd Row K1, * P1, K1, rep from * to end.

Rep 1st and 2nd rows 7 times more. Cast off.

MAKING UP

Sew up left shoulder and neckband seam, fold neckband in half on to RS and stitch in position. Sew sleeves in position. Sew up side and sleeve seams.

HAT

Hat with 3¼mm (No 10) needles and A cast on 79(85:91:97:103:109:115) sts.

1st Row K1, * P1, K1, rep from * to end.

2nd Row P1, * K1, P1, rep from * to end.

Rep 1st and 2nd rows 18(19:20:21:22:23:23) times more.

Change to 4mm (No 8) needles and st st and proceed as follows:

Work from 1st to 20th row of chart A joining in and breaking off colours as required as indicated.

The odd rows are knit and the even rows are purl.

From 15th to 20th row forms patt.

Rep 15th to 20th row 1(1:1:2:2:2:3) times more.

Next Row K1A, * K2 tog A, rep from * to end. 40(43:46:49:52:55:58) sts.

Next Row P0(1:0:1:0:1:0:A), * P2 tog A, rep from * to end. 20(22:23:25:26:28:29) sts.

Slip rem sts onto a thread and draw up and fasten off. Sew up side seam, fold rib in half on to RS and with A make a pom-pom for top and sew in position.

SCARF

With 4mm (No 8) needles and A cast on 79 sts.

With A work 2 rows in st st.

Work from 1st to 20th row of chart A as given for 1st size joining in and breaking off colours as required.

The odd rows are knit and the even rows are purl.

From 15th to 20th row forms patt.

Cont in patt until work measures approximately 86cm (34in) ending with 20th row of patt.

1st Row With B knit to end.

2nd Row P3A, * P1B, P3A, rep from * to last 4 sts, P1B, P3A.

3rd Row K1B, K3A, * K2A, K1B, K1A, K1B, K3A, rep from * to last 3 sts, K2A, K1B.

4th Row P1A, P1B, P1A, * P2A, (P1B, P1A) 3 times, rep from * to last 4 sts, P2A, P1B, P1A.

5th Row (K1B, K1A) twice, * (K1B, K1A) 4 times rep from * to last 3 sts, K1B, K1A, K1B.

6th Row As 4th row.

7th Row As 3rd row.

8th Row As 2nd row.

9th Row As 1st row.

10th Row With A purl to end.

11th Row With A knit to end.

12th Row With A purl to end.

13th Row With A knit to end.

Cast off purlways.

MAKING UP

Fold in half length ways and sew up centre back seam, sew up end seams, and fringe ends with A.

23

Cabled set

This cosy cardigan and hat, worn by Caroline Bates (Diana Davies) is perfect for chilly winter weather. The honeycomb and cable panels add extra interest to the traditional design.

MEASUREMENTS

To fit sizes

86	91	97	102	107	cm
34	36	38	40	42	in

Actual measurement

102	107	112	117	122	cm
40	42	44	46	48	in

Length

66	67	67	69	69	cm
26	26½	26½	27	27	in

Sleeve length

43	44	44	46	46	cm
17	17½	17½	18	18	in

MATERIALS

Granary Aran Tweed

Country Cream (751)	14	15	15	16	17	50g balls

8 buttons

NEEDLES

1 pair 3¾mm (No 9) knitting needles
1 pair 4½mm (No 7) knitting needles
Cable needle

TENSION

19 sts and 24 rows = 10cm (4in), measured over reversed st st on 4½mm (No 7) needles; when worked to the correct tension, the honeycomb and cable panel of 54 sts should measure 22.5cm (8¾in) wide

ABBREVIATIONS

Tw2: twist 2 by knitting into front of second st on left hand needle then knit first st and slip both sts off the needle in the normal way
C4R(L): cable 4 right (left) by slipping next 2 sts onto cable needle, leave at back (front) of work, k2 then k2 from cable needle
C6: cable 6 by slipping next 3 sts onto cable needle, leave at back of work, k3 then k3 from cable needle

HONEYCOMB AND CABLE PANEL

1st Row (RS) *Tw2, P1, (C4R, C4L) twice, P1, Tw2,* P2, K6, P2, rep from * to *.
2nd and every alt row: *P2, K1, P16, K1, P2,* K2, P6, K2, rep from * to *.
3rd Row *Tw2, P1, K16, P1, Tw2,* P2, K6, P2, rep from * to *.
5th Row *Tw2, P1, (C4L, C4R) twice, P1, Tw2,* P2, C6, P2, rep from * to *.

7th Row As 3rd row.
8th Row As 2nd row.
These 8 rows form honeycomb and cable pattern.

BACK

With 3¾mm (No 9) needles, cast on 95(99:105:109:115) sts.
1st Row (RS) K1, *P1, K1, rep from * to end.
2nd Row P1, *K1, P1, rep from * to end.
Rep these 2 rows until work measures 6cm (2½in), ending with a RS row.
Inc row: Rib 11(11:4:4:11) inc in next st, [rib 2(2:3:3:3), inc in next st] 24(25:24:25:23) times, rib 11(12:4:4:11). 120(125:130:135:139) sts. Change to 4½mm (No 7) needles and work in reversed st st with honeycomb and cable panels as follows:
1st Row P3(5:6:8:10), *work across next 54 sts as 1st row of panel patt,* P6(7:10:11:11), rep from * to *, P3(5:6:8:10).
2nd Row K3(5:6:8:10), *work across next 54 sts as 2nd row of panel patt,* K6(7:10:11:11), rep from * to *, K3(5:6:8:10).
Cont in reversed st st with panels as set, starting with 3rd patt row until Back measures 64(65:65:66:66)cm [25(25½:25½:26:26)in from beg, ending with a WS row.

Shape Neck

Next Row Patt 47(49:50:52:53) sts, cast off next 26(27:30:31:33) sts, patt to end. Working on first set of sts and keeping patt correct, dec 1 st at neck edge on next 5 rows.
Cast off remaining 42(44:45:47:48) sts.
Rejoin yarn to remaining sts and patt to end.
Complete to match first side of neck.

LEFT FRONT

** With 3¾mm (No 9) needles, cast on 45(49:51:53:55) sts and work 6cm (2½in) in rib as given for Back, ending with a RS row.
Inc row: Rib 2(6:1:2:1), inc in next st, [rib 2(2:3:3:3), inc in next st] 13(12:12:12:13) times, rib 3(6:1:2:1). 59(62:64:66:69) sts.
Change to 4½mm (No 7) needles and work in reversed st st with honeycomb and cable panel as foll: **

24

1st Row P3(5:6:8:10), work across next 54 sts as 1st row of panel patt P2(3:4:4:5).

2nd Row K2(3:4:4:5), work across next 54 sts as 2nd row of panel patt, K3(5:6:8:10).

Cont in reversed st st with panel as set, starting with 3rd patt row until Front measures 58(59:59:60:60)cm [23(23¼:23¼:23½:23½)in] from beg, ending with a WS row.

Shape Neck

Next Row Patt 51(53:54:56:57), cast off remaining 8(9:10:10:12) sts.

Rejoin yarn to remaining sts and keeping cont of patt, dec 1 st at neck edge on next 6 rows then 1 st at this same edge on following 3 alt rows. 42(44:45:47:48) sts.

Work straight until Front matches Back to shoulder then cast off.

RIGHT FRONT

Follow instructions for Left Front from ** to **.

1st Row P2(3:4:4:5), work across next 54 sts as 1st row of panel patt, P3(5:6:8:10).

2nd Row K3(5:6:8:10), work across next 54 sts as 2nd row of panel patt, K2(3:4:4:5).

Cont in reversed st st with panel as set, starting with 3rd patt row until Front measures 58(59:59:60:60)cm [23(23¼:23¼:23½:23½)in] from beg, ending with a WS row.

Shape Neck

Next Row Cast off 8(9:10:10:12) sts, patt to end. 51(53:54:56:57) sts.

Keeping cont of patt, dec 1 st at neck edge on next 6 rows then 1 st at this same edge on following 3 alt rows. 42(44:45:47:48) sts.

Complete to match Left Front.

SLEEVES

With 3¾mm (No 9) needles, cast on 45(47:49:51:55) sts and work 9cm (3½in) in rib as given for Back, ending with a RS row.

Inc row: Rib 1(0:1:2:4), (inc in next st, rib 1, inc in next st) 14(15:15:15:15) times, inc in next st, rib 1(1:2:3:5) 74(78:80:82:86) sts.

Change to 4½mm (No 7) needles and work in reversed st st with honeycomb and cable panel as follows:

1st Row P10(12:13:14:16), work across next 54 sts as 1st row of panel patt, P10(12:13:14:16).

2nd Row K10(12:13:14:16), work across next 54 sts as 2nd row of panel patt, K10(12:13:14:16).

Cont in reversed st st with panel as set, starting with 3rd patt row, inc and working into reversed st st 1 st at each end of 3rd and every following 5th row until there are 104(108:108:112:112) sts on the needle.

Work straight until Sleeve measures 43(44:44:46:46)cm [17(17½:17½:18:18)in] from beg, ending with a WS row. Cast off loosely.

NECKBAND

Join shoulder seams, taking care to match pattern. With RS of work facing and using 3¾mm (No 9) needles, pick up and K7(8:9:9:11) sts from cast off sts of Right Front neck, 17(19:19:21:21) sts evenly up right side of front neck, 6 sts down right side of back neck, 25(25:29:29:31) sts from cast off sts of back neck, 6 sts up left side of back neck, 17(19:19:21:21) sts evenly down left side of front neck and 7(8:9:9:11) sts from cast off sts of Left Front neck. 85(91:97:101:107) sts.

Work 4cm (1½in) in rib as given for Back, starting with a 2nd row.

Cast off neatly in rib.

BUTTON BAND

With 3¾mm (No 9) needles, cast on 11 sts.

1st Row (RS) K2, *P1, K1, rep from * to last st, K1.

2nd Row K1, *P1, K1, rep from * to end.

Rep these 2 rows until Band measures 59(60:60:61:61)cm [23¼(23½:23½:24:24)in], ending with a WS row, Cast off neatly in rib.

Mark the position of 8 buttons on Band, the first to come 6 rows above cast on edge, the last to come 4 rows below cast off edge and the remainder spaced evenly between.

BUTTONHOLE BAND

Work as for Button Band, making buttonholes to correspond with markers as follows:

1st Buttonhole Row (RS) Rib 4, cast off next 2 sts, rib to end.

2nd Buttonhole Row Rib, casting on over sts cast off in previous row.

MAKING UP

Place marker threads 24(25:25:27:27)cm [9½(10:10:10½:10½)in] either side of shoulder seams to mark armholes. Set in sleeves between markers. Join side and sleeve seams. Sew on Front Bands, stretching bands to fit then sew on buttons.

ARAN HAT

To fit average head

MATERIALS
Granary Aran Tweed
Country Cream (751) 3 50g balls

NEEDLES
1 pair 3¾mm (No 9) knitting needles
1 pair 4½mm (No 7) knitting needles
Cable needle

TENSION
19 sts and 24 rows = 10cm (4in), measured over
reversed st st on 4½mm (No 7) needles

ABBREVIATIONS
Tw2: twist 2 by knitting into front of second st on left
hand needle then knit first st and slip both sts off the
needle in the normal way
C6: cable 6 by slipping next 3 sts onto cable needle,
leave at back of work, k3 then k3 from cable needle

With 3¾mm (No 9) needles, cast on 115 sts.
1st Row (RS) K1, *P1, K1, rep from * to end.
2nd Row P1, *K1, P1, rep from * to end.
Rep these 2 rows until work measures 13cm (5in),
ending with a WS row.
Inc row: Rib 8, inc in next st, (rib 6, inc in next st) 14
times, rib 8. (130 sts)
Change to 4½mm (No 7) needles. Starting with a RS
row to reverse patt for Crown, cont in patt as follows:
1st Row P1. *P1, Tw2, P2, K6, P2, Tw2, P1, rep from *
to last st, P1.
2nd and every alt row K1, *k1, P2, K2, P6, K2, P2, K1,
rep from * to last st, K1.
3rd Row As 1st row.
5th Row P1, *P1, Tw2, P2, C6, P2, Tw2, P1, rep from
* to last st, P1.
7th Row As 1st row.
8th Row As 2nd row.
Rep these 8 rows 3 times more.
Shape Crown
1st Row K1, *K6, K2 tog, rep from * to last st, K1. (114
sts)
2nd Row Purl.
3rd Row Knit.
4th Row P1, *P2 tog, P5, rep from * to last st, P1.
(98 sts)
5th Row Knit.
6th Row Purl.
7th Row K1, *K4, K2 tog, rep from * to last st, k1. (82
sts)

8th Row Purl.
9th Row Knit.
10th Row P1, *P2 tog, P3, rep from * to last st, P1.
(66 sts)
11th Row Knit.
12th Row P1, *P2 tog, P2, rep from * to last st, P1.
(50 sts)
13th Row Knit.
14th Row P1, *P2 tog, P1, rep from * to last st, P1.
(34 sts)
15th Row Knit.
16th Row P1, (P2 tog) 16 times, P1. (18 sts)
17th Row K1, (K2 tog) 8 times, K1. (10 sts)

MAKING UP
Break yarn, thread through remaining sts, draw up and
fasten off securely.
Join seam, reversing seam on ribbed section. Fold
ribbed brim to RS.

Saddle-shouldered sweater

Modelled by Nick Bates (Cy Chadwick) this easy-to-wear, chunky style will look equally good in more conventional colours such as navy, fawn or cream. Team it with blue jeans for a young, casual effect.

MEASUREMENTS

To fit sizes

91	97	102	107	112	cm
36	38	40	42	44	in

Actual measurement

107	112	117	122	127	cm
42	44	46	48	50	in

Length

66	67	69	70	71	cm
26	26½	27	27½	28	in

Sleeve length

46	47	47	48	48	cm
18	18½	18½	19	19	in

MATERIALS

Emmerdale Double Knitting

Gold (022)	8	9	11	12	13	50g balls

NEEDLES

1 pair 3¼mm (No 10) needles
1 pair 4mm (No 8) needles

TENSION

25 sts and 32 rows = 10cm (4in), measured over pattern on 4mm (No 8) needles

ABBREVIATIONS

See page 2

BACK

** With 3¼mm (No 10) needles, cast on 107(115:121:127:133) sts.
1st Row (RS) K1, *P1, K1, rep from * to end.
2nd Row P1, *K1, P1, rep from * to end.
Rep these 2 rows until work measures 8cm (3in), ending with a RS row.
Inc row: Rib 7(11:2:5:8), inc in next st, [rib 3(3:4:4:4), inc in next st] 23 times, rib 7(11:3:6:9) 131(139:145:151:157) sts.
Change to 4mm (No 8) needles and pattern.
1st Row Knit.
2nd Row P1(1:0:1:0), *P2, K1, P1, rep from * to last 2(2:1:2:1) st(s), P2(2:1:2:1).

These 2 rows form pattern.
Cont in patt until work measures 41(41:42:42:43)cm [16(16:16½:16½:17)in] from beg, ending with a WS row.

Shape Armholes

Keeping cont of patt, cast off 13(14:15:16:17) sts at beg of next 2 rows. 105(111:115:119:123) sts. **
Work straight until armholes measure 23(24:24:25:25)cm [9(9½:9½:10:10)in], ending with a WS row.

Shape Shoulders

Keeping continuity of patt, cast off 38(40:41:42:43) sts loosely at beg of next 2 rows. Leave remaining 29(31:33:35:37) sts on a stitch holder.

FRONT

Follow instructions for Back from ** to **.
Work straight until armholes measure 18(19:19:20:20)cm [7(7½:7½:8:8)in], ending with a WS row.

Shape Neck

Next Row Patt 40(42:43:44:45) sts and turn, leaving remaining sts on a spare needle.
Keeping cont of patt, dec 1 st at neck edge on next 4 rows then 1 st at this same edge on every alt row until 33(35:36:37:38) sts remain.
Work straight until Front matches Back to shoulder, ending at side edge. Cast off loosely. Slip centre 25(27:29:31:33) sts onto a stitch holder, rejoin yarn to remaining sts and patt to end.
Complete to match first side of neck, reversing shaping.

LEFT SLEEVE

*** With 3¼mm (No 10) needles, cast on 55(57:59:61:65) sts and work 8cm (3in) in rib as given for Back, ending with a RS row.
Inc row Rib 2(1:2:1:5), inc in next st, (rib 1, inc in next st) 25(27:27:29:27) times, rib 2(1:2:1:5).

81(85:87:91:93) sts.

Change to 4mm (No 8) needles and cont in patt as given for Back, placing this as follows:

1st Row Knit.

2nd Row P 0(2:3:1:2), *K1, P3, rep from * to last 1(3:4:2:3) sts, K1, P 0(2:3:1:2).

Cont in patt as set, inc and working into patt 1 st at each end of 3rd and every following 5th row until there are 125(131:131:137:137) sts on the needle. ***

Work straight until Sleeve measures 46(47:47:48:48)cm [18(18½:18½:19:19)in] from beg, ending with a WS row and marking both ends of last row with a coloured thread.

**** Work a further 16(18:18:20:22) rows in patt as set.

Shape Saddle Shoulder

Keeping cont of patt, cast off 55(58:58:61:61) sts loosely at beg of next 2 rows.

Cont in patt on remaining 15 sts for 43(45:47:49:51) rows.

Shape Neck

Next Row Cast off 8 sts, patt to end.

Keeping patt correct, dec 1 st at shaped edge on next 5 rows then cast off remaining 2 sts.

RIGHT SLEEVE

Follow instructions for Left Sleeve from *** to ***. Work straight until Sleeve measures 46(47:47:48:48)cm [18(18½:18½:19:19)in] from beg, ending with a RS row and marking both ends of last row with a coloured thread. Complete by following instructions for Left Sleeve from ****.

NECKBAND

Join Back and Front to saddle shoulder extensions, leaving left back saddle shoulder seam open. With RS of work facing and using 3¼mm (No 10) needles, pick up and K 15 sts from top of Left Sleeve and 16 sts down left side of front neck, K across 25(27:29:31:33) sts at centre front, pick up and K 16 sts up right side of front neck and 15 sts from top of Right Sleeve then K across 29(31:33:35:37) sts of back neck. [116(120:124:128:132) sts]
Work 5cm (2in) in K1, P1 rib. Cast off loosely in rib.

MAKING UP

Join left back saddle shoulder seam and neckband. Set in sleeves below saddle shoulders by setting cast off sts of sleeve to straight edges of armhole and side edges of sleeve above marker threads to cast off sts of armhole. Join side and sleeve seams. Fold neckband in half to WS and slip stitch loosely in place.

Speckled look

The producer of Emmerdale Farm, Stuart Doughty, is wearing a classically shaped design which will be appreciated by men of all ages – and a lot of women! The intriguing, speckled effect adds a chic touch. For a louder effect, brighter colours can be introduced.

MEASUREMENTS

To fit sizes

76	81	86	91	97	102	107	112	cm
30	32	34	36	38	40	42	44	in

Actual measurement

91	97	102	107	112	117	122	127	cm
36	38	40	42	44	46	48	50	in

Length

58	61	64	66	69	71	71	71	cm
23	24	25	26	27	28	28	28	in

Sleeve length

44	44	46	46	48	48	50	50	cm
17½	17½	18	18	19	19	19½	19½	in

MATERIALS

Emmerdale Double Knitting

Black (037)

A	7	7	7	8	8	9	9	10	50g balls

Silver Birch (029)

B	1	1	1	1	1	2	2	2	50g balls

NEEDLES

1 pair 3¼mm (No 10) needles
1 pair 4mm (No 8) needles

TENSION

24 sts to 10cm (4in) on 4mm (No 8) needles over st st

ABBREVIATIONS

See page 2

BACK

With 3¼mm (No 10) needles and A cast on 107(113:119:125:131:137:143:149) sts.
1st Row K1, *P1, K1, rep from * to end.
2nd Row P1, *K1, P1, rep from * to end.
Rep 1st and 2nd rows 10(10:10:11:12:13:13:13) times more.
Change to 4mm (No 8) needles and proceed in patt as follows:
** With A work 4 rows in st st.
5th Row K 1(0:3:2:1:0:0:2)A, *K1B, K7A, rep from * to last 2(1:4:3:2:1:1:3) sts, K1B, K 1(0:3:2:1:0:0:2)A.
With A work 4 rows in st st.
10th Row P 1(0:3:2:1:0:0:2)A, *P4A, P1B, P3A, rep from * to last 2(1:4:3:2:1:1:3) sts, P 2(1:4:3:2:1:1:3).
***

From ** to *** forms patt. ****
Cont in patt until work measures 58(61:64:66:69:71:71:71)cm (23(24:25:26:27:28:28:28)in) ending with RS facing for next row.
Shape Shoulder
Cast off 8(9:9:10:10:11:11:12) sts at beg of next 2 rows.

Cast off 8(9:9:10:10:11:11:12) sts at beg of next 2 rows.

Cast off 9(9:10:10:11:11:12:12) sts at beg of next 2 rows.

Cast off 9(9:10:10:11:11:12:12) sts at beg of next 2 rows.

Leave rem 39(41:43:45:47:49:51:53) sts on a thread.

FRONT

Work as for Back to ****

Cont in patt until work measures
50(52:55:56:58:61:61:61)cm
(19½(20½:21½:22:23:24:24:24)in) ending with RS facing for next row.

Shape Neck

Next Row Patt 47(50:52:55:57:60:62:65) sts, turn.

Working on these 47(50:52:55:57:60:62:65) sts only proceed as follows:

Work 13(14:14:15:15:16:16:17) rows in patt dec one st at neck edge only in every row.

34(36:38:40:42:44:46:48) sts.

Cont in patt until work measures same as back to Shape Shoulder ending with RS facing for next row.

Shape Shoulder

Next Row Cast off 8(9:9:10:10:11:11:12) sts, patt to end.

Next Row Patt to end.

Next Row Cast off 8(9:9:10:10:11:11:12) sts, patt to end.

Next Row Patt to end.

Next Row Cast off 9(9:10:10:11:11:12:12) sts, patt to end.

Next Row Patt to end.

Next Row Cast off rem 9(9:10:10:11:11:12:12) sts.

With RS of work facing slip first
13(13:15:15:17:17:19:19) sts onto a thread, rejoin yarn to rem sts and patt to end.

Work 13(14:14:15:15:16:16:17) rows in patt dec one st at neck edge only in every row.

34(36:38:40:42:44:46:48) sts.

Cont in patt until work measures same as back to Shape Shoulder ending with WS facing for next row.

Shape Shoulder

Next Row Cast off 8(9:9:10:10:11:11:12) sts, patt to end.

Next Row Patt to end.

Next Row Cast off 8(9:9:10:10:11:11:12) sts, patt to end.

Next Row Patt to end.

Next Row Cast off 9(9:10:10:11:11:12:12) sts, patt to end.

Next Row Patt to end.

Next Row Cast off rem 9(9:10:10:11:11:12:12) sts.

SLEEVES

With 3¼mm (No 10) needles and A cast on
49(51:53:55:57:59:61:61) sts.

1st Row K1, *P1, K1, rep from * to end.

2nd Row P1, *K1, P1, rep from * to end.

Rep 1st and 2nd rows 8(8:8:9:10:11:11:11) times more inc one st at each end of last row.
51(53:55:57:59:61:63:63) sts.

Change to 4mm (No 8) needles and proceed in patt as follows:

** With A work 4 rows in st st.

5th Row K 1(2:3:0:1:2:3:3)A, *K1B, K7A, rep from * to last 2(3:4:1:2:3:4:4) sts, K1B, K 1(2:3:0:1:2:3:3)A.

With A work 4 rows in st st.

10th Row P 1(2:3:0:1:2:3:3)A, * P4A, P1B, P3A, rep from * to last 2(3:4:1:2:3:4:4) sts, P 2(3:4:1:2:3:4:4)A. ***

From ** to *** forms patt.

Cont in patt inc one st at each end of next and every foll 4th row to 99(101:103:105:109:115:117:117) sts, working inc sts in patt.

Cont in patt until work measures
44(44:46:46:48:48:50:50)cm
(17½(17½:18:18:19:19:19½:19½)in) ending with RS of work facing for next row.

Cast off 6 sts at beg of next 14 rows.

Cast off rem sts.

NECK BAND

Sew up right shoulder seam.

With RS of work facing 3¼mm (No 10) needles and A pick up and K 24(24:24:28:28:28:28:28) sts down left side of neck, K 13(13:15:15:17:17:19:19) sts from front neck, pick up and knit 23(23:23:27:27:27:27:27) sts from right side of neck, K
39(41:43:45:47:49:51:53) sts from back neck.
99(101:105:115:119:121:125:127) sts.

1st Row P1, *K1, P1, rep from * to end.

2nd Row K1, *P1, K1, rep from * to end.

Rep 1st and 2nd rows twice then 1st row once.

Cast off in rib.

MAKING UP

Sew up left shoulder and neckband seam. Sew sleeves in position. Sew up side and sleeve seams.

Ethnic polo sweater

Most men love polo necked jumpers. The unusual design on this one, modelled by Joe Sugden (Frazer Hines) is reminiscent of the creative work of North American Indian tribespeople.

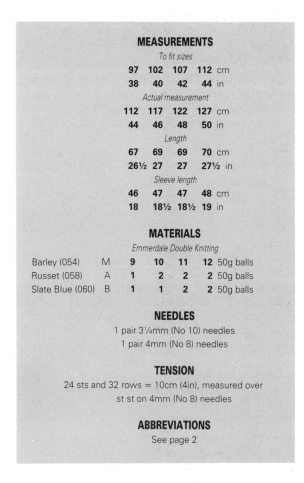

MEASUREMENTS

To fit sizes

97	102	107	112	cm
38	40	42	44	in

Actual measurement

112	117	122	127	cm
44	46	48	50	in

Length

67	69	69	70	cm
26½	27	27	27½	in

Sleeve length

46	47	47	48	cm
18	18½	18½	19	in

MATERIALS

Emmerdale Double Knitting

Barley (054)	M	9	10	11	12	50g balls
Russet (058)	A	1	2	2	2	50g balls
Slate Blue (060)	B	1	1	2	2	50g balls

NEEDLES

1 pair 3¼mm (No 10) needles
1 pair 4mm (No 8) needles

TENSION

24 sts and 32 rows = 10cm (4in), measured over st st on 4mm (No 8) needles

ABBREVIATIONS

See page 2

NB When working from chart, read RS rows from right to left and WS rows from left to right; carry yarn not in use loosely across back of work, taking care to keep tension correct.

BACK

** With 3¼mm (No 10) needles and M, cast on 115(121:127:133) sts.
1st Row (RS) K1, *P1, K1, rep from * to end.
2nd Row P1, *K1, P1, rep from * to end.
Rep these 2 rows until work measures 8cm (3in), ending with a RS row.
Inc row: Rib 6(0:3:6), inc in next st, [rib 5(6:6:6), inc in next st] 17 times, rib 6(1:4:7). 133(139:145:151) sts.
Change to 4mm (No 8) needles and cont in st st, starting with a K row until work measures 47(48:48:50)cm [18½(19:19:19½)in] from beg, ending with a P row. **

Cont in st st and follow chart, repeating the 10 patt sts 12(12:14:14) times across row and working end sts as indicated until 36 rows of Fairisle band have been completed. Using M only, cont in st st until Back measures 66(67:67:69)cm [26(26½:26½:27)in] from beg, ending with a P row.
Shape Neck
Next Row K 49(51:53:55), K2 tog and turn, leaving remaining sts on a spare needle. Dec 1 st at neck edge on next 2 rows.
Work 1 row straight then cast off remaining 48(50:52:54) sts loosely.
Slip centre 31(33:35:37) sts onto a stitch holder, rejoin yarn to remaining sts, K2 tog, K to end. 50(52:54:56) sts.
Complete to match first side of neck.

FRONT

Follow instructions for Back from ** to **.
Cont in st st and follow chart as given for Back until 32 rows of Fairisle band have been completed.
Shape Neck
Next Row Patt 57(59:61:63) sts and turn, leaving remaining sts on a spare needle.
Next Row Using B, P2 tog, P to end.
Next Row Using B, K to last 2 sts, K2 tog.
Next Row Using A, P2 tog, P to end.
Cont in M only, dec 1 st at neck edge on next 3 rows then 1 st at this same edge on following 3 alt rows. 48(50:52:54) sts.

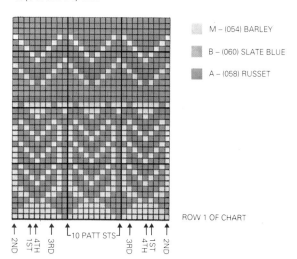

▨	M – (054) BARLEY
▨	B – (060) SLATE BLUE
▨	A – (058) RUSSET

ROW 1 OF CHART

↑ ↑↑ ↑ ⌊10 PATT STS⌋ ↑ ↑↑ ↑
2ND 4TH 3RD   3RD 1ST 2ND
    1ST   4TH

Work straight until Front matches Back to shoulder. Cast off loosely.

Slip centre 19(21:23:25) sts onto a stitch holder, rejoin yarn to remaining 57(59:61:63) sts and patt to end. Complete to match first side of neck, reversing shaping.

SLEEVES

With 3¼mm (No 10) needles and M, cast on 55(59:61:65) sts and work 8cm (3in) in rib as given for Back, ending with a RS row.

Inc row: Rib 3(2:3:2), inc in next st, (rib 2, inc in next st) 16(18:18:20) times, rib 3(2:3:2). 72(78:80:86) sts.

Change to 4mm (No 8) needles. Cont in st st, starting with a K row and inc 1 st at each end of 5th and every following 6th row until there are 86(92:100:96) sts on the needle then 1 st at each end of every following 4th row until there are 126(132:132:144) sts on needle. Work straight until Sleeve measures 46(47:47:48)cm [18(18½:18½:19)in] from beg, ending with a P row. Cast off loosely.

POLO COLLAR

Join right shoulder seam. With RS of work facing, using 3¼mm (No 10) needles and M, Pick up and K 29 sts evenly down left side of front neck, K across 19(21:23:25) sts at centre front, pick up and K 29 sts evenly up right side of front neck and 5 sts down right side of back neck, K across 31(33:35:37) sts of back neck then pick up and K 5 sts up left side of back neck. 118(122:126:130) sts.

Work 8cm (3in) in K1, P1 rib then change to 4mm (No 8) needles and cont in rib as set until Collar measures 15cm (6in). Cast off neatly in rib.

MAKING UP

Join left shoulder seam and collar, reversing seam on turn down section of collar. Place marker threads 27(28:28:29)cm [10½(11:11:11½)in] either side of shoulder seams to mark armholes. Set in sleeves between markers. Join side and sleeve seams. Fold polo collar to RS as shown.

Winter warmer

Knitted in a warm, tweedy yarn, this cosy sweater, modelled by Amos Brearly (Ronald Magill) is perfect for walks in the country. The inset collar adds a distinctive cold-weather touch.

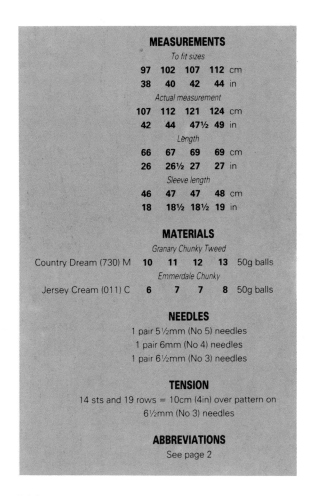

MEASUREMENTS

To fit sizes			
97	102	107	112	cm
38	40	42	44	in

Actual measurement

107	112	121	124	cm
42	44	47½	49	in

Length

66	67	69	69	cm
26	26½	27	27	in

Sleeve length

46	47	47	48	cm
18	18½	18½	19	in

MATERIALS

Granary Chunky Tweed

Country Dream (730) M	10	11	12	13	50g balls

Emmerdale Chunky

Jersey Cream (011) C	6	7	7	8	50g balls

NEEDLES

1 pair 5½mm (No 5) needles
1 pair 6mm (No 4) needles
1 pair 6½mm (No 3) needles

TENSION

14 sts and 19 rows = 10cm (4in) over pattern on 6½mm (No 3) needles

ABBREVIATIONS

See page 2

BACK

** With 5½mm (No 5) needles and M, cast on 69(73:77:81) sts.
1st Row (RS) K1, *P1, K1, rep from * to end.
2nd Row P1, *K1, P1, rep from * to end.
Keeping cont of rib as set, work 2 rows in C and 9 rows in M.
Change to 6½mm (No 3) needles.
Inc row: P4(6:3:10), inc in next st, *P 14(19:13:14), inc in next st, rep from * to last 4(6:3:10) sts, P to end. 74(77:83:86) sts.
Commence pattern.
1st Row Using C, K2, *sl 1P, K2, rep from * to end.
2nd Row Using C, purl.
3rd Row Using M, K1, *sl 1P, K2, rep from * to last st, K1.
4th Row Using M, purl.

These 4 rows form pattern.
Cont in patt until work measures approximately 34(36:36:36)cm [13½(14:14:14)in] from beg, ending with a 4th patt row.
Using M work 6 rows in st st, starting with a K row and marking both ends of last row with a coloured thread to denote armholes. **
Cont in patt, starting with 1st patt row until back measures 64(65:66:66)cm [25(25½:26:26)in] from beg, ending with a RS row.
Shape Neck
Next Row P 29(30:32:33) sts and turn, leaving remaining sts on a spare needle.
Keeping cont of patt, dec 1 st at neck edge on next 3 rows.
Work 2 rows straight then cast off remaining 26(27:29:30) sts loosely.
Slip centre 16(17:19:20) sts onto a stitch holder.
Rejoin yarn to remaining 29(30:32:33) sts and P to end.
Complete to match first side of neck, reversing shaping.

FRONT

Follow instructions for Back from ** to **.
Cont in patt, starting with 1st patt row until Front measures 10 rows less than Back to start of neck shaping, ending with a RS row.
Shape Neck
Next Row P 32(33:35:36) sts and turn, leaving remaining sts on a spare needle.
Keeping cont of patt, dec 1 st at neck edge on next 3 rows then 1 st at this same edge on every alt row until 26(27:29:30) sts remain.
Work straight until Front matches Back to shoulder.
Cast off loosely.
Slip centre 10(11:13:14) sts onto a stitch holder.
Rejoin appropriate yarn to remaining 32(33:35:36) sts and P to end.
Complete to match first side of neck, reversing shaping.

SLEEVES

With 5½mm (No 5) needles and M, cast on

33(35:35:37) sts and work 13 rows in striped rib as given for Back.

Change to 6½mm (No 3) needles.

Inc row: P 1(0:0:0), inc in next st, *P2, inc in next st, rep from * to last 1(1:1:0) st, P 1(1:1:0). 44(47:47:50) sts.

Cont in patt as given for Back, inc and working into patt 1 st at each end of 4th and every following 6th row until there are 48(53:51:60) sts on the needle then 1 st at each end of every following 4th row until there are 74(75:77:78) sts on the needle.

Work straight until Sleeve measures 46(47:47:48)cm [18(18½:18½:19)in] from beg, ending with a RS row. Cast off loosely.

NECKBAND

Join right shoulder seam. With RS of work facing, using 5½mm (No 5) needles and M, pick up and K 18 sts evenly down left side of front neck, K across 10(11:13:14) sts at centre front [marking 3rd and 8th(9th:11th:12th) sts with coloured threads], pick up and K 18 sts evenly up right side of front neck and 7 sts down right side of back neck, K across 16(17:19:20) sts of back neck, then pick up and K 7 sts up left side of back neck 76(78:82:84) sts.

Work 2 rows in K1, P1 rib.

Keeping cont of rib, work 2 rows in C and 2 rows in M then using M, cast off neatly in rib.

COLLAR

With 5½mm (No 5) needles and M, cast on 75(77:79:81) sts.

1st Row (RS) K2, *P1, K1, rep from * to last st, K1.

2nd Row K1, *P1, K1, rep from * to end.

Rep these 2 rows twice more.

Shape Collar

1st Row Rib 47(48:50:51) sts and turn.

2nd Row Sl 1, rib 18(18:20:20) sts and turn.

3rd Row Sl 1, rib 25(25:27:27) sts and turn.

4th Row Sl 1, rib 32(32:34:34) sts and turn.

Cont working 7 sts extra in this way on every row until the row Sl 1, rib 60(60:62:62) sts and turn has been worked.

9th Row Sl 1, rib to end.

Change to 6mm (No 4) needles.

Keeping cont of rib as set, work 12(12:14:14) rows in M, 2 rows in C and 2 rows in M. Using M, cast off neatly in rib.

MAKING UP

Do not press. Join left shoulder seam and neckband. Set in sleeves between armhole markers. Join side and sleeve seams, taking care to match pattern. Sew cast on edge of Collar inside Neckband (to ridge formed by picked up sts), starting and ending at marked sts of front neck.

Cable and rib sweater

This classic cabled sweater, with its dropped shoulders and round neck, will always be a favourite. Worn by Alan Turner (Richard Thorp), its generous proportions make it comfortable and easy-to-wear.

MEASUREMENTS

To fit sizes

97–102	107–112	117–122	127–132	cm
38–40	42–44	46–48	50–52	in

Actual measurement

112	122	132	142	cm
44	48	52	56	in

Length

69	70	70	71	cm
27	27½	27½	28	in

Sleeve length

46	47	47	48	cm
18	18½	18½	19	in

MATERIALS

Granary Aran Tweed

Highlands (754) **16**	**17**	**19**	**20**	50g balls

NEEDLES

1 pair 3¾mm (No 9) needles
1 pair 4½mm (No 7) needles
Cable needle

TENSION

20 sts and 28 rows = 10cm (4in), measured over rib pattern on 4½mm (No 7) needles

ABBREVIATIONS

m1: make one stitch by picking up loop between last st and next st and working into back of it

C6R: cable 6 right by slipping next 3 sts onto cable needle leave at back of work, k3 then k3 from cable needle

C6L: cable 6 left by slipping next 3 sts onto cable needle, leave at front of work, k3 then k3 from cable needle

BACK

** With 3¾mm (No 9) needles, cast on 95(105:115:125) sts.

1st Row (RS) K1, *P1, K1, rep from * to end.

2nd Row P1, *K1, P1, rep from * to end.

Rep these 2 rows until work measures 8cm (3in), ending with a RS row.

Inc row: Rib 4(5:5:6), *m1, rib 3(3:4:4), rep from * twice more, rib 2(3:2:3), (m1, rib 1) 5 times, rib 3(6:2:5), **M1, rib 7(7:9:9), rep from ** 6 times more, m1, rib 4(7:3:6), (m1, rib 1) 5 times, rib 5(6:6:7), ***m1, rib 3(3:4:4), rep from *** twice more, rib 0(1:0:1). 119(129:139:149) sts.

Change to 4½mm (No 7) needles and rib pattern with

cable panels as follows:

1st Row P 0(1:0:1), (K3, P1) 4(4:5:5) times, *K1, P1, K9, P1, K1,* P1, (K3, P1) 15(17:18:20) times, rep from * to *, (P1, K3) 4(4:5:5) times, P 0(1:0:1).

2nd Row K 0(1:0:1), (K1, P1, K2) 4(4:5:5) times, *P1, K1, P9, K1, P1,* K2, P1, (K3, P1) 14(16:17:19) times, K2, rep from * to *, (K2, P1, K1) 4(4:5:5) times, K 0(1:0:1).

These 2 rows form rib pattern and are repeated.

3rd Row Patt 16(17:20:21), *K1, P1, C6R, K3, P1, K1,* patt 61(69:73:81), rep from * to *, patt to end.

4th Row Patt 16(17:20:21), *P1, K1, P9, K1, P1,* patt 61(69:73:81), rep from * to *, patt to end.

5th Row Patt 16(17:20:21), *K1, P1, K9, P1, K1,* patt 61(69:73:81), rep from * to *, patt to end.

6th Row As 4th row.

7th Row Patt 16(17:20:21), *K1, P1, K3, C6L, P1, K1,* patt 61(69:73:81), rep from * to *, patt to end.

8th Row As 4th row.

These 8 rows form cable panel pattern. **

Keeping cont of rib patt and cable panels as set, cont until Back measures 66(67:67:69)cm [26(26½:26½:27)in] from beg, ending with a WS row.

Shape Neck

Next Row Patt 47(51:55:59) sts and turn, leaving rem sts on a spare needle.

Keeping cont of patt, dec 1 st at neck edge on next 3 rows.

Work 2 rows straight then cast off remaining 44(48:52:56) sts loosely.

Slip centre 25(27:29:31) sts onto a stitch holder, rejoin yarn to remaining sts and patt to end.

Complete to match first side of neck.

FRONT

Follow instructions for Back from ** to **.

Keeping cont of rib patt and cable panels as set, cont until Front measures 61(62:62:64)cm [24(24½:24½:25)in] from beg, ending with a WS row.

Shape Neck

Next Row Patt 50(54:58:62) sts and turn, leaving remaining sts on a spare needle.

Keeping cont of patt, dec 1 st at neck edge on next 2 rows then dec 1 st at this same edge on following 4 alt

rows. 44(48:52:56) sts rem.

Work straight until Front matches Back to shoulder. Cast off loosely.

Slip centre 19(21:23:25) sts onto a stitch holder, rejoin yarn to remaining sts and patt to end.

Complete to match first side of neck, reversing shaping.

SLEEVES

With 3¾mm (No 9) needles, cast on 49(53:55:57) sts and work 8cm (3in) in rib as given for Back welt, ending with a RS row.

Inc row: Rib 2(4:1:6), m1, [rib 3(3:4:3), m1] 15(15:13:15) times, rib 2(4:2:6). 65(69:69:73) sts

Change to 4½mm (No 7) needles and rib patt as given for Back, placing this as follows:

1st Row P1, *K3, P1, rep from * to end.

2nd Row K2, P1, *K3, P1, rep from * to last 2 sts, K2.

Cont in patt as set, inc and working into patt 1 st at each end of 3rd and every following 6th row until there are 81(85:85:89) sts on the needle then 1 st at each end of every following 4th row until there are 105(111:111:117) sts on the needle.

Work straight until Sleeve measures 46(47:47:48)cm [18(18½:18½:19)in] from beg, ending with a WS row. Cast off loosely.

NECKBAND

Join right shoulder seam, taking care to match pattern. With RS of work facing and using 3¾mm (No 9) needles, pick up and K 21 sts down left side of front neck, K across 19(21:23:25) sts at centre front, pick up and K 21 sts up right side of front neck and 6 sts down right side of back neck, K across 25(27:29:31) sts of back neck then pick up and K 6 sts up left side of back neck. 98(102:106:110) sts.

Work 6cm (2½in) in K1, P1 rib. Cast off loosely in rib.

MAKING UP

Join left shoulder and neckband seam, taking care to match pattern. Place marker threads 27(28:28:29)cm [10½(11:11:11½)in] either side of shoulder seams to mark armholes. Set in sleeves between markers. Join side and sleeve seams. Fold neckband in half to WS and slip stitch loosely in place.

College-boy sweater

Reminiscent of the American prep look, this sporty sweater looks great when teamed with a favourite pair of jeans. Modelled here by Mark Hughes (Craig McKay), it is a superb casual style for both men and women.

MEASUREMENTS

To fit sizes

91	97	102	107	112	cm
36	38	40	42	44	in

Actual measurement

107	112	117	122	127	cm
42	44	46	48	50	in

Length

66	67	67	69	69	cm
26	26½	26½	27	27	in

Sleeve length

46	46	47	47	48	cm
18	18	18½	18½	19	in

MATERIALS

Emmerdale Double Knitting

Willow Green (018)	10	11	12	14	15	50g balls

5 buttons

NEEDLES

1 pair 3¼mm (No 10) needles
1 pair 3¾mm (No 9) needles
1 pair 4mm (No 8) needles
Cable needle

TENSION

24 sts and 33 rows = 10cm (4in), measured over pattern on 4mm (No 8) needles

ABBREVIATIONS

T2F: slip next st onto cable needle and leave at front of work, P next st then K stitch from cable needle
T2B: slip next st onto cable needle and leave at back of work, K next st then P stitch from cable needle
C2L: slip next st onto cable needle and leave at front of work, K next st then K st from cable needle

BACK

** With 3¼mm (No 10) needles, cast on 109(115:121:127:133) sts.
1st Row (RS) K1, *P1, K1, rep from * to end.
2nd Row P1, *K1, P1, rep from * to end.
Rep these 2 rows until work measures 6cm (2½in), ending with a WS row.
Inc row Rib 0(3:6:0:3), inc in next st, [rib 5(5:5:6:6), inc in next st] 18 times, rib 0(3:6:0:3).
128(134:140:146:152) sts.
Change to 4mm (No 8) needles and pattern.
1st Row (WS) Purl.

2nd Row P1, *T2F, K2, T2B, rep from * to last st, P1.
3rd Row K2, *P4, K2, rep from * to end.
4th Row P2, *T2F, T2B, P2, rep from * to end.
5th Row K3, P2, *K4, P2, rep from * to last 3 sts, K3.
6th Row K3, C2L, *K4, C2L, rep from * to last 3 sts, K3
7th Row Purl.
8th Row K2, *T2B, T2F, K2, rep from * to end.
9th Row P3, K2, *P4, K2, rep from * to last 3 sts, P3.
10th Row K1, *T2B, P2, T2F, rep from * to last st, K1.
11th Row P2, *K4, P2, rep from * to end.
12th Row C2L, *K4, C2L, rep from * to end.
These 12 rows form pattern. **
Cont in patt until Back measures 64(65:65:66:66)cm [25(25½:25½:26:26)in] from beg. End with a WS row.
Shape Neck
Next Row Patt 53(55:57:59:61) sts and turn, leaving remaining sts on a spare needle. Keeping cont of patt, dec 1 st at neck edge on next 5 rows.
Work 2 rows straight then cast off remaining 48(50:52:54:56) sts loosely.
Slip centre 22(24:26:28:30) sts onto a stitch holder, rejoin yarn to remaining sts and patt to end.
Complete to match first side of neck.

POCKET LINING (make one)

With 3¾mm (No 9) needles, cast on 25 sts and work 27 rows in st st, starting with a K row.
Leave sts on a spare needle.

FRONT

Follow instructions for Back from ** to **.
Cont in patt until Front measures 32(33:33:33:33)cm [12½(13:13:13:13)in] from beg, ending with a RS row.
Divide for Front Opening
Next Row Patt 61(64:67:70:73) sts, cast off next 6 sts, patt to end.
Keeping cont of patt, work on first set of sts for left side of Front until work measures 43cm (17in) from beg, ending with a RS row. Place Pocket
Next Row Patt 18(19:21:22:24), slip next 25 sts onto a stitch holder, patt across sts of Pocket Lining, patt to end.
*** Cont in patt across all sts until Front measures

12(12:12:16:16) rows less than Back to start of neck shaping, ending with a WS row. ***

Shape Neck

Next Row Patt 56(58:60:64:66) then cast off remaining 5(6:7:6:7) sts.

Rejoin yarn to remaining sts and keeping cont of patt, dec 1 st at neck edge on next 6 rows then 1 st at this edge on every alt row until 48(50:52:54:56) sts remain. Work straight until Front matches Back to shoulder. Cast off loosely.

Rejoin yarn to remaining 61(64:67:70:73) sts. Patt to end.

Foll instructions for left side of Front from *** to ***

Shape Neck

Next Row Cast off 5(6:7:6:7) sts, patt to end. 56(58:60:64:66) sts

Keeping cont of patt, dec 1 st at neck edge on next 6 rows then 1 st at this same edge on every alt row until 48(50:52:54:56) sts remain.

Complete to match left side of Front.

SLEEVES

With 3¼mm (No 10) needles, cast on 51(55:57:59:63) sts and work 8cm (3in) in rib as given for Back, ending with a WS row.

Inc row: Rib 3(3:6:3:9), inc in next st, (rib 1, inc in next st) 22(24:22:26:22) times, rib 3(3:6:3:9). 74(80:80:86:86) sts.

Change to 4mm (No 8) needles. Cont in patt as given for Back, inc and working into patt 1 st at each end of 5th and every following 6th row until there are 94(104:104:114:114) sts on the needle then 1 st at each end of every following 4th row until there are 120(126:126:132:132) sts on the needle.

Work straight until Sleeve measures 46(46:47:47:48)cm [18(18:18½:18½:19)in] from beg, ending with a WS row. Cast off loosely.

BUTTONHOLE BAND

With RS of work facing and using 3¼mm (No 10) needles, pick up and K 87 sts evenly down left side of front opening from start of neck shaping to cast off sts at centre front.

1st Row K1, *P1, K1, rep from * to end.
2nd Row K2, *P1, K1, rep from * to last st, K1.
Rep these 2 rows once more.

1st Buttonhole Row Rib 15, (cast off next 2 sts, rib 12 including st used in casting off) 4 times, cast off next 2 sts, rib to end.

2nd Buttonhole Row Rib, casting on over sts cast off in previous row.

Work a further 4 rows in rib as set then cast off in rib.

BUTTON BAND

With RS of work facing and using 3¼mm (No 10) needles, pick up and K 87 sts evenly up RS of front opening from cast off sts at centre front to start of neck shaping.

Work to match Buttonhole Band, omitting buttonholes.

COLLAR

Join shoulder seams, taking care to match pattern. With RS of work facing and using 3¼mm (No 10) needles, pick up and K 36(37:38:41:42) sts evenly up RS of front neck from centre of Button Band to shoulder and 7 sts down right side of back neck, K across 22(24:26:28:30) sts of back neck, pick up and K 8 sts up left side of back neck and 36(37:38:41:42) sts down left side of front neck from shoulder to centre of Buttonhole Band. 109(113:117:125:129) sts.

1st Row K2, *P1, K1, rep from * to last st, K1.
2nd Row K1, *P1, K1, rep from * to end.
Rep these 2 rows twice more.

Shape Back Collar

1st Row Rib 66(69:72:77:80) sts and turn.
2nd Row Sl 1, rib 22(24:26:28:30) sts and turn.
3rd Row Sl 1, rib 29(31:33:35:37) sts and turn.
4th Row Sl 1, rib 36(38:40:42:44) sts and turn.
5th Row Sl 1, rib 41(43:45:47:49) sts and turn.
6th Row Sl 1, rib 46(48:50:52:54) sts and turn.
7th Row Sl 1, rib 51(53:55:57:59) sts and turn.
8th Row Sl 1, rib 56(58:60:62:64) sts and turn.
9th Row Sl 1, rib to end.

Change to 3¾mm (No 9) needles and keeping cont of rib as set, work 8cm (3in). Cast off neatly in rib.

POCKET TOP

With RS of work facing and using 3¾mm (No 9) needles, rejoin yarn to sts from stitch holder.

1st Row K2, *P1, K1, rep from * to last st, K1.
2nd Row K1, *P1, K1, rep from * to end.
Rep these 2 rows twice more then cast off neatly in rib.

MAKING UP

Place marker threads 25(27:27:28:28)cm [10(10½:10½:11:11)in] either side of shoulder seams to mark armholes. Set in sleeves between markers. Join side and sleeve seams. Sew Pocket Lining in place to WS of work then sew ends of Pocket Top in place. Lapping Buttonhole Band over Button Band, sew lower ends of bands neatly in place to cast off sts at centre front. Sew on buttons.

Pin-striped sweater

The understated design and clean 'masculine' colours of this sweater make it suitable for both casual and more formal wear. Worn here by Henry Wilks (Arthur Pentelow), with a shirt and tie, it can successfully be teamed with an open-necked cotton shirt for a sporty but smart look.

MEASUREMENTS

To fit sizes					
97	102	107	112	117	cm
38	40	42	44	46	in
Actual measurement					
107	112	119	124	130	cm
42	44	47	49	51	in
Length					
67	67	69	69	70	cm
26½	26½	27	27	27½	in
Sleeve length					
46	47	47	48	48	cm
18	18½	18½	19	19	in

MATERIALS

Emmerdale Double Knitting

Slate (030) M	9	10	11	12	13	50g balls
White (001) C	2	2	2	3	3	50g balls

NEEDLES

1 pair 3¼mm (No 10) needles
1 pair 4mm (No 8) needles

TENSION

26 sts and 32 rows = 10cm (4in), measured over pattern on 4mm (No 8) needles

ABBREVIATIONS

See page 2

BACK

** With 3¼mm (No 10) needles and M, cast on 115(121:127:133:139) sts.
1st Row (RS) K1, *P1, K1, rep from * to end.
2nd Row P1, *K1, P1, rep from * to end.
Rep these 2 rows until work measures 8cm (3in), ending with a RS row.
Inc Row Rib 4(7:0:3:6), inc in next st, (rib 4, inc in next st) 21(21:25:25:25) times, rib 5(8:1:4:7). 137(143:153:159:165) sts.
Change to 4mm (No 8) needles and rib pattern.
1st Row K3 (1:1:4:2), *P1, K4, rep from * to last 4(2:2:5:3) sts, P1, K3(1:1:4:2).
2nd Row P3(1:1:4:2), *K1, P4, rep from * to last 4(2:2:5:3) sts, K1, P3(1:1:4:2).
These 2 rows form pattern. **
Cont in patt until Back measures 65(65:66:66:67)cm [25½(25½:26:26:26½)in] from beg, ending with a WS row.

Shape Neck

Next Row Patt 52(54:58:61:63) sts and turn, leaving remaining sts on a spare needle.
Keeping cont of patt, dec 1 st at neck edge on next and following 2 alt rows.
Work 2 rows straight then cast off remaining 49(51:55:58:60) sts loosely.
Slip centre 33(35:37:37:39) sts onto a stitch holder, rejoin yarn to remaining sts and patt to end.
Complete to match first side of neck.

FRONT

Follow instructions for Back from ** to **.
Cont in patt until Front measures 42cm (16½in) from beg, ending with a WS row.

Shape Neck

Next Row Patt 68(71:76:79:82) sts and turn, leaving remaining sts on a spare needle.
Keeping cont of patt, dec 1 st at neck edge on every alt row 5 times then 1 st at this same edge on every following 4th row until 49(51:55:58:60) sts remain.
Work straight until Front matches Back to shoulder.
Cast off loosely.
Slip centre st onto a stitch holder, rejoin yarn to remaining sts and patt to end. 68(71:76:79:82) sts.
Complete to match first side of neck, reversing shaping.

SLEEVES

With 3¼mm (No 10) needles and M, cast on 57(59:61:63:65) sts and work 8cm (3in) in rib as given for Back ending with a RS row.
Inc row: Rib 7(4:7:4:7), inc in next st, (rib 1, inc in next st) 21(25:23:27:25) times, rib 7(4:7:4:7). 79(85:85:91:91) sts.
Change to 4mm (No 8) needles and rib patt as given for Back, placing this as follows:
1st Row K4(2:2:0:0), *P1, K4, rep from * to last 5(3:3:1:1) sts, P1, K4(2:2:0:0).
2nd Row P4(2:2:0:0), *K1, P4, rep from * to last 5(3:3:1:1) sts, K1, P4(2:2:0:0).
Cont in patt as set, inc and working into patt 1 st at each end of next and every following 4th row until

there are 137(143:143:149:149) sts on the needle. Work straight until Sleeve measures 46(47:47:48:48)cm [18(18½:18½:19:19)in] from beg, ending with a WS row. Cast off loosely.

NECKBAND

Join right shoulder seam, taking care to match pattern. With RS of work
facing, using 3¼mm (No 10) needles and M, pick up and K 70(70:74:74:78) sts evenly down left side of front neck, K stitch from stitch holder (marking this st with a coloured thread), pick up and K 70(70:74:74:78) sts evenly up right side of front neck and 7 sts down right side of back neck, K across 33(35:37:37:39) sts of back neck then pick up and K 7 sts up left side of back neck. 188(190:200:200:210) sts.
1st Row K1, *P1, K1, rep from * to within 2 sts of marked centre st, P2 tog, P centre st, P2 tog tbl, **K1, P1, rep from ** to end.
2nd Row Work in rib as set to within 2 sts of marked centre st, K2 tog tbl, K centre st, K2 tog, rib to end.
3rd Row Work in rib as set to within 2 sts of marked centre st, P2 tog, P centre st, P2 tog tbl, rib to end.
Rep last 2 rows twice then 2nd row once more.
Cast off neatly in rib, dec on this row as before.

MAKING UP

Join left seam and neckband, taking care to match pattern. Place marker threads 27(28:28:29:29)cm [10½(11:11:11½:11½)in] either side of shoulder seams to mark armholes.
Set in sleeves between markers. Using C and chain stitch, embroider stripes up single purl sts of main rib as shown. Join side and sleeve seams.

Super stripes

Stripes are always a favourite, for both men and women. The subtle colours used for this V-necked sweater worn by Seth Armstrong (Stan Richards) give the garment a fresh, 'country' feel.

MEASUREMENTS

To fit sizes

97	102	107	112	cm
38	40	42	44	in

Actual measurement

112	117	122	127	cm
44	46	48	50	in

Length

69	70	70	71	cm
27	27½	27½	28	in

Sleeve length

46	47	47	48	cm
18	18½	18½	19	in

MATERIALS

Emmerdale Double Knitting

Woodland (055) M	7	7	8	9	50g balls
Bottle (027) A	3	3	4	4	50g balls
Barley (054) B	2	2	3	3	50g balls
Scarlet (034) C	2	2	3	3	50g balls

NEEDLES

1 pair 3¼mm (No 10) needles
1 pair 4mm (No 8) needles

TENSION

24 sts and 34 rows = 10cm (4in), measured over pattern on 4mm (No 8) needles

ABBREVIATIONS

S1 = slip purlwise

NB When working slip stitch rows, carry yarn loosely across WS of slipped sts taking care to keep tension correct.

BACK

** With 3¼mm (No 10) needles and M, cast on 115(121:127:133) sts.
1st Row (RS) K1, *P1, K1, rep from * to end.
2nd Row P1, *K1, P1, rep from * to end.
Rep these 2 rows until work measures 9cm (3½in), ending with a WS row.
Inc row: Rib 9(4:7:2), inc in next st, (rib 5(6:6:7), inc in next st) 16 times, rib 9(4:7:2). 132(138:144:150) sts.
Change to 4mm (No 8) needles and pattern.
1st Row Using M, purl.
2nd Row K 3(4:3:4)A, *sl 2, K2 A, rep from * to last 1(2:1:2) st(s), K 1(2:1:2)A.

3rd Row P 3(4:3:4)A, *sl 2, P2 A, rep from * to last 1(2:1:2) st(s), P 1(2:1:2)A.
4th Row Using M, knit.
5th Row P *1B, 1M, rep from * to end.
6th Row K *1B, 1M, rep from * to end.
7th Row Using M, purl.
8th Row K 1(2:1:2)A, *sl 2, K2A, rep from * to last 3(4:3:4) sts, sl 2, K 1(2:1:2)A.
9th Row P1(2:1:2)A, *sl 2, P2 A, rep from * to last 3(4:3:4) sts, sl 2, P 1(2:1:2)A.
10th Row Using M, knit.
11th Row P *1C, 1M, rep from * to end.
12th Row K *1C, 1M, rep from * to end.
These 12 rows form pattern. **
Continue in patt until Back measures 66(67:67:69)cm [26(26½:26½:27)ins] from beg, ending with a WS row.
Shape Neck
Next Row Patt 52(54:56:58) sts and turn, leaving remaining sts on a spare needle.
***

Next Row Cast off 4 sts, patt to end.
Next Row Patt to end.
Next Row Cast off 3 sts, patt to end.
Next Row Patt to end.
Next Row Cast off one st, patt to end. ***
Work 2 rows straight then cast off remaining 44(46:48:50) sts loosely.
Slip centre 28(30:32:34) sts onto a stitch holder, rejoin yarn to remaining sts and patt to end.
Next Row Patt to end. 52(54:56:58) sts.
Work as for first side of neck from *** to ***.
Work 1 row straight then cast off remaining 44(46:48:50) sts loosely.

FRONT

Follow instructions for Back from ** to **.
Cont in patt until Front measures 37cm (14½ins) from beg, ending with a WS row.
Shape Neck
Next Row Patt 65(68:71:74) sts and turn, leaving remaining sts on a spare needle.
Keeping cont of patt, dec 1 st at neck edge on 2nd and every following 4th row until 44(46:48:50) sts remain.
Work straight until Front matches Back to shoulder.

Cast off loosely.

Slip centre 2 sts on to a stitch holder, rejoin yarn to remaining sts and patt to end.

Complete to match first side of neck, reversing shaping.

SLEEVES

With 3¼mm (No 10) needles and M, cast on 55(59:61:65) sts and work 8cm (3in) in rib as given for Back, ending with a WS row.

Inc row: Rib 3(2:3:2), inc in next st, (rib 2, inc in next st) 16(18:18:20) times, rib 3(2:3:2). 72(78:80:86) sts.

Change to 4mm (No 8) needles and cont in patt as given for Back, inc and working into patt 1 st at each end of 5th and every following 6th row until there are 86(92:100:96) sts on the needle then 1 st at each end of every foll 4th row until there are 126(132:132:144) sts on the needle.

Work straight until sleeve measures 46(47:47:48)cm [18(18½:18½:19)in] from beg, ending with a wrong side row. Cast off loosely.

NECKBAND

Join Right shoulder seam. With RS of work facing, using 4mm (No 8) needles and M, pick up and K 105(109:109:113) sts evenly down left side of front neck, K 2 sts from stitch holder (marking these sts with a coloured thread), pick up and K 105(109:109:113) sts evenly up right side of neck and 10 sts down right side of back neck, K across

28(30:32:34) sts of back neck then pick up and K 10 sts up left side of back neck. 260(270:272:282) sts.

1st Row *P1, K1, rep from * to within one st of marked centre sts, P2 tog tbl, P2 tog, **K1, P1, rep from ** to end.

2nd Row Work in rib as set to within one st of marked centre sts, K2 tog, K2 tog tbl, rib to end.

3rd Row Work in rib as set to within one st of marked centre sts, P2 tog tbl, P2 tog, rib to end.

Rep last 2 rows 4 times more AT THE SAME TIME working in stripes of 2 rows B, 2 rows M, 2 rows A, 2 rows M.

Change to 3¼mm (No 10) needles and, dec every row as before, work 2 rows C and 6 rows M.

Using M, cast off neatly in rib, dec on this row as before.

MAKING UP

Join left shoulder and neckband seam, taking care to match stripes. Place marker threads 27(28:28:29)cm [10½(11:11:11½)ins] either side of shoulder seams to mark armholes. Set in sleeves between markers. Join side and sleeve seams, taking care to match pattern.

Grey luxury

This irresistible mohair jacket, modelled by Kate Sugden (Sally Knyvette), is easy to knit and very versatile. It looks great with jeans, as shown here, and can also be worn as a luxurious cover-up with evening clothes.

MEASUREMENTS

To fit sizes		
86–91	97–102	107–112 cm
34–36	38–40	42–44 in
Actual measurement		
102	112	122 cm
40	44	48 in
Length		
71	71	71 cm
28	28	28 in
Underarm length		
46	46	46 cm
18	18	18 in

MATERIALS

Nicole Mohair

Cornish Mist (107)	13	14	15	50g balls

NEEDLES

1 pair 5½mm (No 5) needles
1 pair 5mm (No 6) needles
1 pair 4½mm (No 7) needles

TENSION

16 sts and 21 rows = 10cm (4in) in st st
on 5½mm (No 5) needles

ABBREVIATIONS

See page 2

BACK

Using 5mm (No 6) needles, cast on 81(89:97) sts and work:

1st Row K2, (P1, K1) to last st, K1.

2nd Row K1, (P1, K1) to end.

Rep these 2 rows twice more. (6 rib rows in all).

Change to 5½mm (No 5) needles and st st starting with a K row and work straight to a total length of 71cm (28in) ending with a P row.

Next Row Cast off 28(32:36) sts, mark this point, cast off 25, mark this point, cast off rem 28(32:36).

LEFT FRONT

Using 5mm (No 6) needles, cast on 65(69:73) sts and work 6 rows in rib in the same way as given for back. *
Change to 5½mm (No 5) needles and st st starting with a K row, and work:

Next Row K39(43:47) turn, leaving rem 26 sts on a holder, P to end.

** Cont in st st on these 39(43:47) sts until work measures 46cm (18in) ending at inside neck edge (same edge as the sts on the holder)

Dec 1 st at neck edge only on next, then every foll 4th row until 28(32:36) sts rem.

Work straight until front matches back to shoulder, ending with a P row.
Cast off.

RIGHT FRONT

Work as for left front as far as *.
Next Row Rem on smaller needles, rib 26 sts and place them on a holder, then change to larger needles and K to end.
Work as for left front from ** to end.

SLEEVES

Same for all sizes
Using 4½mm (No 7) needles, cast on 37 sts and work 13cm (5in) in rib in the same way as given for the back, ending with a row 2, and inc by 6 sts evenly across the last row. (43 sts)
Change to 5½mm (No 5) needles and st st starting with a K row and inc 1 st each end of the 3rd, then every foll 4th row until there are 81 sts.
Work straight to a total measurement of 52cm (20½in) ending with a P row.
Cast off loosely.

POCKETS

Using 5½mm (No 5) needles cast on 22 sts and work 27cm (10½in) in st st.
Cast off.

MAKING UP AND BANDS

Do not press or brush.
Join both shoulder seams, matching inner edge of front shoulder to marked points on back shoulder.
Using 5mm (No 6) needles, pick up and rib, keeping rib correct as before, the 26 sts from the holder at the bottom of the left front.
Work straight on these sts only until band, when only slightly stretched, reaches up the complete left front edge as far as the centre back neck.
Cast off.
Work the right front band in the same way.
Attach both bands and join their cast off ends. Double pockets and seam, leaving cast on and cast off edges open. Join all rem seams, matching shaping, ensuring that armholes are 25cm (10in) deep after making up and inserting pockets into side seams, with their bottom edge 13cm (5in) above the bottom edge of the jacket. Turn the ribbed front bands onto the RS and catch down at bottom edge only if preferred. Double back cuffs.

Riviera pearl

This elegant short-sleeved jacket, worn by Dolly Skilbeck (Jean Rogers) is perfect for slipping over a bare-shouldered evening dress. The appliquéd flower motif adds an extra touch of individuality – pearls or sequins could also be used to create a luxurious effect.

MEASUREMENTS

To fit sizes

86–91	97–102	107–112	cm
34–36	38–40	42–44	in

Actual measurement

102	112	122	cm
40	44	48	in

Length

46	46	46	cm
18	18	18	in

Sleeve length

9	9	9	cm
3½	3½	3½	in

MATERIALS

Riviera Double Knitting

White Meringue (341)	5	6	6	50g balls

Appliqué motif (optional)

NEEDLES

1 pair 4mm (No 8) needles
1 pair 3¾mm (No 9) needles
1 pair 3¼mm (No 10) needles
Long circular 3¾mm (No 9) needle

TENSION

24 sts and 32 rows = 10cm (4in) in st st
on 4mm (No 8) needles

ABBREVIATIONS

See page 2

LEFT FRONT

Using 4mm (No 8) needles, cast on 36(42:48) sts and work in st st.

1st Row K to last st, inc 1 st in last st in K.
2nd Row Inc 1 st in first st in P, P to end.
* Rep these 2 rows 5 more times. (48:54:60 sts)
Inc 1 st at the same, inside edge on the next, then every foll alt row until there are 54(60:66) sts.
Work straight to a total measurement, from cast on edge of 18cm (7in) ending at the outside, unshaped edge.

Shape Underarm and Neck

Cast on 14 sts at beg of next row. (68:74:80 sts)
Keeping outside sleeve edge straight, dec 1 st at inside neck edge on next, then every foll 6th(5th:5th) row until 57(62:67) sts rem.

Work straight until sleeve edge measures 25cm (10in) from cast on at underarm, and work therefore measures a total of 43cm (17in) from the first cast on edge, ending at the outside sleeve edge. **
Leave these sts on a holder and break off yarn.

RIGHT FRONT

Using 4mm (No 8) needles, cast on 36(42:48) sts and work in st st:

1st Row Inc 1 st in first st in K, K to end.
2nd Row P to last st, inc 1 st in last st, in P.
Work as for left front from * to ** so ending with a K row and at sleeve edge.
With WS facing, work in P across the 57(62:67) sts of the right front, cast on 35(37:39) sts for the back neck, then work in P across the 57(62:67) sts for the left front from the holder with WS facing. (149:161:173 sts)
Work back:
Work 25cm (10in) straight on these sts, ending with a P row.
Cast off 14 sts at beg of next 2 rows. (121:133:145 sts)
Work 18cm (7in) straight on these sts, ending with a P row, so that back of work now matches front when folded across back neck and shoulders.
Change to 3¾mm (No 9) needles and work:
1st Row K2, (P1, K1) to last st, K1.
2nd Row K1, (P1, K1) to end.
Rep these 2 rows 3 more times. (8 rib rows in all).
Cast off loosely in rib.

ARMBANDS

Both alike and the same for all sizes.
Using 3¼mm (No 10) needles, with RS facing, pick up and K evenly across the whole sleeve edge 120 sts.
Next Row P2, (P2 tog, P3) to last 3, P3. (97 sts)
Work the 2 rib rows as given for the back welt 4 times. (8 rib rows in all).
Cast off loosely in rib.

FRONT EDGE RIB

Using a 3¾mm (No 9) long circular needle,

49

commencing at outside edge of bottom of right front, with right side facing, pick up and K the 36(42:48) cast on sts, then 26 sts around the shaped bottom corner, 26 sts up the straight front edge as far as the beg of the neck shaping, 64(65:66) sts up the right neck slope, the 35(37:39) sts cast on for the back neck, 64(65:66) sts down the left neck slope, 26 sts down the straight front edge as far as the bottom shaping, 26 sts around the shaped bottom corner and the

36(42:48) cast on sts at the bottom of the left front. (339:355:371 sts).
Starting with row 2, work the 2 rib rows as given for the back welt until 8 rib rows have been worked in all, cast off loosely in rib.

MAKING UP

Do not press. Join side seams matching shapings. Stitch on appliqué motif.

Sugar twinset

Knitted in soft, flattering colours, this elegant slip-over and cardigan, modelled by Annie Sugden (Sheila Mercier) are quick and easy to knit. If the weather is warm enough, the slip-over can be worn on its own as a pretty summer top.

MEASUREMENTS

To fit sizes

86–91	97–102	107–112	cm
34–36	38–40	42–44	in

SLIPOVER:

Actual measurement

97	107	117	cm
38	42	46	in

Length

58	58	58	cm
23	23	23	in

CARDIGAN:

Actual measurement

104	114	124	cm
41	45	49	in

Length

61	61	61	cm
24	24	24	in

Sleeve length

44	44	44	cm
17½	17½	17½	cm

MATERIALS

Emmerdale Double Knitting

CARDIGAN:

Jersey Cream (011)	8	8	9	50g balls
Salmon (016)	2	2	2	50g balls

SLIPOVER:

Jersey Cream (011)	1	1	1	50g ball
Salmon (016)	4	5	5	50g balls

9 buttons for the Cardigan

NEEDLES

1 pair 4mm (No 8) needles
1 pair 3¼mm (No 10) needles

TENSION

24 sts and 32 rows = 10cm (4in) in st st
on 4mm (No 8) needles

ABBREVIATIONS

See page 2

BACK

Using 3¼mm (No 10) needles and Salmon, cast on 109(121:133) sts and work:

1st Row K2, (P1, K1) to last st, K1.
2nd Row K1, (P1, K1) to end.

Rep these 2 rows until rib measures 5cm (2in) ending with a row 2 and inc by 6 sts evenly across this last row. (115:127:139 sts).

Change to 4mm (No 8) needles and st st starting with a K row and work:

* Change to Cream and work 4 rows.
Change to Salmon and work 18 rows *.
Rep from * to * until work measures 32cm (12½in) ending with a P row.

Cont to keep stripe pattern correct throughout rem of work, shape armholes:

Cast off 4(5:6) sts at beg of next 2 rows. (107:117:127 sts).

Dec 1 st at each end of next 3 rows, then at each end of every alt row until 97(105:113) sts rem. **

Work straight to a total measurement of 56cm (22in) ending with a P row.

Shape Shoulders

Cast off 9(11:12) sts at beg of next 4 rows, then 10(10:12) sts at beg of next 2 rows.

Place rem 41 sts on a holder.

FRONT

Work as for slipover back as far as **.

Work straight until front is 24 rows shorter than back to start of shoulder shaping, so ending with a P row.

Shape Neck

Cont to keep stripe pattern correct throughout work:

Next Row K 38(42:46) turn, leaving rem sts on a holder, P2 tog tbl, P to end.

*** Dec 1 st at neck edge only on next 4 rows, then on every alt row until 28(32:36) sts rem.

Work 8 rows straight, so ending at armhole edge.

Shape Shoulders

Cast off 9(11:12) sts at beg of next, then alt row.
Work 1 row.
Cast off rem 10(10:12) sts. ***

Rejoin yarn to inside edge of rem sts, K 21 sts and place them on a holder, K to end.

Next Row P to last 2, P2 tog.

Rep from *** to *** noting that 9 rows will be worked straight after neck shaping in order to end at armhole edge.

NECKBAND

Same for all sizes

Press according to ball band instructions.

Join left shoulder seam matching shaping. Using 3¼mm (No 10) needles and Salmon, with RS facing, pick up and K the 41 sts from the back neck holder, inc by 1 st in the middle, 30 sts down left neck slope, the 21 sts from the front neck holder and 30 sts up the right neck slope. (123 sts).

Starting with row 2, work 8 rows in rib in the same way as given for the slipover back.

Cast off in rib.

ARMBANDS

Both alike

Join rem shoulder seam matching shaping.

Using 3¼mm (No 10) needles and Salmon, with RS facing, pick up and K the 4(5:6) sts cast off at the armhole base, 11(12:13) sts around the rem of the armhole base shaping, 50 sts up the rem of the armhole edge as far as the shoulder seam, 51 sts down the armhole edge as far as the top of the shaping, 11(12:13) sts around the base shaping, and the 4(5:6) sts cast off at the armhole base. (131:135:139 sts)

Starting with row 2, work 8 rows in rib in the same way as before.

Cast off in rib.

MAKING UP

Join rem seams matching shaping and stripes.

CARDIGAN

BACK

Using 3¼mm (No 10) needles and Cream, cast on 117(129:141) sts and work 5cm (2in) in rib in the same way as given for the Slipover Back, ending with row 2, and inc by 6 sts evenly across this last row. (123:135:147 sts)

Change to 4mm (No 8) needles and st st starting with a K row and work 8 rows.

**** Change to Salmon and work 4 rows.

Change to Cream and work 18 rows. ****

Rep from **** to **** until work measures 61cm (24in) ending with a P row.

Next Row Cast off 44(49:54) K until 44(49:54) sts rem, place the 35(37:39) sts just worked onto a holder, cast off to end.

LEFT FRONT

Using 3¼mm (No 10) needles and Cream, cast on 65(71:77) sts and work 5cm (2in) in rib in the same way as before, ending with row 2, and inc by 3 sts evenly across this row. (68:74:80 sts).

Change to 4mm (No 8) needles and work next row K 59(65:71), turn, leaving rem 9 sts on a pin for button band and P back.

Cont in st st.: ***** Work 6 further Cream rows.

Rep from **** to **** as given for Cardigan Back until front is 8cm (3in) shorter than the back, ending at neck edge.

Cont to keep stripe pattern correct, shape neck:

Next Row Work 6(7:8) sts and place them on a holder, work to end. Dec 1 st at neck edge on next 4 rows, then on every alt row until 44(49:54) sts rem.

Work straight until front matches back to shoulder, ending with a P row.

Cast off.

RIGHT FRONT

Using 3¼mm (No 10) needles and Cream, cast on 65(71:77) sts and work 4 rows in rib in the same way as before, so ending with row 2.

Next Row Making button hole, rib 3, cast off 3, rib to end.

Next Row Rib, casting on 3 over the 3 cast off on the previous row.

Cont in rib until work measures 5cm (2in) ending with row 2, and inc by 3 sts evenly across this row.

Next Row Rib 9 sts and place them on a pin for the button hole band, change to 4mm (No 8) needles and K rem 59(65:71) sts.

P1 row, then cont in st st as given for Cardigan left from ***** to end.

SLEEVES

Using 3¼mm (No 10) needles and Cream, cast on 51(53:55) sts and work 5cm (2in) in rib in the same way as before, ending with row 2, and inc by 6 sts evenly across the last row. (57:59:61 sts).

Change to 4mm (No 8) needles and st st starting with a K row and work 8 rows Cream, then rep 4 rows Salmon, 18 rows Cream as before throughout, at the same time, inc 1 st, each end of the 3rd, then every foll 3rd row until there are 121(121:121) sts).

Work straight to a total measurement of 44cm (17½in) ending with a P row.

Cast off loosely.

BUTTON BAND

Using 3¼mm (No 10) needles and Cream, with RS facing, pick up and work as for row 1 of rib, the 9 sts from the pin at the top of the left front welt. Work in rib as before until band, when slightly stretched reaches up the whole front edge as far as the beg of the neck shaping, ending with row 2. Leave sts on a pin, break off yarn and attach Button Band evenly to left front edge.

Mark a point 6cm (2½in) below the top of the band, and another point to match the button hole in the right front welt.

Mark 6 further points evenly spaced between these 2, 8 points in all.

BUTTON HOLE BAND

Work as for button band, but work from the 9 sts at the right front welt, and to match each marked point on the button band, work a button hole:

Next Row Rib 3, cast off 3, rib 3.

Next Row Rib, casting on 3 over the 3 cast off on the previous row.

When band is complete, ending with row 2 and therefore at outside edge, leave sts on the needle and do not break off yarn.

NECKBAND

Press according to ball band instructions.

Attach button hole band and join both shoulder seams.

Using 3¼mm (No 10) needles and attached Cream yarn, with RS facing, commencing at right front edge, rib across the 9 sts at the top of the buttonhole band as for row 1 of rib, pick up and K the 6(7:8) sts from the right front neck holder, 24 sts up the right front slope, the 35(37:39) sts across the back neck holder, 24 sts down left front slope and the 6(7:8) sts from the left front neck holder, rib across the 9 sts at the top of the button band as for row 1 of rib. (113:117:121 sts) Starting wth row 2, work 4 rib rows.

Next Row Rib to last 6, cast off 3, rib rem 3.
Next Row Rib, casting on 3 over the 3 cast off on the previous row.
Rib 4 further rows.
Cast off in rib.

MAKING UP

Join rem seams matching shaping and stripes, ensuring that armholes are 25cm (10in) deep after making up. Attach buttons to match buttonholes.

The alphabet

Knitted in shower-proof yarn, this eye-catching design, modelled by Archie Brooks (Tony Pitts) is both practical and comfortable. The sweater also looks good in different colourways, for instance, white out of black or red out of navy.

MEASUREMENTS

To fit sizes

76	81	86	91	97	102	107	112	cm
30	32	34	36	38	40	42	44	in

Actual measurement

91	97	102	107	112	117	122	127	cm
36	38	40	42	44	46	48	50	in

Length

64	64	64	66	66	66	69	69	cm
25	25	25	26	26	26	27	27	in

Sleeve length

44	44	44	44	48	48	48	48	cm
17½	17½	17½	17½	19	19	19	19	in

MATERIALS

Emmerdale Showerproof Double Knitting

Sandstorm (218)

A	7	7	8	8	9	9	10	10	50g balls

School Brown (028)

B	3	3	3	3	3	3	3	3	50g balls

NEEDLES

1 pair 3¼mm (No 10) needles
1 pair 4mm (No 8) needles

TENSION

24 sts and 32 rows to 10cm (4in) on 4mm (No 8) needles over st st

ABBREVIATIONS

See page 2

BACK

With 3¼mm (No 10) needles and A cast on 107(113:119:125:131:137:143:149) sts.
1st Row K1, *P1, K1, rep from * to end.
2nd Row P1, *K1, P1, rep from * to end.
Rep 1st and 2nd rows 10(10:11:11:12:13:14:14) times more.
Change to 4mm (No 8) needles and proceed as foll:
Work 4(4:4:6:6:6:8:8) rows with A in st st.
Work from 1st to 142nd row of Chart A once, joining in and breaking off colours as required and working size required as indicated.
The odd rows are knit and the even rows are purl.
Break off B.
With A work 4(4:4:6:6:6:8:8) rows in st st. **
With A work 28(28:28:32:32:32:36:36) rows in st st.
Shape Shoulder
Cast off 8(9:9:10:10:11:11:12) sts at beg of next 2 rows.
Cast off 9(9:10:10:11:11:12:12) sts at beg of next 2 rows.
Cast off 9(9:10:10:11:11:12:12) sts at beg of next 2 rows.
Cast off 9(10:10:11:11:12:12:13) sts at beg of next 2 rows.
Leave rem 37(39:41:43:45:47:49:51) sts on a thread.

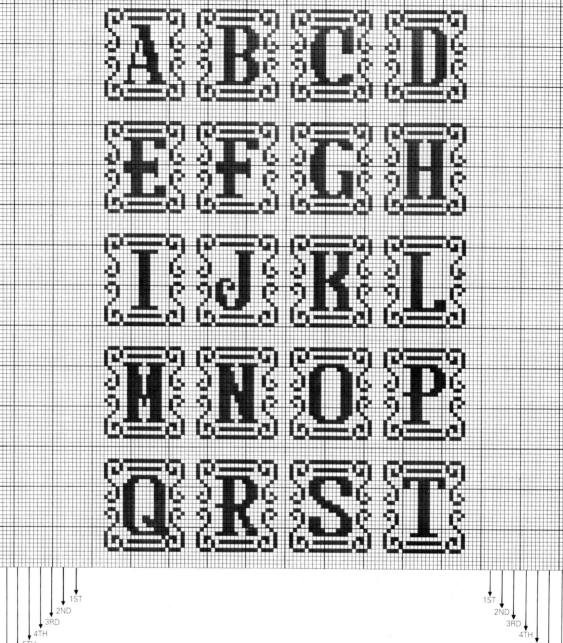

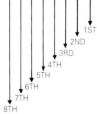

■ B – (218) SANDSTORM

□ A – (028) SCHOOL BROWN

FRONT

Work as for Back to ** with A cont in st st as follows:

Shape Neck

Next Row K 47(50:52:55:57:60:63:66) sts, turn.

Working on these 47(50:52:55:57:60:63:66) sts only proceed as follows:

Work 12(13:13:14:14:15:16:17) rows dec one st at neck edge only in every row

35(37:39:41:43:45:47:49) sts.

Work 15(14:14:17:17:16:19:18) rows in st st.

Shape Shoulder

Next Row Cast off 8(9:9:10:10:11:11:12) sts, knit to end.

Next Row Purl to end.

Next Row Cast off 9(9:10:10:11:11:12:12) sts, knit to end.

Next Row Purl to end.

Next Row Cast off 9(9:10:10:11:11:12:12) sts, knit to end.

Next Row Purl to end.

Next Row Cast off rem 9(10:10:11:11:12:12:13) sts.

With RS of work facing for next row slip first 13(13:15:15:17:17:17:17) sts onto a thread rejoin yarn to rem sts and knit to end.

Work 12(13:13:14:14:15:16:17) rows dec one st at neck edge only in every row

35(37:39:41:43:45:47:49) sts.

Work 16(15:15:18:18:17:20:19) rows in st st.

Shape Shoulder

Next Row Cast off 8(9:9:10:10:11:11:12) sts, purl to end.

Next Row Knit to end.

Next Row Cast off 9(9:10:10:11:11:12:12) sts, purl to end.

Next Row Knit to end.

Next Row Cast off 9(9:10:10:11:11:12:12) sts, purl to end.

Next Row Knit to end.

Next Row Cast off rem 9(10:10:11:11:12:12:13) sts.

SLEEVES

With 3¼mm (No 10) needles and A cast on 53(53:59:59:65:65:71:71) sts.

1st Row K1, *P1, K1, rep from * to end.

2nd Row P1, *K1, P1, rep from * to end.

Rep 1st and 2nd rows 10(10:10:12:12:12:12:12) times more.

Change to 4mm (No 8) needles and with A work 36(36:36:36:44:44:44:44) rows in st st inc one st at each end of 5th and every foll 4th row to 69(69:75:75:85:85:91:91) sts.

Work from 1st to 84th row of Chart B once joining in and breaking off colours as required and working size required as indicated and inc as indicated.

The odd rows are knit and the even rows are purl.

Cast off.

CHART B

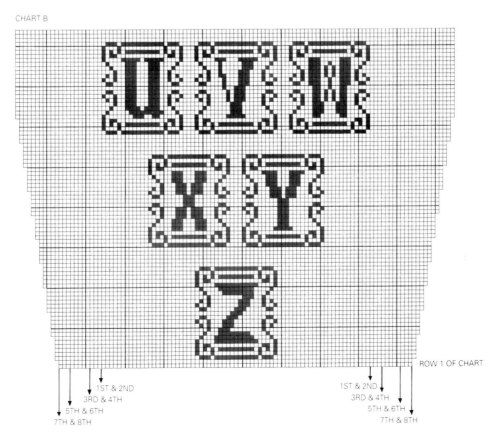

ROW 1 OF CHART

1ST & 2ND
3RD & 4TH
5TH & 6TH
7TH & 8TH

1ST & 2ND
3RD & 4TH
5TH & 6TH
7TH & 8TH

NECKBAND

Sew up right shoulder seam.

With RS of work facing 3¼mm (No 10) needles and A pick up and K 24(24:24:27:27:27:30:30) sts down left side of neck, K 13(13:15:15:17:17:17:17) from front neck, pick up and knit 25(25:25:28:28:28:31:31) sts up right side of neck, K 37(39:41:43:45:47:49:51) sts from back neck. 99(101:105:113:117:119:127:129) sts.

1st Row P1, *K1, P1, rep from * to end.
2nd Row K1, *P1, K1, rep from * to end.
Rep 1st and 2nd rows 8(8:8:10:12:12:12:12) times more.
Cast off.

MAKING UP

Sew up left shoulder and neckband seam, fold neckband in half onto WS and stitch in position. Sew sleeves in position. Sew up side and sleeve seams.

Geometric jumper

Perfect for wearing with jeans or casual trousers, this comfortable, baggy sweater worn by Jackie Merrick (Ian Sharrock) is perfect for everyday wear. Try it in navy and cream for a completely different, crisper effect.

MEASUREMENTS

To fit sizes

76	81	86	91	97	102	107	112	cm
30	32	34	36	38	40	42	44	in

Actual measurements

91	97	102	107	112	117	122	127	cm
36	38	40	42	44	46	48	50	in

Length

58	61	64	66	69	71	71	71	cm
23	24	25	26	27	28	28	28	in

Sleeve length

44	44	46	47	48	48	50	50	cm
17½	17½	18	18½	19	19	19½	19½	in

MATERIALS

Emmerdale Showerproof Aran Parchment (217)

A	10	10	11	11	11	12	12	12	50g balls

Collette Red Pepper (912)

B	2	2	2	2	2	2	2	2	50g balls

NEEDLES

1 pair 3¼mm (No 10) needles
1 pair 4½mm (No 7) needles

TENSION

19 sts to 10cm (4in) on 4½mm (No 7) needles over st st

ABBREVIATIONS

See page 2

BACK

With 3¼mm (No 10) needles and A cast on 87(91:97:103:107:111:115:119) sts.

1st Row K1, *P1, K1, rep from * to end.
2nd Row P1, *K1, P1, rep from * to end.
Rep 1st and 2nd rows 9(9:9:10:10:12:12:12) times more.
Change to 4½mm (No 7) needles and proceed in patt as follows:
With A work 6(6:6:10:10:10:10:10) rows in st st.
With B work 2 rows in st st.
1st Row K 10(12:15:18:20:22:24:26)A, (K1A, K1B, K4A) 5 times, K1A, K1B, K 45(47:50:53:55:57:59:61)A.
2nd Row P 47(49:52:55:57:59:61:63)A, (P1A, P1B,

P4A) 5 times, P 10(12:15:18:20:22:24:26)A.
3rd Row K 10(12:15:18:20:22:24:26)A, (K3B, K1A, K1B, K1A) 5 times, K3B K 44(46:49:52:54:56:58:60)A.
4th Row P 47(49:52:55:57:59:61:63)A, (P1A, P1B, P4A) 5 times, P 10(12:15:18:20:22:24:26)A.
5th Row K 10(12:15:18:20:22:24:26)A, (K1A, K1B, K4A) 5 times, K1A, K1B, K 45(47:50:53:55:57:59:61)A.
6th Row P 45(47:50:53:55:57:59:61)A, P1B, P1A, (P3B, P1A, P1B, P1A) 5 times, P 10(12:15:18:20:22:24:26)A.
Rep 1st to 6th row 6 times more.
With B work 2 rows in st st.
45th Row K 44(46:49:52:54:56:58:60)A, (K1A, K1B, K4A) 5 times, K1A, K1B, K 11(13:16:19:21:23:25:27)A.
46th Row P 13(15:18:21:23:25:27:29)A, (P1A, P1B, P4A) 5 times, P 44(46:49:52:54:56:58:60)A.
47th Row K 44(46:49:52:54:56:58:60)A, (K3B, K1A, K1B, K1A) 5 times, K3B, K 10(12:15:18:20:22:24:26)A.
48th Row P 13(15:18:21:23:25:27:29)A, (P1A, P1B, P4A) 5 times, P 44(46:49:52:54:56:58:60)A.
49th Row K 44(46:49:52:54:56:58:60)A, (K1A, K1B, K4A) 5 times, K1A, K1B, K 11(13:16:19:21:23:25:27)A.
50th Row P 11(13:16:19:21:23:25:27)A, P1B, P1A, (P3B, P1A, P1B, P1A) 5 times, P 44(46:49:52:54:56:58:60)A.
Rep 45th to 50th row 6 times more.
With B work 2 rows in st st **
With A cont in st st until work measures 58(61:64:66:69:71:71:71)cm [23(24:25:26:27:28:28:28)in] ending with RS facing for next row.

Shape Shoulder

Cast off 9(10:10:11:11:12:12:12) sts at beg of next 2 rows.
Cast off 10(10:11:11:12:12:12:13) sts at beg of next 2 rows.
Cast off 10(10:11:12:12:12:13:13) sts at beg of next 2 rows.
Leave rem 29(31:33:35:37:39:41:43) sts on a thread.

FRONT

Work as for Back to **.

With A cont in st st until work measures
50(52:55:56:58:61:61:61)cm
[9½(20½:21½:22:23:24:24:24)in] ending with RS
facing for next row.

Shape Neck

Next Row K 39(41:43:46:47:49:50:52) sts, turn.
Working on these 39(41:43:46:47:49:50:52) sts only
proceed as follows
Work 10(11:11:12:12:13:13:14) rows dec one st at
neck edge only in every row.
29(30:32:34:35:36:37:38) sts.
Cont in st st on rem sts until work measures same as
back to Shape Shoulder ending with RS facing for next
row.

Shape Shoulder

Next Row Cast off 9(10:10:11:11:12:12:12) sts, knit
to end.
Next Row Purl to end.
Next Row Cast off 10(10:11:11:12:12:12:13) sts, knit
to end.
Next Row Purl to end.
Next Row Cast off rem 10(10:11:12:12:12:13:13) sts.
With RS of work facing slip first
9(9:11:11:13:13:15:15) sts rejoin yarn to rem sts and
knit to end.
Work 10(11:11:12:12:13:13:14) rows dec one st at
neck edge only in every row.
29(30:32:34:35:36:37:38) sts.
Cont in st st on rem sts until work measures same as
back to Shape Shoulder end with WS facing for next
row.

Shape Shoulder

Next Row Cast off 9(10:10:11:11:12:12:12) sts, purl
to end.
Next Row Knit to end.
Next Row Cast off 10(10:11:11:12:12:12:13) sts, purl
to end.
Next Row Knit to end.
Next Row Cast off rem 10(10:11:12:12:12:13:13) sts.

SLEEVES

With 3¼mm (No 10) needles and A cast on
43(45:47:49:51:51:53:53) sts.
1st Row K1, *P1, K1 rep from * to end.
2nd Row P1, *K1, P1 rep from * to end.
Rep 1st and 2nd rows 9(9:9:10:10:12:12:12) times
more inc one st at each end of last row.
45(47:49:51:53:53:55:55) sts.

Change to 4½mm (No 7) needles and proceed as
follows:
With A work 6(6:8:10:12:12:14:14) rows in st st inc
one st at each end of 3rd and every foll 4th row.
47(49:53:55:59:59:61:61) sts.
With B work 2 rows in st st.
1st Row K 7(8:10:11:13:13:14:14)A, (K1A, K1B, K4A)
5 times, K1A, K1B, K 8(9:11:12:14:14:15:15)A.
2nd Row P 10(11:13:14:16:16:17:17)A, (P1A, P1B,
P4A) 5 times, P 7(8:10:11:13:13:14:14)A.
3rd Row K 7(8:10:11:13:13:14:14)A, (K3B, K1A, K1B,
K1A) 5 times, K3B, K 7(8:10:11:13:13:14:14)A.
4th Row P 10(11:13:14:16:16:17:17)A, (P1A, P1B,
P4A) 5 times, P 7(8:10:11:13:13:14:14)A.
5th Row K 7(8:10:11:13:13:14:14)A, (K1A, K1B, K4A)
5 times, K1A, K1B, K 8(9:11:12:14:14:15:15)A.
6th Row P 8(9:11:12:14:14:15:15)A, P1B, P1A, (P3B,
P1A, P1B, P1A) 5 times, P 7(8:10:11:13:13:14:14)A.
From 1st to 6th row forms patt, cont in patt inc one st
at each end of next and every foll 3rd row to
91(91:93:95:97:99:101:103) sts, working inc sts in st
st.
Cont in patt until work measures
39(39:41:42:43:43:44:44)cm
[15½(15½:16:16½:17:17:17½:17½)in] ending with
RS facing for next row.
With B work 2 rows in st st.
With A cont in st st until work measures
44(44:46:47:48:48:50:50)cm
[17½(17½:18:18½:19:19:19½:19½)in] ending with
RS facing for next row.
Cast off.

NECKBAND

Sew up right shoulder seam.
With RS of work facing 3¼mm (No 10) needles and A
pick up and knit 18(18:19:19:20:20:21:21) sts down
left side of neck, K 9(9:11:11:13:13:15:15) sts from
front neck, pick up and knit 19(19:20:20:21:21:22:22)
sts up right side of neck, K 29(31:33:35:37:39:41:43)
sts from back neck. 75(77:83:85:91:93:99:101) sts.
1st Row P1, *K1, P1, rep from * to end.
2nd Row K1, *P1, K1, rep from * to end.
Rep 1st and 2nd rows twice more then 1st row once.
Cast off in rib.

MAKING UP

Sew up left shoulder and neck band seam. Sew
sleeves in position. Sew up side and sleeve seams.

Fluffy sheepdog

This adorable sweater, worn by Sam Skilbeck (Benjamin Whitehead), will prove irresistible to children of all ages! The sheepdog motif is knitted in a mohair as a contrast to the flatter texture of the background.

MEASUREMENTS

To fit sizes

66	71	76	cm
26	28	30	in

Actual measurement

71	76	81	cm
28	30	32	in

Length

43	48	55	cm
17	19	21½	in

Sleeve length

32	36	41	cm
12½	14	16	in

MATERIALS

Emmerdale Double Knitting

Main colour (MC)

Jade Green (018)	4	5	5	50g balls
Russett (058)	1	1	1	50g ball

Biarritz Mohair

Steel (381)	part ball
Diamanté (367)	part ball

For all sizes, small quantities of black, white and pink double knitting

NEEDLES

1 pair 4mm (No 8) needles
1 pair 3¼mm (No 10) needles

TENSION

24 sts and 32 rows = 10cm (4in), in st st on 4mm (No 8) needles

ABBREVIATIONS

See page 2

FRONT

Using 3¼mm (No 10) needles and MC, cast on 85(91:97) sts and work:
1st Row K2, (P1, K1) to last st, K1.
2nd Row K1, (P1, K1) to end.
Rep these 2 rows until rib measures 5cm (2in) ending with row 2.
Change to 4mm (No 8) needles and st st starting with a K row. **
Work 6(18:32) st st rows.
Commence chart with next row as row 1 of the chart, placing it as given and work straight until the 88 rows of the chart are complete, so ending the chart with a P row.

Work 4(8:12) further rows.
Shape Neck
Next Row K34(36:38) turn, leaving rem sts on a holder, P2 tog tbl, P to end.
*** Working on these sts only, dec 1 st at neck edge only on next 2 rows, then on every alt row until 29(31:33) sts rem.
Work 14(14:16) rows straight, so ending with a P row. Cast off. ***
Rejoin yarn to inside edge of rem sts, K 17(19:21) sts and place them on a holder, K to end.
Next Row P to last 2, P2 tog.
Rep from *** to ***.

BACK

Work as given for front as far as **.
Work 38(50:64) rows in plain MC.
Starting with row 33, work the next 12 rows from the chart omitting the dog, but working the fence all across.
Work straight in MC in st st until back matches front to shoulder, ending with a P row.
Next Row Cast off 29(31:33) K until 29(31:33) sts rem, place the 27(29:31) sts just worked onto a holder, cast off to end.

SLEEVES

Using 3¼mm (No 10) needles and MC, cast on 43(45:47) sts and work 5cm (2in) of rib in the same way as given before so ending with row 2.
Change to 4mm (No 8) needles and st st starting with a K row and inc 1 st each end of the 3rd, then every foll 4th row until there are 83(89:95) sts, AT THE SAME TIME, when 40(52:68) st st rows have been worked and there are 63(71:81) sts, work the next row:
K 1(0:0) in MC,* K2 MC, K2 brown, K1 MC *, rep from * to * until 2(1:1) sts rem, K2(1:1) MC.
Using this as an establishing row, cont to shape as before, AT THE SAME TIME, work the fence as before, working all inc into the pattern.
When fence is completed, complete inc in plain MC.
Work straight to a total measurement of 32(36:41)cm (12½(14:16)in) ending with a P row.
Cast off loosely.

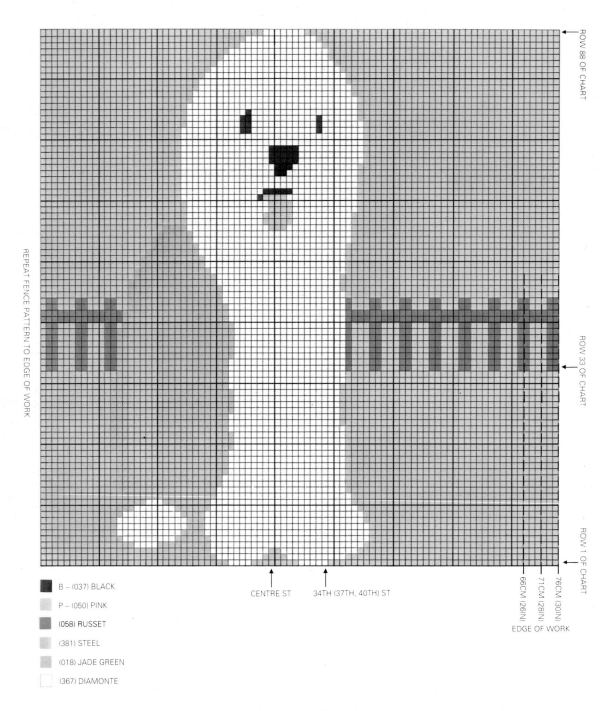

REPEAT FENCE PATTERN TO EDGE OF WORK

ROW 33 OF CHART

ROW 1 OF CHART

B – (037) BLACK

P – (050) PINK

(058) RUSSET

(381) STEEL

(018) JADE GREEN

(367) DIAMONTE

CENTRE ST   34TH (37TH, 40TH) ST

66CM (26IN)
71CM (28IN)
76CM (30IN)
EDGE OF WORK

NECKBAND

Press according to ball band instructions, omitting ribs and mohair.

Join left shoulder seam.

Using 3¼mm (No 10) needles and MC, with RS facing, pick up and K the 27(29:31) sts from the back neck holder working 2 tog in the centre, 22(22:24) sts down the left neck slope, the 17(19:21) sts from the front neck holder, and 22(22:24) sts up the right neck slope. (87:91:99 sts)

Starting with a row 2, work in rib as before until 10 rib rows have been worked in all, ending with a RS row.

K1 row.

Starting with row 1, work 10 further rib rows.

Cast off very loosely.

MAKING UP

Join all rem seams matching shapings and pattern and ensuring that armholes are 18(19:20)cm (7(7½:8)in) deep after making up. Turn neckband onto WS and loosely slip stitch down. The mohair picture may be brushed. Using the picture as a guide embroider detail.